T0330212

Capturing the Innovation Opportunity Space

Capturing the Innovation Opportunity Space

Creating Business Models with New Forms of Innovation

Stephen Flowers
Kent Business School, University of Kent, UK

Martin Meyer
Kent Business School, University of Kent, UK

Jari Kuusisto
University of Vaasa, Finland

With contributions from

Juha Arrasvuori
Sami Berghäll
Jose Christian
Ming Dong
Arja Kuusisto
Liting Liang
Guo Wen
Pirjo Yli-Viitala

Edward Elgar
PUBLISHING

Cheltenham, UK • Northampton, MA, USA

Published by
Edward Elgar Publishing Limited
The Lypiatts
15 Lansdown Road
Cheltenham
Glos GL50 2JA
UK

Edward Elgar Publishing, Inc.
William Pratt House
9 Dewey Court
Northampton
Massachusetts 01060
USA

A catalogue record for this book
is available from the British Library

Library of Congress Control Number: 2017931756

This book is available electronically in the **Elgar**online
Business subject collection
DOI 10.4337/9781783475520

MIX
Paper from
responsible sources
FSC
www.fsc.org   FSC® C013604

ISBN 978 1 78347 551 3 (cased)
ISBN 978 1 78347 552 0 (eBook)

Typeset by Servis Filmsetting Ltd, Stockport, Cheshire
Printed and bound by CPI Group (UK) Ltd, Croydon, CR0 4YY

Contents

Authors

Juha Arrasvuori, SC-Research, University of Vaasa, Finland

Sami Berghäll, Department of Forest Sciences, University of Helsinki, Finland

Jose Christian, Science Policy Research Unit, University of Sussex, UK

Ming Dong, School of Economics and Management, Xidian University, China

Stephen Flowers, Kent Business School, University of Kent, UK

Arja Kuusisto, SC-Research, University of Vaasa, Finland

Jari Kuusisto, University of Vaasa, Finland

Liting Liang, SC-Research, University of Vaasa, Finland

Martin Meyer, Kent Business School, University of Kent, UK

Guo Wen, Institutes of Science and Development Chinese Academy of Sciences

Pirjo Yli-Viitala, SC-Research, University of Vaasa, Finland

Preface

Stephen Flowers, Martin Meyer and Jari Kuusisto

This book is the result of a project funded by Tekes,[1] Finland's funding agency for innovation, that explored user-driven service innovation and co-creation. The aim of the project was to develop new insights and novel perspectives to help us better understand how innovation takes place in the 21st century. Within this huge topic the project focused on new business models that were emerging due to forms of innovation often initiated by those outside of traditional producer firms, including users and online communities. From the outset, the project focused on pioneers working at the boundaries of what is possible, rather than the mainstream (often R&D intensive) innovators that are found in many industries. The project was far more interested in the potential disruptors rather than the incumbents, and this book is an exploration of the new models of business that have begun to emerge.

The material contained within this book is the result of collaborative efforts between a large team of international researchers that worked hard to explore new forms and models of innovation across many different types of industry. As the project progressed and our thinking developed it became clear that many of the labels and frameworks we were trying to employ were often a poor fit in the new context we were exploring. The central idea of this book, the Innovation Opportunity Space (IOS), was a result of this mismatch and provided us with a way of understanding the complex events we were examining. The IOS approach also enabled us to begin to recognise the importance of new innovation actors and highlight the need to collect a new generation of metrics that will help us better understand the emerging world of innovation that has grown up around us. In order to undertake this work the research team was able to draw on a range of academic traditions, frameworks and approaches but, once again, found they were often a poor match with the empirical findings. For those with a forensic turn of mind the traces of this conceptual mismatch can be found throughout this book and are evidence of the long struggle we all face when we try and understand a new reality. The challenges of this struggle are not to be underestimated and old ideas often have a far stronger hold on us than we realise.

As the evidence accumulated what emerged was a pattern of innovation activity that went beyond older classifications and involved many different types of actor. Indeed, what emerged was that a phenomenon we had assumed was only confined to innovation had itself morphed and could also be found in the tasks associated with the day-to-day operation of relatively mundane organisations. In some cases entirely new business models were being developed that drew on resources that were far outside the firm's control. We realised that, in innovation terms, we were privileged to be looking at a Petri dish in which new models and ideas about business were being developed and trialled before our eyes. The many case studies in this book have been carefully selected, and often connected to existing work in the area, in order to provide a series of distinct insights into the new forms of innovation that we have explored. This book provides a new way of thinking about these forms of innovation, the value that is created, and the novel business models that are now being developed.

NOTE

1. We gratefully acknowledge the support of Tekes in undertaking this work. The research was undertaken within the Tekes FiDipro project: 'User-driven Service Innovation and Co-creation Management (NOMAD)', project leader: Affiliate Professor Jari Kuusisto, University of Vaasa.

1. The new frontier of innovation

Stephen Flowers, Martin Meyer and Jari Kuusisto

The old world order is trembling and a new world of innovation is opening up before us. New ways of doing things and new products and services, unimagined and currently unimaginable, will emerge and become ubiquitous. The groups that produce these new ways of working and new products and services will be very different and will likely not fit into the usual easy categories. Immense value will be created but the traditional ideas of finance, firm, property and profit will not always apply in the same way as they have in the past. We are at the new frontier of innovation.

Many researchers and academics excel at joining up the dots whilst looking backwards, and their detailed retrospective analyses have an important part to play in strategic analysis. However, in the context of fundamental change, where the past may no longer be a reliable guide to the future, this approach will have clear limitations for those (for example, managers, policymakers, entrepreneurs) concerned with dealing with such changes. This chapter, and indeed this entire book, is designed to provide those concerned with the 'now' and the future with the tools to help make sense of the fundamental changes in the shape and nature of innovation that are taking place within our economies. This book does look backwards and draws on many ideas taken from a wide range of academic and other sources in order to set the scene, but in recognising that managers, entrepreneurs and policymakers need to act in the present and plan for the future, it also looks forward. This book does not claim to tell you how to act. Rather it is designed to provide you with the insights, understanding and tools to enable you to analyse your own context and to make your own decisions.

The last few decades have seen fundamental shifts in the way in which products and services are created and offered to the world. Firms are no longer the only source of new ideas, products, services and individuals now reach out to each other in a way that creates a critical mass that sparks new ideas and leads to action. These individuals may go on to form the online communities that are now such a feature of the 21st century, and can become major drivers of innovation. Of course, the Internet has played an important part in this but it is important to recognise that individuals, people like us, are the key ingredient in all this. The Internet is just the platform for communication – it is *individuals* that come up with the ideas and work hard to create new products and services. Until recently it was largely the people who worked within firms that drove innovation and were paid to make sure that their firm benefitted from their activities. Of course, a great deal of this still goes on, but the online communities that are now so active will often have different objectives and may have a complicated relationship with firms. In some cases such communities may work closely with firms, but they may also work against, or else want to have nothing do to with firms. In some cases the activities of such communities are so far away from the mainstream that firms find it impossible to publically relate to them in any way at all. Firms, like people, are sometimes trapped in ways of seeing and doing that may once have made sense, but have outlived their usefulness. As far as our understanding of innovation is concerned, this is where we now are.

This book is an exploration of the new frontier of innovation that is slowly but surely changing the world we live in, and the how, what and when of the new things that emerge. You'll have noticed that terms like 'market' and 'commercialisation' have not yet been mentioned, and this is because the new forms of innovation that we will explore in this book may not always be offered to the 'market' in the traditional sense – financial exchange may not take place, firms may not issue shares and no one will necessarily get rich in the traditional sense, although huge value will have been created and shared. That is not to say that some will not seek to create businesses and established firms will not learn to draw on this activity in order to create their own commercial offerings, but the key issue is that we now have a major wellspring of innovative activity that is not primarily concerned with commercial profit in the traditional sense. The communitarian strands of many societies make clear that this a recurrent feature of human existence, and the ability to reach out to others over the Internet means that this is now a feature in the realm of the products and services we use in our everyday lives. As a result many firms are now engaged in communication, challenge, and even competition with their own customers.

What we are seeing at the start of the 21st century is a result of several fundamental changes in the way in which goods and services are produced and consumed. These changes are perhaps most apparent in consumer markets, but what we can see in these contexts is simply the leading edge of the fundamental shifts that will have major implications for all firms, no matter which market they operate in. These fundamental changes are explored in more detail below.

1.1   INDIVIDUALS ARE EMPOWERED

Our attitude to the products and services that we use today in our everyday lives is very different to just a few years ago – there is now an open invitation to join the creative party. There are now whole classes of new 'empty' product that depend on us filling them up with our news, images, ideas, reviews and comments. The organisations that provide these social media services are (at least at the time of writing) some of the most well-known and highly-valued in the world and it is now commonplace for individuals to spend a significant part of each day 'working' on such systems. At the same time, it is now well known that some people will routinely hack, crack and re-engineer the products and services that they use. Admittedly, this is a much more obscure and rare activity than being on social media, but it is now part of our culture and platforms like YouTube provide a window into this world for those who wish to look. Just one example of how prevalent this idea is within our culture is demonstrated by the results of a simple Google search: the terms 'hacking' or 'hacks' deliver 147 million and 136 million hits respectively. Individuals are no longer the passive actors whose role is simply to buy, consume, and buy again and there has been a sea change in attitudes – individuals feel valued and their opinions and needs are valued and can have an impact.

At the same time there is a much wider recognition that traditional rules, norms and accepted ways of doing things can be challenged or set aside. Hacking is not necessarily widespread, but it is certainly a mainstream idea that has found its way into many areas. For example, some parts of the video games industry now encourage their customers to 'hack' or 'mod' their products and may even provide a marketplace for the sale and distribution of their hacks and mods. Such firms effectively invite consumers into their New Product Development process and change the architecture of their products to make it easier to gain access and make changes.

1.2   INDIVIDUALS MAKE THINGS HAPPEN

As a result of the changes made to product and service architecture and the easy access to resources (see below) the barriers faced by dissatisfied individuals are no longer very great. On a very simple level, individuals can now directly send feedback and comments to firms concerning the quality of their products and services, their ethical standards or any other matter that they feel is important. Social media has become a powerful force for change and firms now pay great attention to their image and presence in this sphere. At the same time some individuals are able to call upon the knowledge, skills and resources required to hack, modify or repurpose a firm's product or service. Design choices and performance parameters will be examined and changed and, in some cases entirely new uses will be created that its original designers had not pursued or else had not considered. This phenomenon is a recurrent feature of technology and it can lead to the creation of new products and services and the opening up of entirely new markets that were pioneered by users, not producers.

1.3 INDIVIDUALS CAN JOIN AN ONLINE COLLECTIVE

One of the biggest changes in the 21st century has been the emergence of the huge online collective made up of individuals who have a range of interests almost as diverse as humanity itself. It is not unusual to search for the most apparently obscure question or topic only to find that a vast reservoir of knowledge, advice and information created by thousands of others, opens up before you. Sometimes this material is fragmentary and its currency is hard to assess, but often it has been sorted, structured and codified by the invisible workers of the online collective. In some cases, for example, healthcare, this work will have been done by trained professionals, but in many others experts (often specialist amateurs or hobbyists[1]) will have performed the tasks.

This is now so commonplace it is easy to forget that this is also totally unprecedented and one can fall into the trap of ignoring the wider implications of what has been created around us. These are explored in more detail below.

1.3.1 Online Communities Emerge

It is now very easy for individuals to seek out and become part of an online community of like-minded others that share their interests. This is a fundamental shift since we are now restricted by the limits of Internet connectivity rather than geographical boundaries – we can now reach out to the several billion people around the world that use the Internet. As a result the potential pool of others who have the same needs or share the same interests is huge, and continuing to grow every year. Of course, most people will not be interested in the things that you or I may be, but the scale of the Internet means that it is far more likely to achieve a viable community around any specific interest. This is why there are so many wildly diverse special interest groups, radically different online communities and seemingly obscure topics that excite devotees. An illustration of this state of affairs can be obtained by a simple experiment: take five minutes and use Google or your preferred search engine to see if you can find a topic or a subject that has not excited discussion or comment. The chances are that you will not be able to do so. However, even if you can it is likely that you could build a community around your topic within a short time.

1.3.2   Innovation Resources are Widely Available Online

One of the major differences in all the information, images, video and comment that are shared on the Internet is what appears to be a temporary, intangible, disposable medium turns out to be highly robust and (to date, at any rate) as near-permanent as it is possible to be. And all at the same time as being easily accessible to a large proportion of the world's population. Using the Wayback Machine (a digital archive) it is even possible to go back in time to look again at websites and other materials as they were in the past. As a result a vast and continually growing pool of resources – information, images, video and comment – are available to those individuals who wish to draw on them.

1.3.3   Non-traditional Innovators are Involved

One of the fascinating things about much of the material that has been made available on the Internet by individuals is that it is openly and freely shared. It may be that the material is a short video of kittens playing (and there is a lot of this kind of thing available) or, more interestingly from an innovation point of view, it may be a detailed technical discussion or 'how-to' that explains in precise detail to the non-technical how to perform a complex procedure. What we are observing is the creation, accumulation and sharing of a vast pool of resources, only a small proportion of which will go on to form inputs to innovative activity. However, the scale of such activity on the Internet means that, in innovation terms, this is a hugely significant resource. Further, the often visual nature of this information makes it accessible to a still wider audience and enlarges the pool of potential innovators to include groups outside those with traditional technical backgrounds and skills.

1.4   UNDERSTANDING INNOVATION AT THE FRONTIER

This book provides a detailed account of the way in which goods and services are produced and consumed at the new frontier of innovation.

Each of the chapters in this book will explore different aspects of this developing frontier and provide detailed case studies of the different forms the processes of creation and consumption are now taking. This is not an exercise in prediction, rather it holds up a mirror to what is happening around us and provides a new toolkit to help make sense of complex and confusing situations. The exciting, or disturbing, reality is that the real-world cases presented throughout the book provide illustrations of possible futures for firms, sectors and entire industries. In the words of renowned author William Gibson, 'the future is already here, it's just not very evenly distributed'.[2]

This is not to claim that the future of *all* innovation will look like the cases and examples presented in this book, rather that firms need to understand their place in this developing world of innovation before they can make informed strategic decisions. Although the likelihood is that the future will *look* a lot like the past – for example, we are still waiting for the wide availability of long-promised personal jetpacks and flying cars – it is also likely that the world that *surrounds* the goods and services we use will be totally transformed. The part of that world that is concerned with the creation and supply of goods and services is also likely to be transformed. In order to ensure that we better understand the wider context of the changes we are exploring, we must guard against falling into the trap of claiming everything will look like the cases and the ideas contained within this book. However, even though the proportion of innovative individuals is always likely to be small, the connected nature of the Internet means that they are likely to have a disproportionate impact on firms and markets. An illustration of this is in the events that are continuing to unfold in the recorded music industry – tiny numbers of innovators that pioneered the sharing of music led to a fundamental reshaping of an entire industry that is still ongoing. This is clearly not the future for many (or even most) firms and industries, but it is an important example of how a determined group of innovators and their supporters can undermine an established business model. Although there are always risks in change, this book contains many examples of the ways in which firms are learning to benefit from working with outsiders to create and supply goods and services at the frontiers of innovation.

The implications of the fundamental changes in the way in which goods and services are produced and consumed are explored throughout the book. It is clear that in some areas innovation is becoming far more of a socially-driven phenomenon and firms may be reflecting rather than driving this change. In some areas the development of the new ideas that are the basis of novel goods and services are flowing from non-commercial online communities rather than businesses. This creation of new ideas – ideation – is often played out in the 'open' space of online communities that are unencumbered by corporate and regulatory restrictions and provide an opportunity for the development of really new ideas. Such online communities are perhaps the most significant new groups on the innovation frontier and although they are most apparent in business–consumer settings, it is likely that their influence will begin to develop in business–business and other contexts as well. One of the key shifts – the spread of 'open' products and services – is an example of how pervasive ideas that emerge from such communities can be. Emerging from the strong libertarian traditions of the west coast of the USA, and as a direct reaction to the idea that software code could be locked down and 'closed', the idea that code can be 'open' to all has become highly influential. The idea that an item of complex technology can be open to all to participate in its creation and development is now a central part of our innovation culture and will be an important driver of innovation in many industries. We are familiar with Open Source software, but many product architectures are now fully or partially open, and the implications of opening the vast quantities of data held by public sector organisations (open data) are just beginning to be explored. The opening up of the innovation process is fundamental and a clear recognition that external groups – often online communities – play a key role in value creation.

Although this is widely understood in many industries, all firms need to recognise that these fundamental changes are happening and learn the lessons that can be applied in their own particular context. Established practices, policies, theories and concepts will need to be reviewed and refreshed so that they will remain relevant in the new contexts. It is clear that the old rules and certainties of innovation are changing and it is important to recognise that the past will no longer be an accurate predictor of the future. This is new territory for everyone and a clear map of the new terrain that we are moving into does not exist – traditional ways of thinking about and measuring innovation will need to be refreshed and likely extended to deal with what has previously been viewed as largely invisible. These themes will be explored in detail, with each chapter focusing on particular aspects of this larger phenomenon.

1.5 CHAPTER 2: INNOVATION PIONEERS: THE ESSENTIAL ROLE OF USERS, ONLINE COMMUNITIES AND THE CROWD

Chapter 2 provides a lively and informative exploration of the language and concepts that have been developed over many years to describe how new products and services are created and brought to the marketplace. In particular, this chapter explores how the language and ideas that have been developed in the context of old forms of innovation often fail to capture and can serve to mislead when one thinks about the 'new' forms of innovation explored in this volume. The chapter explores the emergence and evolution of the traditional forms of innovation and examines how the users of technology can have major impacts on its development over time. The new forms of innovation that are emerging are also examined and a series of case studies that illustrate the many different approaches to the creation of products and services are outlined. The developing roles of online communities are also explored and the creation of Safecast – the international innovation community established following the Fukushima nuclear disaster in 2011 to deal with the lack of reliable radiological information – is presented.

1.6 CHAPTER 3: EXPLORING THE CHANGING LANDSCAPE OF INNOVATION: THE RISE OF USERS, ONLINE COMMUNITIES AND THE CROWD

Chapter 3 focuses on the part played by users of technologies and online communities in the creation of new goods and services. Taking as its starting point some of the earliest recorded mentions of innovation by users of technologies, the chapter charts the role of technology users in the invention and and innovation of new machines, consumer products and services. It explores how practical people, and not scientists, were at the leading edge of invention in years gone by and highlights the importance of users' knowledge and experience in the processes of invention and innovation. The way in which the recent growth of online communities and the crowd is revolutionising the creation and consumption of goods and services is also examined and a series of case studies are used to illustrate the impact of this phenomenon. Ideas around different forms of use and types of user are unpicked and analysed and the value of such users to firms that produce goods and services is outlined. Some users and online user communities may find and promote unexpected applications of technologies, and this is also explored within the chapter, using Machinima as an example.

1.7 CHAPTER 4: MAPPING THE NEW WORLD OF INNOVATION: THE INNOVATION OPPORTUNITY SPACE

Chapter 4 introduces a new approach to thinking about the parts played by non-traditional actors in innovation, for example, online user communities. The Innovation Opportunity Space is a new conceptual framework designed to provide strategic managers, entrepreneurs, policymakers and academics with an improved way of viewing innovation-related issues. Rather than starting with firms and focusing on products, as so often is the case, the Innovation Opportunity Space takes a more neutral starting point – the space into which an innovation will be introduced. Developed in response to difficulties in understanding how non-firm actors like users create value from their innovation activities, the Innovation Opportunity Space approach allows managers to better comprehend the opportunities that exist. The chapter makes very clear that Innovation Opportunity Spaces can vary wildly and the characteristics of the main types of Innovation Space are presented and their characteristics and the strategic implications analysed. The chapter outlines how the key features of an Innovation Opportunity Space may be analysed – focusing on the Architecture, Actors, Activities and Aftershocks within an IOS – and how different forms of data may be required to more fully understand the innovation activity that is underway. These ideas are applied to four case studies and the chapter concludes with a technical appendix.

1.8 CHAPTER 5: DEFENDING TERRITORY: CHANGING FORMS OF INTELLECTUAL PROTECTION

Chapter 5 explores the important part played by the creation (and protection) of intellectual property (IP) within the innovation process. The growth in importance of IP within the modern business world is clearly laid out and the different forms of IP are defined and their importance explored. The emergence of new forms of IP in areas like online media are also explored and emerging tensions between 'closed' and more collaborative and 'open' forms of IP are examined. Mainstream approaches to the protection of IP are contrasted with the new forms of IP protection that are beginning to emerge. With much of the IP in these contexts emerging from online communities these new forms of IP protection also tend to be characterised by their non-commercial nature and their openness. The chapter explores the challenge this creates within the traditional approaches towards IP that are central to many firms' business models. Traditional 'closed' and newer 'open' models of IP protection are compared and new forms of business model based on IP are laid out in detail, including many examples. The chapter concludes with a technical appendix that relates the ideas presented to a range of policy, business and academic sources.

1.9 CHAPTER 6: NEW FRONTIER BUSINESS MODELS: CREATING VALUE THROUGH INNOVATION

Chapter 6 examines how firms are developing business models that work in concert with the new 'open' approaches that are being pioneered within online innovation communities. The chapter explores how these new business models require a step-change in their relationship with their users and the developing roles they can play. The part played by online communities in business start-ups and in the renewal of existing businesses is also explored with reference to a large number of recent examples. The emergence of crowdfunding and its developing role in business models is explored and the impact of peer-to-peer lending on innovation is also examined. Business models that focus on making use of the resources that individuals are willing to share with others for payment is also explored. The growth of this 'sharing economy' is examined in some detail and provides the basis of a detailed case study. The chapter concludes with a technical appendix that maps the ideas explored back to a range of academic and other sources.

1.10 CHAPTER 7: EMERGING BUSINESS MODELS IN SETTLED CONTEXTS

Chapter 7 presents two in-depth case studies that explore the challenges of developing new business models in mature or settled contexts. These cases provide very different responses to the quite different strategic and operational challenges that are faced in the two contexts – one a traditional agricultural sector, the other a mobile telecommunications service provider. The Finnish forest industry is an example of a very mature and stable extractive industry that has changed little over many decades and has very clear structures around 'user' and 'producer'. This is a classic example of a process industry in which there should be very little opportunity for users and online communities to make any impact. However, this case study provides insights that show how the industry is in the process of reimagining and reinventing what it can offer and opening up a new Innovation Opportunity Space that draws in users and others and creates new value. The second case in this chapter – giffgaff – is an example of how a new entrant to the mature mobile telephony service market in the UK reimagined the service model and drew in its users to help provide core aspects of its sales, marketing and customer services.

1.11 CHAPTER 8: EMERGING BUSINESS MODELS IN FRONTIER CONTEXTS

Chapter 8 presents two in-depth case studies of new business models that are being developed on the frontiers of innovation. The cases explore the two quite distinct forms of Innovation Opportunity Space that have emerged and the business models that are being developed in order to benefit from them. The first case study examines the move to make the vast stores of, often publically held, data available to firms and others in order to provide a basis for new forms of value creation and, potentially, new types of business model. This move, to what is popularly called open data, is a potentially fundamental shift in the way data that has been collected for other purposes and can be used to create new and different forms of value. The second case is a detailed case study of an organisation that emerged specifically to create and supply what was, at the time, a new class of product – a user-developed version of the Android smartphone operating system. The case explores the foundation and development of the CyanogenMod project, and how the collective development of its products, takes place in concert with its large and active user base. Unlike many more traditional firms CyanogenMod represents a new organisational form – the User Organisation – in which extensive volunteer labour has been drawn into the core of its operations.

1.12 CHAPTER 9: CAPTURING THE INNOVATION OPPORTUNITY SPACE

Chapter 9 draws together the many strands in this book and provides a roadmap for managers who wish to develop new business models to benefit from new sources of ideas and effort characterised by new forms of innovation. The chapter links the Innovation Opportunity Space approach, a strategic mapping tool, to the forms of innovative activity that currently exist, or may be developed, around novel and innovative products and services. Starting with the IOS approach the chapter explores how managers can begin to think about their interactions with the external groups that drive the new forms of innovation, and move them to a context in which optimal value is obtained by both the firm and those involved. In order to better understand the fundamental shifts that have taken place in the innovation landscape the chapter makes a clear distinction between the source of the resources required for innovation (within the firm or external to the firm) and the primary intent of the innovation itself (commercial or non-commercial). This provides the basis for a detailed analysis of the cases presented within the book as a whole and highlights the scale of the potential innovation opportunities available to managers who work in traditional 'old' innovation contexts. Building on this analysis the chapter presents a four-stage action-oriented approach that managers can utilise as they seek to capture an Innovation Opportunity Space.

NOTES

1. The term 'amateur' or 'hobbyist' is often used by 'professionals' to denigrate those who undertake this form of unpaid work in their spare time. However, it is important to recognise that the collective nature of this output means that it tends to improve in quality and reliability over time. It is also important to be clear that professional status and expert knowledge may not always be synonymous. Significantly, it is only the amateur or hobbyist that is so passionate about something that they are prepared to pursue it in their spare time – not because it will make them rich, but because it will make them happy.
2. Taken from a radio interview in August 1993.

BIBLIOGRAPHY

Benkler, Y. (2007) *The Wealth of Networks: How Social Production Transforms Markets and Freedom*, New Haven, CT: Yale University Press.

Callon, M. and Rabeharisoa, V. (2003) Research 'in the wild' and the shaping of new social identities, *Technology in Society*, vol. 25, pp. 193–204.

Castells, M. (1996) *The Rise of the Network Society, The Information Age: Economy, Society and Culture Volume 1*, Oxford: Blackwell.

Christian, J. (2015) The User Organisation, unpublished PhD thesis, University of Brighton.

Edgerton, D. (2007) *Shock of the Old: Technology and Global History Since 1900*, London: Profile Books.

Harhoff, D., Henkel, J. and von Hippel, E. (2003) Profiting from voluntary information spillovers how users benefit by freely revealing their innovations, *Research Policy*, vol. 32, no. 10, pp. 1753–1769.

Keen, P. (2007) *The Cult of the Amateur: How Blogs, MySpace, YouTube and the Rest of today's User-generated Media are Killing our Culture and Economy*, London: Nicholas Brealey Publishing.

Keynes, J.M. (1936) *The General Theory of Employment Interest and Money*, London: Macmillan & Co, p. 383.

Kuhn, T. (1962) *The Structure of Scientific Revolution*, Chicago: University of Chicago Press.

Leadbeater, C. (2008) *We-Think: Mass Innovation, Not Mass Production*, London: Profile Books.

Lessig, L. (2005) *Free Culture: The Nature and Future of Creativity*, London: Penguin Books.

McLuhan, M. and Nevitt, B. (1972) *Take Today: The Executive as Dropout*, New York: Harcourt Brace Jovanovich.

Postigo, H. (2003) From pong to planet quake: post-industrial transitions from leisure to work, *Information, Communications and Society*, vol. 6, no. 4, pp. 593–607.

Ritzer, G. and Jorgenson, N. (2010) Production, consumption, prosumption: the nature of capitalism in the age of the digital 'prosumer', *Journal of Consumer Culture*, vol. 10, no. 13, pp. 13–36.

Schumpeter, J. (1942) *Capitalism, Socialism and Democracy*, London: Impact Books.

Tapscott, D. and Williams, A.D. (2006) *Wikinomics: How Mass Collaboration Changes Everything*, New York: Portfolio.

Toffler, A. (1980) *The Third Wave*, New York: Pan Books.

von Hippel, E. (1986), Lead users: a source of novel product concepts, *Management Science*, vol. 32, no. 7, pp. 791–806.

von Hippel, E. (1988) Sources of Innovation, Oxford: Oxford University Press.

von Hippel, E. (1994) Sticky information and the locus of problem solving: implications for innovation, *Management Science*, vol. 40, no. 4, pp. 429–439.

von Hippel, E. and Katz, R. (2002) Shifting innovation to users via toolkits, *Management Science*, vol. 48, no. 7, pp. 821–833.

von Hippel, E. (2005) Democratizing Innovation, Boston: MIT Press.

von Hippel, E. (2007) Horizontal Innovation Networks – by and for users, Industrial and Corporate Change. Vol. 16, no. 2, pp. 293–315.

von Hippel, E. (2016) Free Innovation, Boston: MIT Press.

TECHNICAL APPENDIX

Arguably we are at an inflection point in the study of innovation at which the long-established understandings of its primary actors, and the processes and dynamics by which new products and services become widespread, will be swept away. In this account it is argued that we are in the process from switching from the current dominant 'producer-centric' paradigm towards a new understanding that includes users and online communities and is focused on ideas around co-production. We are in the process of making a Kuhnian shift (Kuhn, 1962) towards a new innovation paradigm.

In the current paradigm innovation producer firms are at the centre of the analysis and all other actors and groups (for example, individual users of goods and services, online user communities) are thrown into deep shadow. Although this may have been a useful working approximation at one point, this model no longer describes the reality of many industrial contexts and, as a result, has been under increasing pressure for some time.

In this new context the producer firm is no longer the sole or, in some contexts, even the most important source of innovation, with users and online user communities becoming far more important. The important role played by the user of technology within innovation has been recognised for a very long time (see Chapter 3 for a more detailed account), and a number of writers have anticipated the impact that new technologies would have on this role. For example, Marshall McLuhan observed that under certain circumstances users would become producers (McLuhan and Nevitt, 1972), and the futurist Alvin Toffler predicted that a certain kind of professional consumer, the Prosumer, will play a very active part in the design of the products that they buy (Toffler, 1980). In his highly influential work the sociologist Manuel Castells also predicted that in certain circumstances 'users' would become 'doers' (Castells, 1996). Toffler's idea of the consumer who is also an active innovator has been further developed by a number of others (for example, Tapscott and Williams, 2006; Ritzer and Jorgenson, 2010) but the core idea – that the individual consumer has become an important actor in the innovation process – remains the same. The work of von Hippel has explored the important parts played by users of technology in the innovation process (for example, von Hippel, 1988, 2005, 2016). This work has provided a series of detailed insights and much of the conceptual underpinnings for the current understandings of user activity including the lead user (von Hippel, 1986), free revealing (Harhoff et al., 2003), sticky information (von Hippel, 1994), and innovation toolkits (von Hippel and Katz, 2002).

The potential for online communities to become important sources of innovation has come to the fore largely as a result of the emergence and growth of Open Source software. The clear demonstration that online groups were able to produce, maintain and continue to develop highly complex software products (for example, Linux, but there are many more recent examples) was a clear demonstration that (at least in software, and probably other areas as well) producer firms are no longer the sole source of goods and services. The implications of this shift has been explored by a number of authors who have examined what this means for various aspects of the way innovation is managed within modern economies (for example, Lessig, 2005), how this will impact innovation (Leadbeater, 2008), the diminishing role of professional expertise (Keen, 2007), and the economics of this new situation (Tapscott and Williams, 2006) and the potential for individual users to be co-opted into undertaking unpaid work (sometimes called Playbour) within their leisure time (Postigo, 2003). Despite its focus on a series of disparate aspects of this phenomenon the emergence and growth in the importance of online communities of users as producers of new goods, services and knowledge is a recurring theme in this literature. This is a very new phenomenon and remains under-explored but it has been recognised that the aims, processes and outputs of innovation within such communities is likely to be quite different from what would take place in traditional firm-led processes. Paraphrasing Callon and Rabeharisoa (Callon and Rabeharisoa, 2003) this is 'innovation in the wild', innovation that takes place outside of the Research and Development process and where the traditional understandings of the supposed 'rules' of innovation are no longer likely to apply.

The conceptual and theoretical underpinnings of this new world have begun to be explored and concepts like Horizontal User Networks (von Hippel, 2007), 'Social Production' (Benkler, 2007) and the 'User Organisation' (Christian, 2015) have been developed. Each of these approaches seeks to highlight different aspects of this large and complex phenomenon, but they all emphasise the role of online communities as an important source of innovation. This supplements the Schumpeterian account that places the entrepreneur and the firm as the motor of innovation and the source of the creative destruction within capitalist economies (Schumpeter, 1942). Arguably, online innovation communities may in certain circumstances replace the role of the entrepreneur, but in others may simply provide the ideas and inspiration that are the foundation for creativity and subsequent innovative activity.

However, although this book takes as its starting point the emergence of a new and developing source of innovation, it is important to recognise that such activity is not an accurate reflection of what happens most commonly within even the most modern economies. In any account of innovation it is important to recognise that it is far too easy to over-focus on the leading edge and overlook that fact that the bulk of products and services in use will not be at the leading edge and be far more likely to belong to older generations of technology (Edgerton, 2007). This is also likely to apply to every aspect of an economy and the organisations that operate within it, such that many (possibly most?) business models, organisational structures and management approaches will be drawn from earlier generations of industrial organisation and will not reflect the leading edge of practice. Looking inward, it is also likely that many mental models and rules of thumb will tend to be based on long-held, possibly outdated, ideas and experience.[1] The Innovation Opportunity Space is designed to move us to a new starting point and open up a new understanding of innovation possibilities involving external groups.

NOTE

1. Indeed, the eminent British economist John Maynard Keynes observed that 'ideas . . . are more powerful than is commonly understood. Indeed the world is ruled by little else. Practical men, who believe themselves to be quite exempt from any intellectual influences, are usually the slaves of some defunct economist. Madmen in authority, who hear voices in the air, are distilling their frenzy from some academic scribbler of a few years back' (Keynes, 1936, p. 383).

2. Innovation pioneers: the essential role of users, online communities and the crowd

Stephen Flowers and Ming Dong

2.1 INTRODUCTION

Users, online communities and the crowd show us the way to a new future, to a new way of seeing the world. The work of these innovation pioneers starts with a want, a need, an unmet desire that is then combined with the means to do something about it. There is likely to be much latent innovation in the world – unmet wants, needs and desires that may never be fulfilled because there are not the resources to do so. However, when unmet wants, needs and desires are put together with the relevant resources, an innovation pioneer is created.

This often starts with a bold, creative, energetic and well-resourced individual – someone who wants to change the world, to make a difference, to make something. They may wish to make money from their efforts, or they may be motivated to try and make the world a better place. At one time, in the years before the Internet, such individuals would labour long and hard and the creation of a community of like-minded individuals would grow only slowly, if at all. History is littered with examples of brilliant minds who never saw their ideas taken up. But that was then. Today, bold, creative, energetic and well-resourced people can share their ideas, link to like-minded people and either build or join an online community that will help develop their ideas.

To borrow a term from economics, the barriers to entry for innovation participation have been lowered dramatically: more people are now involved in innovation than ever before. But this involvement is often largely absent from our everyday lives, often existing only as invisible palaces of software to which only the initiated gain access. This is a democratic and meritocratic world in which you can, if you so wish, become involved, with hierarchy and prestige largely the result of effort and contribution. But just like any human endeavour, such efforts require a wide range of people and skills – most or all of which will be available from users, online communities and the crowd.

Although much of the writing and comment about innovation is largely focused on commercial innovation, there is another source of innovation – innovation for one's community, and recent history has provided many examples of this form of activity. Indeed, it can be argued that the emergence of the Internet has provided us with an unrivalled window into this world. Of course, most column-inches in newspapers are devoted to the comings and goings of commercial innovation, and despite the Internet facilitating the emergence of entirely new firms whose relentless focus is on exploiting their commercial innovations, there are many more smaller more community-focused initiatives out there. This chapter will explore how we think about innovation and how our perspective on what is occurring may be distorted so that we struggle to see what is in front of our eyes – the emerging new world of innovation.

2.2   INNOVATION PIONEERS

The world is full of needs that cannot be satisfied and Innovation Pioneers are the small group that have the means to do something about it. In this context such Innovation Pioneers will often, at least in the first instance, not be driven by commercial issues but will focus rather on the need, challenge or simply the opportunity. In many cases they will not be commercially-minded at all and simply want to make their part of the world a better place. As a result, whilst this form of 'pioneer' innovation contains examples of ideas that have gone on to be commercialised, it also contains many instances of innovations that are simply offered to the wider community at no cost. In some cases such innovations may be actively protected from commercialisation, whilst in others they may be non-commercial by their very nature.

Pioneering innovative activity often takes place out of mainstream sight and involves a wide array of individuals, groups and communities who have mobilised to tackle a problem, achieve a goal or meet a challenge. These problems, goals and challenges may often be pretty niche and, in many cases, appear slightly irrelevant to the outsider, but such activity can involve the highly skilled contributions of thousands of volunteers and has become an important aspect of the wider innovation story within many economies.

Despite the disparate nature of the innovative activity that takes place, the two factors that are common to all Innovation Pioneers are that they possess both a desired end – a problem, goal or challenge – and also have the means to do something about it. Innovation Pioneers can be found amongst users of existing goods and services, but they may also be true pioneers and go on to create things that are are not available commercially. As a group, and depending on the end they wish to pursue, Innovation

Pioneers may be composed of a varying mix of users of existing goods and services, members of online communities, and elements of the larger crowd of Internet users who wish to offer assistance. The precise composition of these three groups will clearly vary according to the end that is being pursued, and how close a group of pioneers is to achieving their desired end. However, it may be that the nature of the desired end is quite small and tightly defined such that it does not permit wider involvement, or the Innovation Pioneers involved may be highly individualistic and have no wish to reach out to others, with the result that pioneering efforts may simply be undertaken by a group of one. Such individuals, often dismissively called hobbyists, may be outliers but will often be passionate about what they want to do, possessed of many ideas, skills and abilities and are likely to be an essential part of the larger grouping of Innovation Pioneers.

In this context what we are faced with is not a simple category in which everyone looks much the same – for example, they are all users of the same commercial good or service – rather we are presented with an innovation ecosystem that has within it users, online communities, and elements of the wider crowd, all of whom are collaborating around a shared goal. Within this ecosystem there will be varying degrees of skill, ability and commitment, and hence varying degrees of contribution, to the shared goal. In some cases the level of commitment displayed may result in a high degree of momentum so that the shared goal is realised quickly, whilst in others momentum may falter and the desired end may not be achieved. However, even when a new good or service has been created, a key challenge remains: the widespread adoption by its intended user base. This is a challenging stage for all forms of innovation and the failure rate, even for commercial goods and services, is high. The same challenges (although possibly not the same odds) are likely to apply to many different forms of innovation activity, so that for every Wikipedia success there are likely to be many earlier systems that did not reach a critical mass of users. However, the cases presented later in this chapter are all examples of successful innovations that emerged from pioneering activity.

2.3 FOCUSING ON EXTERNAL RESOURCES AND VALUE

The case studies that will be presented in this book show that the novel business models built around the new forms of innovation that have emerged are about two things: *resources* and *value*. Put simply, many organisations have begun to learn how to create commercial value by drawing on a range of external resources, often at little or no cost.

Structuring ideas into a 2x2 matrix is a good way to crystallise any

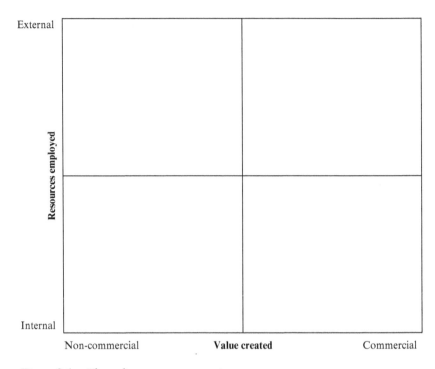

Figure 2.1   The value resources matrix

analysis and considering Figure 2.1 helps to focus on these two factors: Resources and Value. Resources include such valuable things as time, money, knowledge, experience, practised routines and processes, but can also include things like ideas, suggestions, proposals, prototypes, comments and videos. Value includes commercial and monetary factors, but also social, communitarian and reputational aspects. Further focusing on the sources of the resources employed (do they come from within the firm, or are they obtained externally?) and the value created (is it commercial and monetary value, or is the value social, communitarian and reputational in nature) enables a structured analysis to be undertaken.

For simplicity the four quadrants have been labelled in Figure 2.2 and it is clear that there is a division between what we shall term Old Form and New Form innovation. In essence, Old Form innovation is characterised by its use of internal resources and processes, whilst New Form innovation makes use of external resources drawn from a range of sources. Although straightforward, the distinction has huge implications for how firms organise themselves, how they are managed and how they create and capture value – in other words, their business model. The terms 'Old' and

---

BOX 2.1   OLD FORM AND NEW FORM INNOVATION

The way in which new ideas, goods and services are created continues to evolve and the ease with which individuals and groups can communicate using the Internet means that innovators are able to access a far wider spread of resources. This represents a major shift away from older models of innovation in which resources needed to be owned and controlled by the innovating organisation. This developing reality is the result of a number of factors including of the emergence of the Open Source approach, a resource-rich environment, and the acceptance of Internet communication norms. This shift has unlocked a new and largely untapped source of resources and value and resulted in the creation of both commercial and community-based organisational models that make use of these resources and access this value. This is New Form Innovation. However, much of the industrial world and the majority of businesses still create value by owning and controlling the resources they require to innovate. This is Old Form Innovation. However, many firms that have grown and prospered in the Old Form Innovation world have developed approaches that enable them to access external resources held by users, online communities and the crowd. Indeed, as the case studies throughout this book show, some commercial organisations have developed entirely new types of business model on such resources.

Old Form Innovation is an approach to the creation of new and improved goods and services based on the ownership and control of the required resources. This has been the dominant model of innovation for a very long time and many of the largest and most successful commercial firms are based on this model. This is a widespread commercial model with financial value flowing back to the resource owners.

New Form Innovation makes use of a wide range of external resources in order to create new goods and services. These resources will tend to be provided by external groups like users, online user communities and members of the crowd and innovating organisations have developed processes for creating value in this new context. The forms of value created will tend to be quite broad and may be financial but may also be social, reputational or communitarian in nature.

'New' should also not be taken to imply 'bad' or 'good', but rather refer to the quite different approaches to innovation that may be selected by different types of organisation. Many of the largest and most successful firms in the world are the result of Old Form innovation and operate according to an Old Form Innovation business model. However, as will be explored throughout this book, there are many new organisations that base their operation on New Form innovation and have developed a New Form innovation business model. This is a fundamentally new phenomenon that means that organisations are able to create entirely novel business models without the need to own the resources they require to operate.

As we have seen, these new models of innovation can create a huge

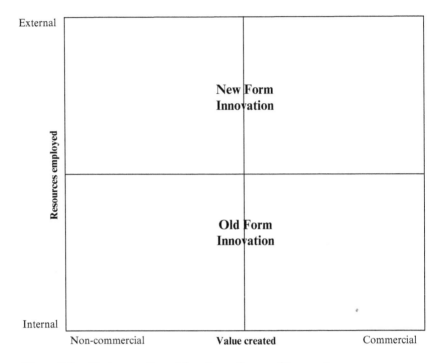

Figure 2.2   Understanding old and new forms of innovation

amount of value for those involved, but they may not necessarily be designed to operate commercially. In some areas – for example, digital information-based systems – the skills and technologies required are now widespread, and the barriers to entry relatively low, with the result that there are many examples of New Form innovations that are non-commercial.

2.4   OLD FORM INNOVATION

Old Form innovation typically involves the creation and development of products and services for commercial ends. This form of innovation tends to monopolise popular thought and modern economies have many incentives, tax breaks and protections to promote this activity. The most prominent firms in the world have often based their success on Old Form commercial innovation and invest large amounts of money in the ongoing research and development (R&D) required to maintain their success. Such firms will often cite their large number of patents (a form of time-limited protection for their work) as evidence of their success, and introduce a stream of new products and services into the marketplace. This is perhaps most apparent in consumer electronics (for example, mobile phones), but is widespread across all sectors of our economies and Old Form Commercial Innovation remains the dominant force for the creation of new products and services in modern industrial economies. Firms like Apple, Samsung, Microsoft, and Dyson are all examples of organisations that have benefitted from their own commercial R&D operations, although we could also add manufacturing firms like Airbus, Boeing, Rolls-Royce, Pratt and Witney, BMW, Ford and Jaguar Land Rover. To this list we could also add pharmaceutical firms like GlaxoSmithKline, Pfizer, AstraZeneca, Novartis, Roche, Bayer and Novo Nordisk. Although these are impressive lists these firms represent only a small sample of the many thousands of firms that operate within the Old Form commercial approach, all of whom share an industrial approach towards the creation of new products and services. What this means in practice is that such firms operate a series of systematic R&D processes that are designed to produce and refine new ideas, designs and knowledge that can be commercially exploited. Although this is now common practice in many industries one of the earliest and most famous exponents of this highly commercial approach was Thomas Alva Edison (Figure 2.3).

What we now see around us is the commercial, legal and political

Figure 2.3   Picture of Thomas Edison[1]

BOX 2.2   THOMAS EDISON AND MENLO PARK

Menlo Park in New Jersey was the location selected by Thomas Edison in 1876 to be the site of his research laboratory. This was close enough to New York to enable access when required, but also far enough away to provide for a focused environment for the work that was to be undertaken there. Menlo Park was the one of the world's first commercial Research and Development (R&D) laboratories and it was from Menlo Park that Edison was to invent both the Phonograph and a commercially viable incandescent electric light bulb filament. Initially demonstrating his incandescent bulbs within his laboratory, in one of the first large-scale demonstrations of the possible use of electricity for public lighting, a street in the town of Menlo Park was also illuminated, attracting large crowds in the process. Although the Menlo Park laboratory was only in operation for the ten years between 1876 and 1886 it was the systematic organisation of the scientific R&D activities to the solution of highly targeted commercial ends that mark it out as a landmark institution. Edison was also very careful to ensure that all his creations were protected by patents and such was the flow of invention and innovation from Thomas Edison's laboratory that he was nicknamed 'The Wizard of Menlo Park' by the media of the time.[2]

---

infrastructure that has evolved over many years to support, promote and protect innovation for commercial purposes. The creation of new ideas, designs and knowledge for commercial ends is likely as old as civilisation itself, and examples of modern approaches can be found in many places. For example, in order to attract and support innovative people and industries by offering legal protection for their inventions the Venetian state began offering patents as early as 1474,[3] creating in the process the first statutory patent system in the world. Similarly, examples of systematic R&D processes are found in many firms active during the Industrial Revolution including Wedgwood (ceramics), Boulton and Watt (steam engines), Abraham Darby (iron and brass), and Richard Arkwright (weaving). Since this period in industrial history modern systems and processes for protecting commercial innovations have been become increasingly sophisticated and these are explored in greater detail in Chapter 5. However, the widespread focus on commercial innovation has tended to throw a shadow over the part played by the users of technologies in the creation of new products and services, something that is very important to many firms. For example Elekta Medical Systems, a Swedish medical technologies firm, works extensively with hospitals and the medical staff that use its technologies to co-develop new systems and services (see Box 2.3). This is now a widespread industrial practice and although users may not always create new products, services or technologies, they can often drive the direction of their subsequent development. This is perhaps most easily

---

BOX 2.3 ELEKTA MEDICAL SYSTEMS' LINEAR ACCELERATOR

Elekta Medical Systems works in the healthcare sector and produces a range of high-technology systems and services for treating cancer and disorders of the brain. Elekta is a Swedish company with its headquarters in Stockholm, but employs around 3,500 worldwide, including in the UK. Elekta's digital linear accelerator is a world-leading device for the treatment of cancer and is built in Crawley in South East England. In order to develop and refine such high-technology medical devices Elekta maintains ongoing partnerships with a small number of research-intensive hospitals in different parts of the world. As part of Elekta's Research and Development process the users of technological solutions, in this case the linear accelerator, play a key role in refining and co-developing final technologies. Elekta can also support external, user-led, research by providing access to research hardware or software, information, or research funding. In return for this, Elekta benefits by access to the intellectual property and research results that are generated.[4]

---

seen in the creation and subsequent development of modern technologies, the mobile phone.

The mobile phone is an example of a complex modern device that integrates many different technologies and is simultaneously both a product and a service. Although mobile phones were launched commercially in the early 1980s it was not until the early 2000s that they began to be ubiquitous devices. By this time the short messaging service (SMS) based on messages up to 160 alphanumeric characters in length had become widely adopted by users and led to the development of new compressed ways of communicating, with spin-off services like Twitter being launched on the back of its popularity. The creation of small images to express emotions was another user-driven spin-off from this form of usage, starting with simple text-based images and moving onto the creation of complex emoticons, with many services now offering extensive libraries of emoticons that each seek to convey a subtle variation in emotional impact. Similarly, the addition of cameras to mobile phones led to many new forms of behaviour and commercial spin-offs like Instagram and other social media services. The emergence of front-facing cameras, and their increasing quality, was in direct response to user behaviour and the emergence of the 'selfie' is a good example of innovation in which users have driven the direction in which a technology continues to be developed. Although at the time of writing the 'selfie' is hugely dominant, with spin-off devices like the 'selfie stick' becoming widely used, it is important to realise that this form of user-driven innovation is continually evolving and will doubtless continue to develop into new and unexpected areas. The patterns of user-driven innovation that are evident with the mobile phone is a useful way into a phenomenon that can often be lost in the context of commercially focused activity – the role of challenge and fun in determining the direction of innovation.

However, much of the activity around mobile phones remains commercial innovation that has been driven by the innovative behaviours of users, with the final decisions on the form and function of commercial products being chosen by the firms that make them, not the users. In this form of commercial innovation the final decisions on form and function will always be made by the commercial supplier and, as a result, there is always likely to be a gap between what users really want and what suppliers are able and willing to provide. As will be explored below, this is the gap in which Innovation Pioneers tend to operate.

2.5   NEW FORM INNOVATION

Some elements of New Form Innovation are driven by the wish to make some small part of the world a better place – innovation that is not commercially motivated but rather driven by the desire to provide a service to the wider community. This form of innovation has strong links to the traditions of charitable and voluntary contribution that has taken many forms and is present (in one way or another) in many areas of modern life. Such innovation tends to have a very different character from its commercial cousin and operates in areas in which businesses are unwilling or unable to operate or in which there is little or no money to be made. This form of innovation will create huge value to those involved but will depend on the efforts of volunteers, sponsors and others to cover the cost base of its operations. This form of innovation is also quite distinct from the many 'free' services that are provided by large operators like Google who have a commercial interest in user data or attracting Internet traffic to their core systems. Community activity is simply the result of individuals and groups who want to make some small part of the world a better place and the examples illustrated below explore how this form of innovation has emerged.

Non-commercial New Form Innovation tends to be most visible in the digital arena, with many non-commercial digital products and services emerging from this source. Software is perhaps best known for its wide array of Open Source projects[5] but the practices and norms associated with that world have had a wide impact on many other forms of community activities, not least because software is often now at the core of many innovations. New Form Innovation will often (although not always) be liberated from the rules, regulations, standards, structures and expectations to which commercial operators have to respond. It can operate effectively in areas that will often be off-limits in commercial terms and, in the process, may develop a distinctly edgy feel and character. If the underlying agenda of commercial innovation is simply to make money, arguably the agenda of many examples of New Form Innovation is to change the world for the better. Of course, defining what is better in this context may have within it a political stance and many of the examples shown below may be considered to be challenging the status quo in some form. These examples are of great interest not simply because they challenge the status quo, but because they have attracted sufficient supporters and users to be widely adopted and, as such, provide a window into areas that are either closed to, or have been overlooked, by the commercial mainstream. However, as will be seen below, in many cases non-commercial and commercial offerings can operate in parallel by simply occupying different niches and appealing to different groups.

However, many of the ideas, norms and practices have been employed as the basis for the commercialisation of New Form Innovation, as shown in Figure 2.4. Not only does New Form Innovation continue to provide many new products and services, it also acts as a feedstock for a large number of commercial innovations that also depend on external resources for their existence.

The following are all good examples of non-commercial New Form Innovation. Freecycle (see Box 2.4) was created as a simple community solution to the problem of disposing of the things that you no longer want, simply by giving them away. Similarly, Parkrun (see Box 2.4) is a grassroots initiative focused on running that grew into an international organisation that stages weekly 5k runs in a number of countries around the world. OpenStreetMap is a mapping initiative that has been developed by a large community of contributors that integrate a range of data sources with a special focus on local knowledge. In contrast, mySociety is an e-democracy project that collects and publishes data on democratic processes with the intention of enabling citizens to improve the public realm and hold their representatives to account. However, in the face of a devastating tsunami and the collapse of infrastructure, the Safecast system took the idea of communitarian innovation to the next level by creating an entire radiological monitoring and mapping system.

It will be clear that New Form Innovation covers a wide range of activities and often sits alongside mainstream commercial activity, it is important to emphasise the distinct difference between commercial and communitarian innovation. In essence, the former is concerned with

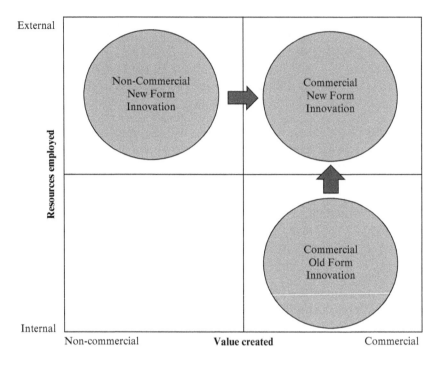

*Figure 2.4   Understanding the emergence of Commercial New Form
               Innovation*

money, whilst the latter is concerned with making the world a better place, although both may seek to offer services in similar areas. Looking across the continuum it is clear that innovation will often emerge in the gaps between the commercial and the community-based.

2.6   CONCLUDING REMARKS

Innovation is now a far more complex phenomenon than it once was and it is no longer the sole preserve of traditional firms and other commercial providers. The creation and growth of the Internet and the widespread diffusion of Internet norms and behaviours means that innovation has been opened up to many more groups than it ever has been. In addition, these groups can reach out to interested others, interact online, coordinate their actions and draw on their own resources to create the new goods and services that can satisfy an unmet need. Innovation has escaped from the R&D lab and is now out there, 'in the wild', and the

---

BOX 2.4 NON-COMMERCIAL NEW FORM INNOVATION: FREECYCLE/PARKRUN

Each of these cases of non-commercial New Form Innovation was created in response to a wish to change the world for the better in some small way. The first two of these examples focus on lifestyle and aim to have an impact on our use of resources and support running at the local level. In contrast, OpenStreetMap has the grander aim of creating a free and editable map of the entire world that is free from corporate and proprietary restrictions. All three are good examples of the way in which some forms of innovations need to grow in scale and draw in a large number of active members in order to be successful. Although building scale and drawing in contributions from individual users and the crowd is clearly important, the heart of any innovation remains the core idea.

Freecycle is a free to use network that acts as an intermediary for those who wish to dispose of unwanted possessions by giving them away at no cost to the recipient – recycling for free. Founded on a very small scale in Arizona in 2003 it has since gone global and now has over 9 million members organised within more than 5,000 town- or district-based groups around the world. Members can register at no cost and can post brief details of either what they want or what they want to give away, with viewing and collection being arranged separately between the parties, so that it is not dissimilar to eBay, craigslist or any of the online marketplaces that exist. However, the main difference of Freecycle is that it acts as a clearing house for things that are no longer wanted and that can be gifted to others. Conceived as an online alternative to old possessions going to landfill, it has developed a niche around the non-financial transfer, or gifting, of goods. Freecycle is a registered non-profit based in Tucson Arizona and depends upon a large network of volunteers for its day-to-day operations.[6]

Parkrun is a free, largely volunteer run, initiative that organises 5km timed running events every week on Saturday mornings. Started in the UK it is free to sign up and since its creation in 2004 its 3,656 clubs have organised more than 61,000 events in nearly 400 locations for something like 1,000,000 runners. Parkrun events have also been organised in many other countries including the USA, South Africa, Italy, Russia and Australia. The operation of Parkrun is intentionally simple, requiring runners to register only once and take part wherever they want to. The identifying barcode that each runner receives is at the heart of the operation and enables data to be easily collected on participation and times, so that every participant can keep track of their performances. Relying on volunteer support at the local level Parkrun has also attracted support from a number of commercial and other partners, including the International Amateur Athletics Federation (IAAF).[7]

---

implications of this change surround us all every day. But much of the thinking around innovation is trapped in old ways of thinking, old ways of working.

This chapter has begun the process of opening up our eyes to the new

BOX 2.5   NON-COMMERCIAL NEW FORM INNOVATION:
USHAHIDI/SAFECAST

These are three very different examples of non-commercial New Form Innovation that are all designed to shape and influence the civic space by providing the kind of detailed information that is not easily available. In this way each one of these innovative systems throws new light on the processes and outcomes of government and the political process, and through this openness applies pressure on politicians, governments and government agencies. Such systems are some distance away from commercial systems and are, by their very nature, more the core territory of non-commercial New Form Innovation activity. In common with the lifestyle innovation outlined above these three systems also rely on the core/volunteer model of operation that is common with many information-based systems.

Ushahidi was created in the aftermath of the political violence that followed the 2007 presidential election in Kenya as a means of collecting eyewitness reports of incidents and publishing where they took place on a map. The word Ushahidi is Swahili and translates to 'testimony' and the approach is based on the core/volunteer model outlined above in which reports come in from their crowd of volunteers via a range of sources including SMS, email and Twitter, before being analysed, geolocated and published. Ushahidi's systems have been deployed over 90,000 times, received over 6.5 million reports or 'testimonies', and has been used in many countries around the world. In addition to their core open source systems Ushahidi also offers services to help firms and others to map and visualise complex datasets. Based in Nairobi, Ushahidi partners with many international organisations and has received many awards for its work.[8]

Safecast[9] was established in response to the 11 April 2011 tsunami in Japan and the subsequent meltdown at the Fukushima Daiichi nuclear power plant. Following this disaster and widespread devastation there was a lack of accurate and reliable radiological information and local populations had no way of knowing how dangerous the environment had become. What followed was swift international action by a group of concerned individuals to respond to the crisis that formed the foundation for the creation of Safecast. This involved the rapid production and deployment of GPS-enabled Geiger counters to the volunteers whose data was mapped and published. Safecast now styles itself as a 'global volunteer-centred citizen-science project working to empower people with data about their environments' and has expanded its reach to include air quality as well as radiological information. The collection of data is at the heart of Safecast and it makes available a huge dataset of radiological information that contains more than 35 million individual measurements. Safecast is based in Tokyo but relies on a large and growing group of international supporters.[10]

world of innovation that has grown up, largely unnoticed, around us. Whilst the old ways of creating new goods and services are characterised by internal resources often being applied to commercial ends – Old Form Innovation, the new world of innovation draws on external resources, often

---

BOX 2.6 NON-COMMERCIAL NEW FORM INNOVATION:
WIKILEAKS/THE PIRATE BAY

WikiLeaks and The Pirate Bay are two prominent examples of extreme New Form Innovation in which the creators, supporters and users of the services are in direct conflict with commercial and policy interests. This stance is highly controversial and the actions may be illegal but given the nature of the Internet is very hard or impossible to stop.

WikiLeaks specialises in analysing and placing in the public domain large datasets of confidential or restricted materials concerning spying, war and corruption. Going some way beyond systems like mySociety (see above), WikiLeaks achieved worldwide notoriety for its handling of the Edward Snowden leak of many thousands of US National Security Agency documents and the subsequent revelations concerning US intelligence activities. Linked to more than 100 important media organisations worldwide it has received widespread recognition for its work. A brief review of the leaked documents they publish includes everything from emails from Sony Pictures Entertainment, to transcripts from a parliamentary enquiry into National Security Agency activities in Germany to diplomatic cables from Saudi diplomats. Given the nature of this system, although the core group of activists is widely known, the scale and scope of the volunteers who provide the leaked material is unclear.[11]

The Pirate Bay goes one step further than WikiLeaks and is an example of a New Form Innovation in which both the core and the volunteers involved would prefer to remain anonymous. Although technically The Pirate Bay is simply an online index of digital materials that can be downloaded anonymously at no cost, the fact that most of the digital content is copyrighted music and films places it, and its users, in direct conflict with firms and governments around the world. Founded in 2003 by a Swedish anti-copyright organisation The Pirate Bay has been one of the main sources online for free copyright music and films for many years. As a result it has been a target for firms and governments and many attempts have been made to permanently close it down. To date these attempts have largely been unsuccessful, although individual members of staff have been successfully prosecuted and jailed. The Pirate Party in Sweden, and its many international spin-offs, has no direct links to The Pirate Bay but does focus on issues including civil rights, copyright and patent law.[12]

---

applied to non-commercial end – New Form Innovation. This distinction is intended to help us perceive the many changes in innovation that are now taking place around us and, clearly, is not intended to link 'Old' and 'New' with 'Bad' and 'Good'. Old Form innovation has brought the world many fundamental and positive innovations and, no doubt, will continue to do so. However, New Form innovation has opened up entirely new vistas of opportunity in which new goods and services can emerge from a combination of resources drawn from many different sources.

BOX 2.7   COMMERCIAL NEW FORM INNOVATION: THE GEEKBRIDGE DRONE/VALVE CORPORATION

Geekbridge Drone: The part played by users in innovation is perhaps most effective when a strong interest or need is combined with the innovation tools to do something about it – this is how the Geekbridge Drone was created. Hiye Electro Co., the manufacturer of the Geekbridge Drone, is a medium-sized electronic remote control designer and manufacturer located in Hangzhou, China. They have been designing and manufacturing remote controls for over 20 years and the decision was made to develop and mass produce an affordable high performance drone, due to the strong interest of the son of the founder – an enthusiastic drone user. Although Hiye did not have the required drone technologies in-house it was able to draw on the skills and technologies of a large group of other enthusiasts (some of whom were user-firms) by opening up the development process. The propeller, control module, motors, camera module and shell were designed and supplied on a collaborative basis and combined with Hiye's core manufacturing capabilities to design and create a product in 15 months – from initial conception to manufacturing.

Valve Corporation is a US-based video game developer that made its name with the Half-Life and Counterstrike series of PC-based games. Founded in 1996 the firm grew to become a highly successful video game enterprise and was one of the first commercial organisations to pioneer mechanisms to draw on the skills and expertise of their extensive user base. Video games, especially PC-based video games, provide an unusual context in which the users of such games develop an intimate product knowledge and, in some cases, are able to provide detailed insights into how the game could be improved. Exceptionally, some users possess the resources necessary (knowledge, skills and so on) to re-programme the game and make their own improvements, which can then be shared with other users online. Such user-developed improvements (often called 'mods', a compression of the term 'modifications') are quite common in some forms of video games and, as a whole, the industry has embraced this phenomenon. In the case of Valve Corporation one of their major games (Counter-Strike) was originally a full mod created by highly skilled users of their video game Half-Life, with Valve subsequently acquiring the intellectual property of the new game and employing the talented user who created it. Valve were later to launch an online distribution platform, Steam, and provide users with an official means to create, share (and potentially profit from) their work. This is a huge, although largely hidden, activity with more than 100 million gamers registered for this one site and a very active user-based 'modding' industry.

However, this book is concerned with exploring the commercialisation of the ideas and practices that underpin New Form Innovation in which firms have developed approaches that allow them to create enormous commercial value from external resources. As we will see in the cases that are included in the rest of this book, the business models that have been developed are based on resources which are held by users, online communities and the crowd, something that may change as these models develop further. However, such models only succeed by developing approaches that allow the value that is created – financial and non-financial – to be shared in some form. How this occurs will be explored in far more depth in the remainder of this book.

NOTES

1. Public domain image downloaded from Wikipedia, https://en.wikipedia.org/wiki/Thomas_Edison#/media/File:Thomas_Edison2.jpg.
2. More information on Thomas Edison and Menlo Park can be found in Stross, R. (2007) *The Wizard of Menlo Park: How Thomas Alva Edison Invented the Modern World*, New York: Three Rivers Press.
3. Ackroyd, P. (2010) *Venice Pure City*, London: Vintage Books.
4. More information can be obtained from www.elekta.com.
5. For a brief insight into the scale and scope of this activity it is worth taking a look at SourceForge, probably the main repository for open source projects and software. The scale of the activity revealed is staggering, with thousands of forum posts, tens of thousands of software code updates and tens of millions of software downloads occurring every week.
6. For more information refer to www.freecycle.org.
7. To get involved, or for more information, refer to www.parkrun.com.
8. For more information, refer to www.ushahidi.com.
9. With thanks to Peter Svensson of Vinnova for introducing this case.
10. For more information refer to blog.safecast.org.
11. For more information refer to wikileaks.org.
12. For more information refer to The Pirate Bay website or its mirror websites if the main site is blocked.

3. Exploring the changing landscape of innovation: the rise of users, online communities and the crowd

Stephen Flowers and Martin Meyer

3.1 INTRODUCTION

Users, online communities and the crowd are not just a target market, but are also a source of valuable resources. Many firms have learnt to make money by routinely drawing on these resources and some business models now depend on users, online communities and the crowd to do some of the 'work' associated with innovation. Users, online communities and the crowd are no longer passive recipients for producers but will often actively engage in all of the stages required to bring a product or service to the market. But this was not always so, and this chapter will explore the background to what has been a major shift in the involvement of such groups to become an important aspect of commercial business models.

This chapter will draw on many years of research to provide a detailed picture of who users are, what they do, why they do it, and how they can be valuable. Key concepts and ideas from research and practice will be outlined and explored and a series of short case studies will be used to illustrate key ideas. As research follows practice (often only very slowly) and external involvement in innovation is continuing to develop the chapter will also draw on recent ideas and examples in mainstream business and management to provide as clear a picture as possible of this evolving phenomenon.

3.2 IDENTIFYING THE USER

In a simple world innovation would be made up of two main groups, producers and users. Producers (usually firms) creating goods and services, whilst users would acquire (usually by buying) these goods and services so that they can make use of them. This is a really useful starting point, and makes a clear distinction between those who produce goods and services

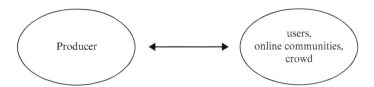

Figure 3.1   The classical producer/user relationship

(producers) and those who acquire them (users). In order to understand the evolving world of innovation it is very useful to be able to refer to these two simple definitions of user and producer (see Figure 3.1):

> Producer – an organised operation (*usually a firm*) that supplies goods or services.

> User – an individual unit that acquires (*usually by buying*) and uses goods and services.

At the most basic level users are individuals that make use of goods and services in order to obtain some benefit. They may do this as part of their everyday lives (in which case they are an individual consumer) and they may share their ideas with other consumers as part of an online community. Of course many individuals will make use of goods and services (for example, capital goods, commercial services) as an employee of a firm (in which case they act on behalf of the firm) and in this case we will also refer to the firm as the user. So, individual consumers will be users of consumer goods and services, and firms will be users of commercial goods and services. All producers, but especially small ones, have a tendency to specialise and it is common to focus on providing goods or services to particular business markets. In such cases the users will be firms. In contrast, the users of producers that focus on consumer markets will be individual consumers, with some firms dealing with both firms and individual consumers. This is illustrated in Figure 3.2. This separation is very useful when trying to make sense of innovation by users as research has shown that the behaviour of firms and consumers can be very different, something that will be explored in more detail later in this chapter.

This is further elaborated in Figure 3.3 which has four main groups within it: two forms of user (user-firms and user-consumers), online communities and the crowd. user-firms are legal entities that are often, but not necessarily, commercial in nature and organised around the supply of products and/or services. By contrast, user-consumers tend to be individuals that acquire products and services for their own use. Both user-firms

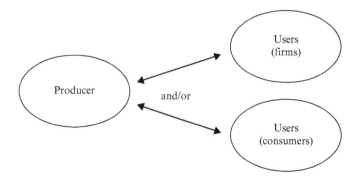

Figure 3.2   Users can be either firms or consumers

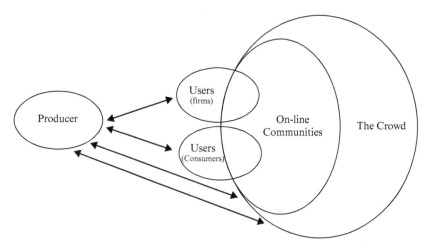

Figure 3.3   Complex linkages between producers, users, online communities
*   and crowds*

and user-consumers may participate in one or more online communities that tend to be focused around particular products, services or interests. In contrast, the crowd (in terms of innovation) is a diffuse, online entity composed of users, experts, fans and volunteer workers that can be the source of expert solutions to problems, feedback, advice, and casual labour.

Of these five groups the user-firm has historically been the object of the most scientific research over a longer period and, as a result, far more is known about the role of firm-based users. Innovation by consumers and online communities is relatively recent and has been the subject of far less research, with the role of the crowd in innovation being the least well understood.

Moving beyond these idealised models it will be no surprise that real life is not quite so compartmentalised or so simple and often presents us with examples that don't fit very well in these straightforward categories – producers who are also users, users who are also producers, producers who co-produce with users, users who co-produce with producers. The case studies in this book explore these complex and evolving relationships, but this chapter is intended to provide an overview of what we know about users of all types. The remainder of this chapter will explore why, in innovation terms, users and the crowd are important and how new forms of innovation are emerging from new types of collaboration.

3.3 USERS' ROLE IN INVENTION AND INNOVATION

In this section we will further explore what it is that makes users so interesting and such a potentially valuable source of ideas, knowledge and innovations. In order to do this we will draw the findings of a body of scientific research that has been built up over many years, as well as insights that have only recently emerged.

Individuals who *use* a good or service will often have ideas about how it can be improved and will sometimes be in a position to see if their ideas work in practice. If these ideas are found to be effective they can result in new or improved products and services. At its simplest level this is how innovation by users happens. Innovation by users is a basic feature of our day-to-day lives and, in addition to the mass of commercial products and services now available, the world is full of things that have been crafted, hacked, or kludged together.[1] These things are not 'products' or 'services' in the formal sense, since they were not created for sale – rather, they are ideas, modifications and inventions made real, that may be widely shared.[2]

This is probably as true now as it has ever been and if we could go back in time it is certain that we would find innovation by users across all types of good and service. However, looking at the scientific literature in this area does not necessarily reflect this common-sense view as much of the early work that noted innovation by users tended to focus on industrial products by user-firms. Partly this was because many scholars at that time were more concerned with industrial development, and partly because it was written before the modern period of mass-produced consumer goods. As a result, the early work in this area tended to focus on user-firms, with work on user-consumers following far later, and work examining the role of online communities and the crowd later still.

The effect of such phases in research is that our understanding of the innovation by users is layered and subtle and draws on work that has explored user-firms, user-consumers, online communities and, most recently the crowd, with the result that this concept is far less developed. The brief review that follows will provide an overview of our understanding of the importance of each of these forms of innovation by users.

3.3.1   Users Invent and Improve Technology

This section will explore how users can improve or invent technologies and will draw on a broad range of research insights that stretch back to the Industrial Revolution in the UK. The main focus of this section is to explore how user-firms innovate and examine the cumulative importance of such innovation activity. The section will draw on insights made by early economists as well as more recent evidence that have explored many of the same issues in the contemporary industrial context.

Innovation by users is not a new phenomenon, and nearly 250 years ago the Scottish moral philosopher and pioneer of political economy, Adam Smith (Figure 3.4), famously observed that 'common workmen' had invented many of the machines that were employed in manufacturing in the 18th century:[3]

Figure 3.4   Adam Smith[4]

A greater part of the machines made use of in those manufactures ... were originally the inventions of some common workman, who, being each of them employed in some very simple operation, naturally turned their thoughts towards finding out easier and readier methods of performing it.

Nearly 60 years later the English polymath and designer of the first programmable computer, Charles Babbage, also noted that 'operative workmen' were perhaps the most successful in 'contriving tools and simplifying processes'[5] in manufacturing. These observations and ideas continued to be developed and more than 100 years later the American economic historian Abbott Payson Usher observed that:

At the lower levels, mechanical invention involves little more than some improvement in the skills required for the making of simple tools ... even the development of relatively complex mechanisms does not seem to involve abstract thought or organized scientific knowledge.[6]

Similarly, in his exploration of 'Useful Knowledge' the contemporary American historian Joel Mokyr noted that many of the technological innovations made in the early part of the Industrial Revolution were not grounded in science and that 'Tacit artisanal savoir faire, experience driven insights, trial and error, and serendipity'[7] were the basis for many novel inventions. By the same token, the Cambridge Economist Ha-Joon Chang has observed that 'the technologies of the industrial revolution ... [were] invented by practical men with good intuition.'[8]

According to these authors, many inventions made during the British Industrial Revolution were not science-based and did not emerge from an R&D system. Simply, this was because the science underlying many of the technologies in use (for example, steam) was not properly understood and the modern system of systematic research and development had yet to be invented. Although it has been argued that the enlightenment played a key role in building the foundations of the science-driven approaches to research that led to many of the advances made from the latter part of the Industrial Revolution,[9] it is not likely that 'practical men' or 'tacit, artisanal savoir faire' has disappeared in the modern context.

Another perspective on the importance of users within the processes of invention and innovation can be obtained from the work of American economist Jacob Schmookler. As one of the first researchers to explore the economics of technological innovation, he clearly established the importance of users in this process. In Schmookler's view the role of the user was key as it was only they who would recognise, and have to live with, the defects of a technology in the context of its intended application. Linking this to the waves of investment and diffusion in firms, he noted that:

[O]ne would expect that the new equipment introduced during expansion will exhibit defects under special, local circumstances, or otherwise evoke dissatisfaction in the breasts of inventive men. Thus ... relatively rapid technical change may stimulate invention among those who make, sell, use or service the new equipment.[10]

But not all inventions are the same and Schmookler distinguished between new to the world inventions and a lesser form of invention termed a subinvention. He defined an invention as a 'prescription for a producable product or operable process so new as not to have been "obvious to one skilled in the art" at the time the idea was put forward'.[11] By contrast a subinvention was an obvious change to a product or process that results from 'relatively straightforward applications of engineering knowledge and from acts of skill by workers, supervisors, [and] users'.[12] This form of low-level invention, subinvention, includes the routine innovation that arises from a 'modification which a skilled practitioner in the art can be expected to make in a product or process to adapt it to minor changes in the materials, functions, site and so on',[13] broadly according with American sociologist S. Colum Gilfillan's notion of a 'routine invention'.[14]

Similar observations were made by the American economist Richard Nelson, who noted that (within firms) 'most inventions are based on common practical experience and knowledge of persons well acquainted with a particular industry or a particular machine'.[15] English scholar of Science and Technology Policy, Keith Pavitt, in his work on the sectoral patterns of technical change also commented that firms in assembly and continuous process industries tend to concentrate relatively more of their innovative resources on process innovations[16] and observed that production and process engineers can:

[D]evelop the capacity to identify technical imbalances and bottlenecks which, once corrected, enable improvements in productivity. Eventually they are able to specify or design new equipment that will improve productivity still further.[17]

From this discussion it is clear that innovation by the users of process technologies in firms – Smith's common workmen, Babbage's operative workmen, and Pavitt's process engineers – is a well-established phenomenon. However, from the language employed to describe their activities – 'routine inventions' or 'subinventions' – it is easy to take away the impression that their innovative activities are less important than those that emerge from R&D labs. Certainly, the terms applied would suggest that this is the case. However, the work of the American economists Samuel Hollander and Fritz Machlup provide some interesting insights into the relative importance of these different forms and sources of innovation.

In his work Hollander was provided with access to detailed cost and investment data concerning the production of rayon by Du Pont across a number of different factories, covering a period of some 30 years. This in-depth study enabled him to identify and measure the contribution of different sources of improvement towards the overall efficiency of each factory. In line with previous work in this area Hollander distinguished between major and minor technical changes, noting that although major technical changes may be considered 'difficult' to those skilled in the pertinent arts, and minor changes 'simple', minor changes are likely to be occurring more or less continuously.[18] The cumulative effect of this continuous regime of minor technical changes, punctuated by episodic major changes, was that minor technical changes had a far greater overall impact on production efficiency. In his study the minor technical changes based on simple innovations undertaken by plant personnel, accounted for over two-thirds of the unit cost reductions attributable to technical change in the plants studied.[19] Similarly, in his study of the production and distribution of knowledge in the United States, Fritz Machlup noted that a 'succession of many minor improvements add up to a big advance in technology'[20] and that 'the sum total of all minor improvements, each too small to be called an invention, has contributed to the increase in productivity more than the great inventions'.[21]

Returning to the modern economic context, recent studies have reported that the kind of user-firm innovation that we have been examining continues to take place, with firms routinely modifying and creating technologies. Although the way in which these activities are described has changed (minor inventions or subinventions = modifications; new to the world inventions = creations) research suggests that firms remain a fertile location for such innovation. Certainly, the evidence indicates innovation by user-firms is widespread and likely to be a valuable source of innovative activity. It is clear that, when faced with innovation challenges, users within firms either modify or create technologies in order to solve the problems they face. This form of problem-solving by user-firms is likely a standard feature of many commercial contexts and, as we have seen, it is well documented as a phenomenon. However, this form of innovation is paradoxical in that although it depends on rare and specialist forms of knowledge, users will sometimes freely share their ideas without payment. It is this aspect of the user innovation phenomenon that we will now explore.

3.3.2   Users Develop, and Sometimes Share, Specialist Insights

Prior to the emergence of user innovation as a distinct area of enquiry writers had observed that the user, rather than the supplier, of a product tended to be in a better position to assess its effectiveness and improve on its performance. This not a recent insight and over two thousand years ago the Greek philosopher Plato noted that in assessing the excellence of a device:

> [T]he user of them must have the greatest experience of them, and he must indicate to the maker the good or bad qualities which develop themselves in use; for example, the flute-player will tell the flute-maker which of his flutes is satisfactory to the performer; he will tell him how he ought to make them, and the other will attend to his instructions.[22]

This is a good illustration of the different forms of information and knowledge that are required to produce or to use a device, and it allows us to apply a new perspective to the phenomenon of innovation by users. It was the ground-breaking work of American innovation scholar Eric von Hippel that began the detailed exploration of innovation by users in the modern era.[23] His work established the conceptual clarity that underpins much of our understanding and provided the sound foundation for the significant subsequent research that has taken place, including the creation and sharing of information. The recognition that users and producers possess distinct forms of information, and that the information possessed by users is hard to transfer is key to understanding the part played by users in innovation. Taking the example of the flute above, there is always likely to be a natural gulf in understanding between producers and users of such things and users will possess far more detailed information concerning their own needs than would a producer. Further, such information is likely to be 'sticky' and potentially difficult for producers to access or, if they can, to draw on effectively.[24] To paraphrase von Hippel: Users . . . are firms or individual consumers that possess information concerned with *using* a product or service, in contrast, manufacturers possess information concerned with creating and *selling* a product or service.[25] It is the gap between this difference in focus that can sometimes make it very hard for producers to fully appreciate user needs and then design and build the products that users really want.

In certain circumstances users will create their own products and services and, in the process, they will often freely share the technical, design and other information concerning how this was achieved. This phenomenon is known as 'free revealing' and has been observed in a range of contexts. Such free exchange of information between innovators has been observed in several settings and was an essential precondition for what became known as 'collective invention'.[26] This open sharing of information between innovators was observed during the Industrial Revolution in UK iron and mining user-firms[27] and led to significant developments in the process technologies in both of these industries. Such sharing of information has also been observed in the early stages of the development of the home computer[28] and powered flight[29] and, for user-firms at least, appears to occur when they:

> [G]enerated technical material as a by-product of their normal investments . . . As long as the rate of investment was high, the rate of experimentation and the discovery of new technical knowledge was also high.[30]

Such free revealing of information can be very valuable for user-firms in an emerging industry since all stand to gain. The usual commercial pressures mean it is not likely to persist over the longer term, but can still be observed in the modern practice of industry benchmarking, where subscribing firms can benefit from the anonymised performance data of peer firms. However, this pattern tends to be quite different for user-consumers as they may have a different commercial orientation and may benefit, both directly and indirectly, from involvement.[31]

3.3.3 Users can Self-organise, Work with Producers or Join the Crowd

Users, especially user-consumers, will often form communities around an interest, product or service. There are many such communities on the Internet and the emergence of online culture and the growth of social media often makes such communities highly visible. This is perhaps most obvious around Open-Source projects, video games, or fan communities, but it is likely that there are few areas of interest remaining for which some form of online community does not already exist. The growth in such online communities amongst user-consumers has led to a re-shaping in the innovation landscape to include online communities and the diffuse, online mass of users, experts, fans and workers that makes up the crowd. Indeed, producer firms are now able to draw on many sources of research and ideas 'provided by various non-commercial actors – the government, universities and charitable foundations. The whole society is now involved in innovation'.[32] The whole society, that is, including users, online communities and the crowd.

One of the most impressive developments of recent years is the emergence and growth of self-organising groups of users. Perhaps the most famous of these is the community that formed around Linux, the PC operating system. The continuous development of the core components of the Linux operating system (sometimes called the kernel) is one of the largest software projects ever undertaken. Initially launched in 1991 the Linux kernel moved from being a small user-led initiative to being a major enterprise that users of all kinds (individuals and firms) were engaged with. Since its creation Linux has undergone continual development with recent versions being the result of major collaborative efforts, with each new release being the work of more than 1,000 programmers based in more than 200 firms. For example, between 2005 and 2013 nearly 10,000 individual programmers (based in over 1,000 firms) contributed to developing the Linux kernel, with each of the new releases containing more than 90,000 changes. Bearing in mind that new releases emerge every 2–3 months this represents a colossal undertaking.[33]

Linux is perhaps the most famous example of a user-led development that self-organised to produce something that has been widely diffused. It is also interesting to note that many of those now involved are *producer* firms that have found that it is in their interest to support an initiative that originally emerged from a user-consumer who was seeking to satisfy his own needs, Linus Torvalds. The complex 'volunteer' organisation we can now observe that supports the development of Linux did not emerge on day one, but has rather evolved over more than 20 years of hard work by a large number of users, both consumers and firms. In this sense the example of Linux is illustrative but is not necessarily representative, and we should seek further examples to better understand how and why users can self-organise to innovate. Some of these examples are to be found elsewhere in this book but the following is a brief summary of a range of cases where users have formed online communities in order to innovate:

> *Audacity* is an open-source audio editor that was designed and developed as part of research project at Carnegie Mellon University. Originally launched in May 2000 it has won many prizes and been downloaded more than 70 million times, Although it was created by two developers, it is now supported by a worldwide network of users[34] and is also obtains finance from donations and advertising.[35]

> *Moodle* is an open-source learning platform that has been designed for use in education and is an example of a service model based around open-source software. The Moodle software is available for free download, the project as a whole is led and coordinated by a commercial firm that derives income from a network of firms that sell services to Moodle users.[36]

> *Vuze* is a BitTorrent client that is used to transfer digital files using the BitTorrent communications protocol. It was originally released in June 2003 and is one of many clients that can be used to transfer digital content. It enables video and music downloads to be played on a range of devices including Xbox, PS3, iTunes, iPhone and TiVo. Information concerning the size of the developer community is not easily available.[37]

Project Gutenberg is an online community whose aim is to digitise and archive cultural works. Founded in 1971 and built on the efforts of volunteers its primary aim is to encourage the creation and distribution of ebooks. Project Gutenberg offers over 45,000 freely downloadable ebooks from the *Adventures of Huckleberry Finn* by Mark Twain to *The Jungle Book* by Rudyard Kipling and *The Story of My Life* by Helen Keller.

The scale of these user efforts can be impressive and the cases above illustrate how producer firms have slowly learnt how to draw such activity into their innovation processes, or build commercial services around them. Another mechanism that is widely used is to provide users with some form of 'toolkit' that can influence and shape user activity and enable it more easily drawn upon.[38] Another is to draw on the broad range of expertise that exists within the crowd[39] using crowd-sourcing systems like InnoCentive or large-scale innovation contests[40] that offer financial incentives like cash prizes.

3.3.4 Users' Demands and Behaviour can Drive Producer Innovation

Users of a technology may also drive innovation in producer firms by being demanding and 'tough' customers and research has also provided insights into the importance of users in innovation processes. For example, the American sociologist Everett Rogers' notion of reinvention, describes the degree to which an innovation is changed or modified by a user in the process of its adoption and implementation.[41] Although Rogers was primarily concerned with diffusion of organisational practices, he later extended his ideas to apply to products and technologies as well, noting that a higher degree of reinvention leads to a higher degree of sustainability for an innovation.[42] This form of active user involvement has also been termed re-innovation[43] and such an approach can offer significant advantages to both the producer and the user firm. For the producer these advantages include the reduction in costs associated with development, testing, training and launch. Users also benefit by lower adoption costs and the opportunity to influence how the technology is developed.[44] However, it is important to recognise that this research revealed the value of user involvement in two quite distinct contexts: first in the creation of a new product, and second in the further development of an existing product.

In the context of the creation of a new product firms can often work with one or more lead clients to identify key performance characteristics, a practice that is common with high-value complex products like airliners and military hardware. Although this is a common practice in capital goods industries it is often a difficult, protracted, and high-risk venture, but one that can also yield huge benefits if successful. The development of

---

BOX 3.1   BOEING 747

The Boeing 747 (Figure 3.5), often known as the Jumbo Jet, has its origins in the growth of air travel in the 1960s and was designed in collaboration with its first customer – the (now defunct) US carrier Pan Am. Originally intended as an aircraft that would be quickly superseded by the expected emergence of supersonic passenger travel, the design also had to facilitate the expected conversion to freight operation when the time came. Pan Am's exacting demands on weight, speed, capacity and overall performance drove the technical development the of 747 which went on to become one of the most successful commercial aircraft of all time.[45]

Source: Photograph by Adrian Pingstone.

Figure 3.5   Boeing 747 in British Airways livery

---

the Boeing 747 is a good example of this (Box 3.1), first flying in 1970 and going on to become one of the world's most successful aircraft.

When new technologies are introduced it is often the case that the longer-term performance profile is not fully known to producer firms. As a result such producer firms will take a great interest in how technologies perform in day-to-day operation, and can use this information as a basis of further development. This has been observed in many contexts by researchers, with American historian of technology Nathan Rosenberg terming this process learning by doing, although the 'learning' he was referring to was by the producer firm, and the 'doing' was being done by

---

BOX 3.2   THE CREATION OF THE VIDEO GAME DESTINY

Released in late 2014 Destiny was, at its launch, one of the most expensive video games ever made. The extract below[46] outlines how they worked with their user community in the development process:

> Like most online games these days, Destiny has been released in a limited demo form to gamers – once in June as an 'alpha build' to a small closed group, and again in August as a 'beta' to a much larger audience. But the studio says it also listens to – and takes on board – feedback through its website and social media. 'I think Bungie [the firm that has developed Destiny] has led the charge in improving the lines of communications between developers and gamers,' says community manager, David 'DeeJ' Dague. 'Through our user research programme we're making this game in conjunction with our community. We have a database of willing test subjects – sometimes they're answering questions about games from the other side of the world, sometimes we're luring them into the lab to get their hands on it and give us a fresh perspective. That's not something we shy away from.' Indeed, deep within Bungie's huge office, a converted multiplex cinema, there is a UI room, where gamers can come in, play and talk about the game. The key though, is in interpreting the feedback without simply handing over the creative process to the players. 'The community informs development, but the act of creation begins with us and our ideas,' says Dague. 'Over time we iterate on that by studying the behaviour of people who infiltrate this living social world, sort of observe the way they behave with each other and pick out the forms of behaviour that we think will be most interesting. This is important. Take Halo – we could never have anticipated that something like Rooster Teeth's Red vs Blue would come along. We need to learn from that.'

---

the user of the technology. Writing in the context of transport systems like airliners, Rosenberg observed how the full performance of such systems only revealed themselves over the longer term and enabled producers to reduce costs, increase loads and otherwise improve overall performance.[47] Although this is an important and valuable feature of user involvement in innovation, it implicitly assumes that the part played by users is largely passive and their main role is to utilise the technology and allow the producer to collect data on their usage. This approach may at first sight seem a little old-fashioned, but it is important to recognise that this role has, if anything, dramatically increased in recent years.

The growth and near ubiquity of software in everything from mobile phones to laptops, printers and vehicles to the widespread use of apps and search engines and e-commerce means that the volume of data generated by users is both huge and hugely valuable. The availability of large volumes of user data that can be used for advertising and other purposes has become the basis for the relatively new 'free' business models adopted by firms like Google and Facebook. But this is, once again, an approach that places a clear division between the producer firm and the user, with the user providing the raw material (in this case, data) that forms the basis for innovation by the producer firm. It is the producer who determines the shape and direction of future innovation with the user, once again, being a passive provider of data.

The user as a passive actor is valuable and important to firms and fits well with the more traditional, linear, approaches to innovation. However, in the context of innovation users can be very active indeed and one of the shifts in recent times has been the opening up of firm innovation processes to draw in innovative users. This will be further explored in the next section.

3.3.5   Certain Types of User are of Great Interest to Producer Firms

The users of a product are those that derive benefit through its *use* and have been distinguished from the producers of a product who derive benefit by selling it. At the simplest level, it has been established that firms can benefit from identifying and working with a certain kind of user – termed a lead user – whose activity can point to the shape of the future market. The concept of the lead user was developed by Eric von Hippel and it describes a user who is unable to satisfy their needs from what is available in the market and has the resources to create their own product, something that could potentially serve as a prototype for a commercial product.[48] Lead users may be very important actors in the innovation process, but it is important to be clear about the range of users that a producer firm may face. These are listed in Table 3.1.

In seeking to better understand the entirety of the users a producer firm may face it is important to explore beyond the lead user as a driver

Table 3.1   A typology of users

User type	Resources
Passive User: Does not seek to innovate	Valuable source of use data
Collaborative User: May possess an unmet need and will collaborate with others to innovate	Valuable source for collaborative innovation activities
Lead User: Possesses an unmet need and will take initiative to innovate	Valuable source of new ideas and prototypes
Non User: Does not use product as has no need or else need met by competitor product	Valuable source of skills, experience and knowledge outside current product focus

of innovation. The passive user is so-called because they appear largely content with the product in its current state and are not active in seeking to improve it, either on their own account or in collaboration with others. In contrast, the collaborative user is a form of user that is willing to work with the producer firm and/or fellow users within their innovation process. Unlike the lead user who takes the initiative to satisfy their unmet need by innovating on their own account, the collaborative user prefers to work with others in order to innovate. In this context 'others' may be either the producer firm or other users. In common with a lead user the collaborative user will have a need that is not met by existing products or services but, unlike the lead user, they will not seek to innovate on their own account, either because the need is not so acute or because they lack the resources to do so. The key differentiator from the lead user is that the collaborative user does not take the initiative, but they will collaborate with others. It is likely that many online communities will contain many collaborative users who are willing to participate in innovation activities but who may not contribute without such structures.

The second important form of user is the non user.[49] Non users do not, by definition, use the product and it might appear paradoxical that they should be important to producer firms. However, the non user is important since it is a strong reminder to producer firms that they may sometimes need to look beyond their existing user base in order to identify the resources they need in order to innovate. However, it is also important to recognise that the users of a product are not static and their engagement with the product, and with the innovation opportunities that emerge, are likely to change over time in response to changes in individual circumstances. Indeed, it is possible that some users will rotate between user types over time, whilst others become locked into one type. Conceptually, it is arguable that the users of a particular product may be only one component of the entire population of users, actual and potential. Of the groups shown in Figure 3.3 – users, online communities and the crowd – the online communities and the crowd are likely to include a significant number of individuals who do not use a particular product, as shown in Figure 3.6.

Figure 3.6 shows that within any population of users it is likely that only a few will be either lead or collaborative users. Any online community will tend to be populated of collaborative and lead users, plus other non users who may have an interest in the area. The crowd is likely to be primarily composed of non users, but these may be possessed of many other valuable innovation resources. A comparatively small number of users are likely to have a presence in both the online community and the wider crowd. Clearly, the proportions of each category will vary in different areas and over time, but looking at it in this way serves to emphasise the overlapping

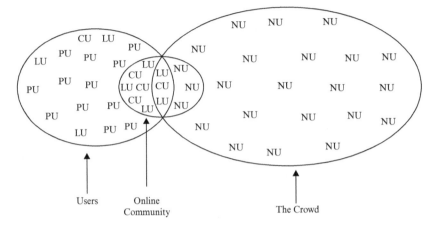

Figure 3.6   Understanding the complex context of potential online innovators

nature of the terms user, online community and crowd. It also emphasises the potentially large scale of the potential resources that are available to innovators.

3.3.6   Users Can Find New and Unexpected Uses for Technologies

New technologies, products and services will tend to be designed with a particular user group in mind – sometimes referred to as the target market. This product will be designed around the needs and the expected use patterns of this user group, and users will be directed to utilise it in a particular way. In other words the designers likely work with an idealised 'user' in mind, the product is built around this profile, and real users are expected to operate according to the designer's 'script'. This process has been called 'configuration'[50] and it is a useful way of understanding how products get designed and why users will often end up doing unexpected things with them.

In this account the design may contain all forms of barriers and limitations that are intended to ensure that the user will only operate the product in the manner that is approved and encouraged by the producer. These limitations may be put in place for all kinds of reasons including product liability, reliability, health and safety, protection of intellectual property or protection of a particular business model. Some of these reasons (for example, health and safety) may be held in common with many users, but

---

BOX 3.3　MACHINIMA

Machinima is a relatively recent genre of film that makes use of the graphics within video games to create scripted animations. Red vs Blue, a comic science fiction series based on the computer game Halo, first launched in April 2003 and went on to become one of the most watched machinima series. Machinima (the term came from the contraction of the term Machine Cinema) was a user-led activity that slowly emerged from the video games industry over many years to become an important element of the industry and an art form that is recognised in its own right.

---

others (for example, intellectual property, protection of the producer firm's business model) may be of less importance to users. As a result, users and producers may have different interests when it comes to the use of a product and, fundamentally, they will be facing a set of innovation opportunities of which the producer firm is unaware or else does not wish to support or encourage. Such unexpected user-led activity has led to many activities that are now considered commercial and mainstream including the creation of custom cars, modding video games and machinima, see below.

3.3.7　Users can Change a Market

If innovation by users is driven by an unmet need,[51] then it is the discontented users who are likely to drive such activity, to make things work the way they want them to. To paraphrase the English writer and playwright George Bernard Shaw:

> The reasonable user adapts himself to the product: the unreasonable one persists in trying to adapt the product to himself. Therefore much progress depends on the unreasonable user.[52]

Innovation by users is not neutral. Individual users can be very innovative and their activities may be of great value to producer firms, but it is important to recognise that the interests and intentions of some users may not necessarily align with such firms. Many users of a product or service, possibly the vast majority, will be content to use it in the manner intended and be largely content to focus their energies on other matters. Others, however, will be discontented and will seek to modify or make changes in order to make it do things the designers either do not wish it to do or else have not considered. Such changes may turn out to be valuable to the producer firm or they may be viewed as something that should not be encouraged or else prevented. In certain circumstances the interests of users can be in direct opposition to those of the producer firm and there are many examples where innovative users have driven fundamental changes in the way a market operates. Perhaps the most earth-shattering of these is in the market for digital content.

This market (for example, music, film, images, software) has undergone a series of fundamental changes in the last few years largely due to the actions of its users. The original business models for these sectors have been swept away with the actions of innovative users being a major factor in this revolution. Clearly, much of this activity violated existing IP restrictions and was illegal but it emphasises that the technical and organisational capabilities within users, as a whole, can either be viewed as a threat, or else as a potentially valuable resource. Many firms, especially those who develop digital products, have learnt how to draw users into their innovation processes and many products and services have been designed around all forms of user activity, up to and including innovation[53] – something that is explored in greater detail later in this book.

3.4　CONCLUDING REMARKS

It is clear the valuable ideas, insights, skills and capabilities that form the wellspring of commercial innovation do not reside solely inside organisations that create commercial products and services. Such firms are important but do not have a monopoly of the good ideas and other resources required to produce successful innovations. To paraphrase Bill Joy:[54]

> No matter who you are, most of the smartest people are innovating somewhere else, and some of them will be individual users, belong to on-line user communities or else be part of the crowd.

Innovation is no longer the sole preserve of industry and although commercial producers form an essential part of the innovation landscape, it is clearly a myth that they are the source of all the best ideas that lead to the most valuable innovations. The internal, formalised, in-house research and development operation remains a vital and important aspect of many modern industries, but it is just one part of a more complex innovation ecosystem that now also includes individual users, online communities and the crowd.

As a result, many industries now inhabit an entirely new and more complex market context in which users, online user communities and the crowd can have huge influence on the rate and direction of innovation. Some commercial organisations have to learn fast how to cope in a new context in which individual users and online user communities can have an unprecedented impact on sales. At the same time, huge and influential organisations can emerge from online user communities and act as 'invisible' pressure groups affecting the rate and direction of product or service development. In some cases such 'invisible' organisations can even morph into competitors and challenge a firm's business model.

This may sound extreme, but it is true and this chapter (and this entire book) is aimed at helping managers and others to better understand the fundamental shift that has taken place in our industrial landscape. But, as has been explored in this chapter, the 'New' often has many roots in the 'Old' and the review of earlier work in this area has made clear the many ways in which echoes of our current understanding of New Forms of innovation can be found in the observations of authors over many hundreds of years. This understanding is important as being effective at managing the Old Forms of innovation that have been so dominant for so long is no longer enough: firms must now also understand New Forms of innovation and the potential that it offers.

NOTES

1. The Jugaad phenomenon in India is a good example of this.
2. The model T Ford is a good example of a product that was often extensively modified by users over time – see Kline, R. and Pinch, T. (1996) Users as agents of technological change: the social construction of the automobile in the rural United States, *Technology and Culture*, vol. 37, no. 4, pp. 763–795.
3. Smith, A. (1776) *An Inquiry into the Nature and causes of the Wealth of Nations*, Book I, Chapter 1, p. 20.
4. Public domain image drawn from Wikipedia https://en.wikipedia.org/wiki/Adam_Smith#/media/File:Adam_Smith_The_Muir_portrait.jpg.
5. Babbage, C. (1832) *On the Economy of Machinery and Manufactures*, Chapter 19, section 225. The full quote is as follows: 'When each process has been reduced to the use of some simple tool, the union of all these tools, actuated by one moving power, constitutes a machine. In contriving tools and simplifying processes, the operative workmen are, perhaps, most successful.'
6. Usher, A.P. (1966) *A History of Mechanical Invention*, Cambridge, MA: Harvard University Press, p. 56.
7. Mokyr, J. (2009) *The Enlightened Economy: An Economic History of Britain 1700–1850*, New Haven: Yale University Press, p. 60.
8. Chang, H.J. (2014) *Economics: The User's Guide*, London: Pelican, p. 65.
9. For example, Mokyr, J. (2002) *The Gifts of Athena: Historical Origins of the Knowledge Economy*, Princeton, NJ: Princeton University Press.
10. Schmookler, J. (1962) Changes in industry and in the state of knowledge as determinants of industrial invention, in Universities-National Bureau (eds) (1962) *The Rate and Direction of Inventive Activity: Economic and Social Factors*, p. 214.
11. Schmookler, J. (1966) *Invention and Economic Growth*, Boston, MA: Harvard University Press, p. 6.
12. Schmookler, J. (1966) *Invention and Economic Growth*, Boston, MA: Harvard University Press, p. 6.
13. Merrill. R.S., quoted in Schmookler, J. (1966) *Invention and Economic Growth*, Boston, MA: Harvard University Press, p. 6.

14. Gilfillan, S.C. (1935) *Inventing The Ship: A Study of the Inventions Made in Her History between Floating Log and Rotorship*, Westchester, IL: Follett Publishing.
15. Nelson, R.R. (1959) The economics of invention: a survey of the literature, *The Journal of Business*, vol. 32, p. 103.
16. Pavitt, K. (1984) Sectoral patterns of technical change: towards a taxonomy and a theory, *Research Policy*, vol. 13, p. 353.
17. Pavitt, K. (1984) Sectoral patterns of technical change: towards a taxonomy and a theory, *Research Policy*, vol. 13, pp. 358–359.
18. Hollander, S. (1965) *The Sources of Increased Efficiency: A Study of Dupont Rayon Plants*, Cambridge, MA: The MIT Press, p. 53.
19. Hollander, S. (1965) *The Sources of Increased Efficiency: A Study of Dupont Rayon Plants*, Cambridge, MA: The MIT Press, p. 204.
20. Machlup, F (1962) *The Production and Distribution of Knowledge in the United States*, Princeton, NJ: Princeton University Press, p. 164.
21. Machlup, F (1962) *The Production and Distribution of Knowledge in the United States*, Princeton, NJ: Princeton University Press, p. 164.
22. Plato, *The Republic*, Book X, 360 BC.
23. For an overview of some of von Hippel's work in this area please refer to von Hippel, E. (1988) *The Sources of Innovation*, Oxford: Oxford University Press and von Hippel, E. (2005) *Democratizing Innovation*, Cambridge, MA: The MIT Press. These are both available as a free download from his website evhippell.mit.edu.
24. von Hippel, E. (2005) Sticky information and the locus of problem solving: implications for innovation, *Management Science*, vol. 40, no. 4, pp. 429–439.
25. von Hippel, E. (2005) *Democratizing Innovation*, Cambridge, MA: The MIT Press, p. 3.
26. Allen, R. (1983) Collective invention, *Journal of Economic Behaviour and Organization*, vol. 4, p. 3.
27. Nuvolari, A. (2004) Collective invention during the British Industrial Revolution: the case of the Cornish pumping engine, *Cambridge Journal of Economics*, vol. 28, no. 3, pp. 347–363.
28. Meyer, P.B. (2003) Episodes of Collective Invention, BLS Working Papers, Office of Productivity and Technology, Working Paper 368.
29. Meyer, P.B. (2012) Open Technology and the Early Airplane Industry, conference paper, EHA conference, September.
30. Allen, R. (1983) Collective invention, *Journal of Economic Behaviour and Organization*, vol. 4, p. 3.
31. Harhoff, D., Henkel, J. and von Hippel, E. (2003) Profiting from voluntary information spillovers: how users benefit by freely revealing their innovations, *Research Policy*, vol. 32, pp. 1753–1769.
32. Chang, H.J. (2014) *Economics: The User's Guide*, London: Pelican, p. 145.
33. Corbet, J., Kroah-Hartman, G. and McPherson, A. (2013) The Linux Kernel Development: How fast it is going, who is doing it, what they are doing, and who is sponsoring it. Annual Report, Linux Foundation.
34. http://audacity.sourceforge.net/about/credits.
35. http://audacity.sourceforge.net.
36. https://moodle.org.
37. http://sourceforge.net/projects/azureus/.
38. Franke, N. and von Hippel., E (2003) Satisfying heterogeneous user needs via innovation toolkits: the case of Apache security software, *Research Policy*, vol. 32, no. 7.
39. Boudreau, K.J. and Lakhani. K.R. (2013) Using the crowd as an innovation partner, *Harvard Business Review*, vol. 91, no. 4, pp. 61–69.
40. Boudreau, K.J., Lacetera, N. and Lakhani, K.R. (2011) Incentives and problem uncertainty in innovation contests: an empirical analysis, *Management Science*, vol. 57, no. 5, pp. 843–863.
41. Rogers, E. (2003) *Diffusion of Innovations*, 5th edition, London: Free Press, p. 180.
42. Rogers, E. (2003) *Diffusion of Innovations*, 5th edition, London: Free Press, p. 183.

43. Rothwell, R. and Gardiner, P. (1985) Invention, innovation, re-innovation and the role of the user: a case study of British hovercraft development, *Technovation*, vol. 3, no. 3, pp. 167–186.
44. Rothwell, R. and Gardiner, P. (1989) The strategic management of re-innovation, *Technovation*, vol. 19, no. 2, pp. 147–160.
45. Irving. C. (1993) *Wide-Body: The Triumph of the 747*, London: William Morrow & Co.
46. Stuart, K. (2014) Destiny: how a universe was assembled by craftspeople and their community, *The Guardian*, 5 September.
47. Rosenberg, N. (1976) *Perspectives on Technology*, Cambridge: Cambridge University Press.
48. von Hippel, E. (1986) Lead users: a source of novel product concepts, *Management Science*, vol. 32, no. 7, pp. 791–805.
49. Wyatt, S. (2005) Non-users also matter: the construction of users and non-users of the Internet, in N. Oudshoorn and T. Pinch (eds), *How Users Matter: The Co-construction of Users and Technology*, Cambridge, MA: The MIT Press, pp. 67–80.
50. Woolgar, S. (1990) Configuring the user: the case of usability trials, *Sociological Review*, vol. 38, S1, pp. 58–99.
51. von Hippel, E. (1986) Lead users: a source of novel product concepts, *Management Science*, vol. 32, no, 7, pp. 791–805.
52. Original quote: The reasonable man adapts himself to the world; the unreasonable one persists in trying to adapt the world to himself. Therefore all progress depends on the unreasonable man. In Shaw, G.B. (1903) *Man and Superman, Maxims for Revolutionists*, Boston, MA: Cambridge University Press, p. 124.
53. Flowers, S. (2008) Harnessing the hackers: the emergence and exploitation of Outlaw Innovation, *Research Policy*, vol. 37, no. 2, pp. 177–193.
54. Quoted in Anderson, C. (2013) *Makers: The New Industrial Revolution*, London: Random House, p. 143. However, the original source of the quote goes back to some time in 1990. The original quote is as follows: 'No matter who you are, most of the smartest people work for someone else.'

4. Mapping the new world of innovation: the Innovation Opportunity Space

Stephen Flowers

4.1 INTRODUCTION

This chapter will introduce the idea of the Innovation Opportunity Space, a conceptual framework that is intended to provide strategic managers, policymakers and academics with a new way of thinking about innovation. As explored earlier in this book much of the thinking about the creation of new products and services tends to focus on Old Form innovation, with producer firms being located at the centre and users, online communities and the crowd being largely ignored. In this world Old Form innovation is dominant and occurs within 'regulated' and 'governed' spaces, with the result that much of the thinking about innovation is trapped in its own narrow space. This chapter shows how to break free from such restrictions.

We have to start by recognising that innovation isn't what it used to be, and the patterns of future innovation will also be different. Many of the strict 'rules' about how the world worked have become 'guidelines' that are subject to interpretation and negotiation and, as a result, the opportunities for innovation have opened up. Firms, individual users and online communities now routinely create entirely new innovation spaces that challenge the status quo and the old 'rules' of how the world works. The guiding assumptions under which many firms work are continually questioned and reassessed both externally and internally and the dynamics of many markets, and the actors within them, are subject to continual adjustment. Firms need a means to better understand their broader innovation context and examine who is doing what, and what it might mean for them. The starting point for such an approach is not the products or services that already exist, or the 'rules', or competitors, but the *Innovation Opportunities* that are emerging. Clearly, the idea that an opportunity can be a useful focusing device for a discussion concerning innovation is not, in itself, new. However, the idea that an *Innovation Opportunity* can itself form the basis for detailed strategic analysis is what sets this approach apart.

Societies and the economies that underpin them run on sets of rules that are intended to be helpful and generally maximise overall wellbeing. Some of these rules – for example, driving on one side of the road – make a lot of sense and are easy to understand. Other forms of rule are concerned with aspects of economic activity and often place boundaries on what firms and individuals are allowed to do. Such rules are often based on a particular understanding of how the world works which, in turn, often tend to be based on the technologies in use when the rules were formed. For example, before the widespread application of computers and the Internet the idea that goods or services could be entirely digital in nature was the stuff of science fiction – books were printed and bound and only sold in bookshops; recorded music was stamped on vinyl and only sold in record stores; taxis were hailed on the street; movies were only shown in movie houses; private enthusiasts only shared their home movies with small numbers of friends and family; written communication was mostly in the form of a letter delivered by a postman; people did not routinely share their personal information with large numbers of other people; specialist teams worked in research and development labs to develop new products and services and often found it hard to effectively engage with the intended customer base before launch; innovative activities of private individuals faced large obstacles and often tended to be small scale, and mostly invisible; the sheer physicality of everyday life meant that the rules were clear.

Of course, the growth of the computer industry and the explosion of the Internet changed all that: many goods and services are now entirely digital; most books are now digital and can be downloaded onto e-readers; most music is sold in digital form; taxis can be 'hailed' using an app; movies are widely distributed over the Internet on streaming services; millions of private individuals share their own clips and movies on specialist sharing sites; the email has largely replaced the letter as a form of written communication; many millions of people routinely share their personal information; research and development labs can now work with large online communities to develop new products and services; innovative private individuals can now reach large markets; the physical world has become wrapped in a digital cloak that is largely invisible, but which affects everything we do. As a result, many of the old certainties have been swept away and many of the assumptions about the way the world should work, and the 'rules' that were created have been changed, or called into question. And as these old 'rules' have been challenged, changed, or questioned, new innovation opportunities have emerged and our settled physical world has been disrupted by successive waves of innovative products and services. Some of these new things have come from established firms and brands that we recognise, whilst many others have emerged from an entirely new form of organisation that is not exactly a firm, nor an individual, but is some kind of loosely coordinated group of volunteer workers. Still others have emerged from organisations that operate in a seemingly traditional way, but rely on such groups of volunteers who make their extensive resources available or act as workers. The nature of innovation has changed fundamentally, just as the nature of the innovation opportunities that now present themselves to firms, individuals, and online communities have also changed. The following section will explore how we might better analyse and understand such changes using the Innovation Opportunity Space approach.

4.2   THE INNOVATION OPPORTUNITY SPACE

An innovation opportunity is the potential to create something (for example, a new technology or technological application, an organisational innovation, a product, a service, or some combination of all of these) that has hitherto not existed in its proposed form. An Innovation Opportunity Space (IOS), or the space for a new product or service to be created, may emerge due to a technological or other change, or it may be latent but unrecognised and have only emerged due to a reframing of the context. At the same time an Innovation Opportunity Space (IOS), may exist and be widely recognised but effectively be closed off due to regulation, market structure, inadequate technology, or a lack of market readiness. Shifts in any of these factors may lead to a re-assessment of the Innovation Opportunity Space and enable innovators to emerge. It must be stressed, however, that economic factors are not always the primary determinants of the viability of an Innovation Opportunity Space and a new IOS may emerge (or an old IOS be reframed) due to a wide range of non-market factors. An IOS is also likely to be in a state of constant flux as contextual factors change key influences that affect its scale, scope and depth. As a result the study of any individual IOS will provide insights into the dynamics of innovation and the parts played by the actors involved.

4.2.1   Origins of the Innovation Opportunity Space Approach

The idea underlying the development of the Innovation Opportunity Space is that exploration of innovation is better approached in a neutral way. The core of the approach is a focus on the *innovation opportunity* that either currently exists, has just emerged, or is in the process of emerging.

The Innovation Opportunity Space approach was developed in response to difficulties in framing research concerning how non-firm actors like users create value from their innovation activities. The mainstream approaches employed in understanding innovation drew on ideas like firm size, the primary sector in which a firm operates, and whether a firm supplies products, services or a combination of both. These are important factors and, although they are a necessary feature of any analysis, when it comes to non-firm actors like users, they are not very useful and fail to capture key contextual factors (for example, the role of regulation, technical standards, product/service architecture and so on) that are often central to the way in which innovations emerge and develop. In addition, framing enquiries according to a relatively small number of organisational features (however dominant they may be in policy and other discourses) provides a very limiting framing.

The primary intention of the concept is to provide a jump-off point for the examination of an innovation that starts with the Opportunity Space itself, rather than the products, services, firms, sectors or the policies that surround or inhabit it. The unit of analysis is the innovation opportunity space. The starting point is the innovation opportunity space. By providing a different starting point (and a different unit of analysis) it is intended that any enquiry is approached more neutrally and without the framing that is often present in the supply-side discourse that is dominant in much of the innovation literature (and in policy analysis).

This will enable a more neutral approach to analysis in which the actions of different actors (producers, policy, users, communities) can be examined and their role in enabling, developing, exploiting, or co-creating value within an Innovation Opportunity Space can be explored. Within this approach users (firms and individual consumers), communities of users, and the crowd can be viewed as key actors within a larger constellation of actors – but they will be considered from the outset, rather than at a later stage. This is an important factor in re-focusing our efforts and it will result in different approaches to the analysis of innovation processes and outcomes and have significant implications for discussions of innovation policy, practice and management.

4.2.2 Understanding Innovation Opportunities

An Innovation Opportunity is the productive gap to create something new (for example, a new technology or technological application, an organisational innovation, a product, a service, or some combination of all of these). A new Innovation Opportunity may emerge due to a technological or other change, or it may be latent but unrecognised. An Innovation

Opportunity may also emerge due to a reframing of the context as a result of a regulatory, demographic, perceptual or other shifts. At the same time, a potential Innovation Opportunity may exist but be closed off due to regulation, market structure, inadequate technology, or a lack of market readiness. Shifts in any of these factors may lead to a re-assessment of the potential of an Innovation Opportunity and enable innovators to emerge to seek to take advantage of the opportunities they have identified.

The creation and application of new technologies will always tend to open up new Innovation Opportunities, as will changes in regulations or consumer behaviour. For example, the development and widespread adoption of computer technology has revolutionised industrial production, and opened up extensive Innovation Opportunities in the computerisation of things like lathes, process control equipment and cash registers. Entirely reshaped industries emerged to manufacture these machines and to collect and analyse the data they generate. Similarly, new regulations concerning the opening up of access to some of the data collected by governments – often termed open data – has created a whole host of Innovation Opportunities that are just beginning to be explored. Changes in consumer behaviour can also create Innovation Opportunities, as seen in the emergence and growth of the social media industry that depends of individuals freely sharing their personal content online.

The emergence of new Innovation Opportunities is very likely to cause conflict. In a stable and mature context conflict is likely to arise due to shifts in power and influence and its implications for the business models of those involved. In contrast, with new and emerging Innovation Opportunities conflict may focus on attempts by different groups to annex and defend key segments of the Innovation Space, with the aim of future exploitation and monetisation. For example the widespread emergence and huge growth of illegal digital music downloading in 1999 is an example of an Innovation Opportunity that drew in new actors to a stable and mature Innovation Space, reshaped a mature industry and created huge conflict that has yet to be resolved. The launch of Uber in 2010 is an example of a conflict within an established industry that has been caused by the attempt to exploit an innovation opportunity in a highly regulated context.

Innovation may be disruptive but it may also be an incremental, gradual, process in which Opportunities are recognised and combined with an existing product, service or activity. Unrecognised Innovation Opportunities may become visible due to changes in behaviour or reductions in cost. For example, the emergence and growth of DIY skate parks (see Box 4.1) is the result of a combination of changes in the practice of skateboarding and in the willingness of skateboarders to take direct action to create their own skate parks that was likely fuelled by the Internet and social media.

In direct contrast, some Innovation Opportunities have been around for such a long time that they are largely ignored and viewed as part of the landscape, something that is largely accepted as a fact of life. As a result such Innovation Opportunities can exist for a long time until the spell is broken and innovation takes place within the firm, the sector, the industry, amongst individuals, or across the economy as a whole. All of these have re-set Innovation Opportunities by an incremental shift in the accepted norms and practices of their industries.

The exploitation of a complex Innovation Opportunity (for example, the creation of an app-based transportation coordination system) may require many complementary forms of knowledge, but less complex Innovation Opportunities (for example, using a webcam to show the length of a queue in a barber shop) may be far less knowledge intensive. Exploiting complex Innovation Opportunities is likely to require the specialist knowledge and skills possessed by a wide range of actors including producers, users, user communities, and policy groups. Different forms of knowledge will be created by these actors and different forms of value will be generated and appropriated. Given that the notion of an IOS is simply a neutral unit of analysis, a neutral starting point for exploring the creation, diffusion and appropriation of resources and value, it is possible to make use of the technical and conceptual approaches that have been developed in traditional analytical approaches.

4.2.3 Understanding Innovation Opportunity Spaces

It is easy to think of an Innovation Opportunity Space as a market, and although this is true in the broadest sense, it would also be misleading since an Innovation Space may be far more than that. An Innovation Opportunity Space is an area of unexploited potential. Such unexploited potential may relate to commercially supplied goods and services that are offered in the market, but it may also relate to goods and services that are made available non-commercially. An Innovation Opportunity Space is likely to involve far more actors than a narrow commercial market – potentially, it may also contain Open-Source activity, online user communities, fan communities, hackers, commentators, all connected by a complex web of online forums, news websites and social media. If we add commercial actors like manufacturers, retailers, customers, users, marketing and PR firms, plus regulators, standards bodies and policy groups we can see that Innovation Opportunity Spaces can be very complex and crowded indeed. Certainly, although many mature mainstream products and services face such complexity, many new (and especially digital) services have a far less complex Innovation Opportunity Space. However, even with mature mainstream products and services the Innovation Opportunity Space tends not to be quite so complex as innovation tends to be localised and incremental. Nonetheless, an Innovation Opportunity Space can be a volatile context.

The key factor concerning an Innovation Opportunity Space is that it is a neutral initial frame of reference that enables the mapping of the actors seeking to obtain value from unexploited potential. The starting point is not the idea of a market for a commercial product, but rather an Innovation Space within which different types of resource (for example, knowledge, experience, skills, buildings, machinery, finance) and different forms of value (for example, financial, reputational, community, public service, brand) may be obtained from a range of actors (for example, third-party institutions, firms, individual users, online communities, the crowd) and created, destroyed, translated or transferred. It is useful simplification to think of Innovation Opportunity Spaces as being of three main types: Stable, Unstable and Emerging:

> A *Stable Innovation Opportunity Space* is likely to be characterised by mature products and services that are well known and understood by those who use them, a small number of dominant suppliers, and clear and enforced norms and practices around use (possibly embedded in standards or enforced by regulation). Innovation pathways will be apparent, clearly communicated and widely accepted.

> An *Unstable Innovation Opportunity Space* will occur when the guiding assumptions that make apparently mature products and services attractive are called into question. Dominant suppliers may be challenged by new entrants, norms and practices around use may be set aside or widely questioned, standards and regulation may be ignored or challenged. Innovation pathways are no longer clear and different versions and visions of the future compete for dominance.

> An *Emerging Innovation Opportunity Space* occurs when existing norms, practices, standards or regulation are questioned or set aside or when new technologies, or novel applications of existing technologies, are created. This provides fertile ground for the creation of a range of new products, services, norms and practices that are likely to lead to unpredictable innovation outcomes. Many innovation pathways appear to be possible and there are many voices and visions seeking to influence how things will develop.

In modern economies many of the products and services we consume emerge from an apparently Stable Innovation Opportunity Space, and commercial firms often take great care to cultivate norms and practices around use and to communicate a clear vision of their innovation pathways. However, such firms operate in a competitive market and innovation is a dynamic force that can sometimes undermine the stability of their Innovation Opportunity Space and call into question its guiding assumptions. For example, the emergence of Open Source software swept away much of the commercial software industry that had developed around the growth of the personal computer in the latter part of the 20th century. Perhaps more significantly, it also led to the widespread adoption of very different set of norms and practices around the creation and distribution of software that continues to be a source of instability in sections of that industry.

Emerging Innovation Opportunity Spaces tend to be associated with the 'new' – for example, new technologies, new uses of older technologies, new/old technology combinations, new norms or practices, new social movements, new access to data collected by old technologies. In this context individuals, groups and collectivities will explore innovation possibilities, start-ups will be founded, venture capital may support new firms, and a new innovation ecosystem will emerge. Regulation will struggle to keep pace with often unpredictable innovation outcomes. The presence of venture capital may result in a drive for growth and an early return on investment. The new organisations that inhabit this space will drive for early market stability or be absorbed by larger entities.

One final word about Innovation Opportunity Spaces concerns the 'rules' that govern them. The 'rules' (accepted norms and practices, standards and regulations) are an important part of any Innovation Opportunity Space since they structure the activity of users, online communities and the commercial actors that inhabit the Space. However, breaking or setting aside the 'rules' are often an important part of innovation and there is often an uneasy tension between those actors that benefit from the Innovation Opportunity Space as it is (since they have often influenced or helped to create the 'rules') and those who wish to change things.

4.3 UNDERSTANDING AN INNOVATION OPPORTUNITY SPACE

The Innovation Opportunity Space approach is intended to be an inherently neutral starting point for an examination of how resources can be mobilised and value created, co-created, and appropriated. Unlike many frameworks of this sort it does not focus on one group of actors nor does it focus on one form of value and, as a result, it can enable a broader examination of value creation that can include but goes beyond economic returns. It can also permit a wider examination of knowledge creation and exploitation that can go beyond (but also include) a narrow focus on IP and patenting.

Innovation is often a complex and uncertain process and a structured

Table 4.1 The four major aspects of the Innovation Opportunity Space

	Definition	Key Initial Questions
Architecture	Norms, practices, behaviours, rules, standards and regulations that govern the Space.	What is the architecture of the innovation opportunity space? (e.g. how is it structured or configured to facilitate or prevent innovation activity? What are the legal structures? What are the technical/non-technical facilitating factors or blockages? What are the accepted norms or practices?) How has this changed/is changing?
Actors	Individual users, online communities, firms and other bodies (e.g. regulators) that are active in the Space.	Who are the main actors in the innovation opportunity space? (e.g. producers, users, consumers, policy actors, non-firms actors like pressure groups, etc.) How has this changed/is changing?
Activities	Individual and collective activities taken by the individual users, online communities, firms and other bodies that are active in the Space.	What are the activities of the actors in the innovation opportunity space? (e.g. who has done what to whom or with whom, and for what reason?) How has this changed/is changing?
Aftershocks	The impact and outcomes of the actions taken by the actors within the Space.	What are the outcomes of the actions that have taken place? (e.g. what has happened in the innovation opportunity space and how has this acted to promote or inhibit innovation?) What might the next shock be?

analysis of an Innovation Opportunity Space focuses on four major aspects: its Architecture, including the accepted norms, practices and rules; the Actors that inhabit the Space; the Actions of the different actors within the Space; and the impact of the actions, also called the Aftershocks. The intention underlying the analysis of an Innovation Opportunity Space is to facilitate a high-level strategic examination of a particular context and enable Areas of Opportunity to be identified. Table 4.1 provides a summary of the main elements of the Innovation Opportunity Space and provides some key initial questions.

As can be seen the intention is to provide a small number of questions that are designed to provide a neutral starting point for any analysis. This does not preclude discussion of policy or producer issues like standards, regulation, copyright, patents or R&D investments, all of which are pertinent to any full analysis of an Innovation Opportunity Space. However, the main point is that any examination does not *start* with such a focus, something that is likely to frame and limit such a discussion, and potentially blind-side strategic managers, policymakers and others in their analyses.

A detailed analysis of an Innovation Opportunity Space is not a trivial undertaking and will require extensive data. The more stable and well-established an Innovation Opportunity Space, the better the data is likely to be, and the more refined the accompanying analyses. As may be expected, an emerging Innovation Opportunity Space is likely to be accompanied by data that is incomplete, poorly focused and unreliable, together with poorly informed and sometimes excitable analyses. Any analysis of an Unstable Innovation Opportunity Space is likely to be quite hard to understand as it will likely be a combination of subtle and detailed analysis of its earlier stable form together with poorly informed and excitable speculations. Such is the reality of analysis of complex phenomena. By contrast, the analysis of a Stable Innovation Opportunity Space needs to guard against being overly influenced by its apparent stability.

4.3.1 Analysing an Innovation Opportunity Space

The analysis of an Innovation Opportunity Space moves through a series of stages and will require access to many forms of data and information drawn from traditional, and non-traditional sources. Managers, policy groups and many academics will be very familiar with the traditional sources of data and information since they are the quantitative DNA of modern economic activity.

The metrics of this world may include sectoral, firm or divisional data, they may include GVA (Gross Value Added) indicators, R&D spending, patents granted and so on. They may also concern data concerning market size and share, customer demographics, purchasing intentions, social media and other online activity around a product, service or brand. There may also be data that provides insights into emerging technologies and market trends. This is familiar to many organisations and an entire commercial research industry has developed to provide this material. What is more complex and difficult to describe are the non-traditional sources of data that managers and organisations need to access other than to state it emerges from non R&D systems that are typically associated with *use*, not production or supply.

Users of products, systems or services can be an excellent source of valuable new ideas, working prototypes and novel applications. As explored in Chapter 3, users and online communities and the crowd approach innovation in a very different way to firms and they will often come up with something that firms have not considered, or have overlooked. This may be because users, online communities and the crowd possess rare insights, but it may also be that they simply see the world in a different way. Much like the DIY skaters who build their own skate parks, where one group sees as a nasty scrap of ground under a noisy flyover, DIY skaters see a building opportunity. Similarly, in the case of giffgaff, where one group sees a crowded market with few opportunities, others see an opportunity to reinvent a service organisation around social media and online communities. In this context, non-traditional sources of information must be employed to provide insights into this world in order to supplement traditional data sources. These non-traditional data sources will not be as polished and apparently reliable as the mainstream sources as they are, almost by definition, fragmentary, incomplete and partial. But they are also the source of insights and, in innovation terms, this is often where the surprises and breakthroughs come from. As a result it is important for managers and policy groups to devote some of their energies to acquiring and understanding both traditional and non-traditional sources of data. Examples of these two sources of data are summarised below:

Traditional sources of data (outward looking, commercial):

- Number of firms, employment, firm entry and exit
- Market size and structure, M&A activity
- Technological pathways and trajectories
- Technological standards
- Customer demographics, purchase intentions
- Marketing and advertising spend, brand awareness
- Social media activity and positioning
- Regulatory structure.

Non-traditional sources of data:

- Size of related online community
- Scale of related online community activity
- Nature of activity – positive/negative
- Nature of activity – experimental/activist
- Nature of activity – recombinatory
- Nature of activity – rule breaking
- Characterisation of *behaviours*

- Application of new technologies
- New (hard/soft) technological solutions
- New (hard/soft) technological phenomenon.

It is pretty clear that the Traditional sources of data tend to be quantitative and technocratic, and derived from standard systems for the research and analysis or *markets*. In contrast, the non-traditional sources of data may be drawn from more ethnographic approaches that provide different forms of insight into possible futures rather than the measured present. As a result it is important to recognise that each of these forms of data provide different insights – the traditional sources measure the current context, whilst the non-traditional sources provide insights into the possible routes the next waves of innovation may take.

An Innovation Opportunity Space analysis gains its focus from three key questions:

1. What is the Space to be examined?
2. What Innovation Opportunities are we looking for?
3. What is the status of my own organisation's innovation readiness?

The IOS template is shown in Figure 4.1. As you can see the template has been designed in order to provide summaries of the four major elements, with Actors and Actions being structured to enable direct linkages to be made. Each of the major case studies examined later in the book will make use of this template.

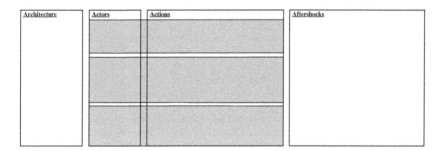

Figure 4.1   The Innovation Opportunity Space template

4.4   THE CASE STUDIES

These case studies have been selected in order to provide the reader with an introduction to the Innovation Opportunity Space approach. Each of the case studies is designed to provide particular insights that inform how we might think about innovation, where innovations might come from, and how organisations might seek to take the lead in, or react to, innovations. These are all 'live' cases and, as with many innovations, there are no clear answers and no neat solutions. These case studies are simply designed to provide the reader with the opportunity to engage with the Innovation Opportunity Space approach.

BOX 4.1   THE PHENOMENON OF DIY SKATE PARKS: DIY
SKATE PARKS – REFRAMING AN INNOVATION
OPPORTUNITY SPACE

This is an example of an Emerging Innovation Space within a civic context. To much of the world skateboarding may be a largely invisible activity that is populated by marginalised young males. In fact, skateboarding is a global phenomenon with a recent report estimating that there are over 11 million skateboarders around the world participating in a world market that is worth nearly $5 billion (Montgomery, 2009), but this may well now be much larger. Although this activity largely revolves around sale of the boards, trucks, bearings, shoes, magazines, clothing and accessories that make up the Opportunity Space of a traditional product-based market, there is also an active DIY (Do-It-Yourself) subculture when it comes to the creation and use of skate parks. This DIY culture is good example of the way in which an Opportunity Space can emerge simply by a reframing of an existing context – faced with a lack of good places to skate, skaters simply went out and built their own skate parks. The DIY skate park is now a recognised global phenomenon and a search on Google will reveal skater-built parks in every continent, apart from Antarctica.

A key aspect of this phenomenon is a culture in skating that celebrates transgression and encourages skaters to push the boundaries. Skateboarding is not a regulated, formalised, activity that is characterised by structures like clubs and societies, but is an individualistic pursuit that celebrates activists and creative rule breaking. At the same time, the product-based market of skateboarding is heavily branded and commoditised and the space for innovation has largely been closed off or is absent. However, it is in the creation of DIY skateboard 'spots' or parks in unused or abandoned locations that skaters' creative rule-breaking enables them to identify Innovation Opportunity Spaces that have been made invisible by the norms, practices and rules of the mainstream.

DIY skate parks – created by skaters themselves – have been built under flyovers, in abandoned buildings, in old tunnels, and on many otherwise overlooked or ignored scraps of urban space. Often there has been no permission asked or granted and activist skaters will simply build it, and then use it until it is either destroyed or accepted. London's South Bank is an example of a found space that became a skate park, with Burnside in Portland, Oregon and Suvilahti DIY in Helsinki, Finland being prime examples of skater-built parks.

Skaters have a particular interest and view of the world that enables them to re-frame the resources they see around them – to re-frame their Innovation Opportunity Space. Once issues like ownership, permissions, permits, and other regulations have been set aside they are able to identify a far greater set of Innovation Opportunities and can act to explore and exploit them. This may, and often has, led to conflict with local residents, landowners and local government, but they can be adopted and (in time) become celebrated by the mainstream. In certain circumstances skateboarding and DIY culture become a celebrated part of the urban scene and the mainstream Opportunity Space adjusts and absorbs what was once an illegal and antisocial activity. For example, in Helsinki skateboarding has been embraced and has been celebrated in the Kiasma National Museum of Contemporary Art, skating is a big part of the urban scene, and the city has some of the best skate parks anywhere in the world.

From and Innovation Opportunity Space perspective it is clear that actions of skaters have been successful in reframing the Architecture of their Opportunity Space, altering norms and practices, but also challenging and changing the over-arching regulations that govern their activities (Figure 4.2).

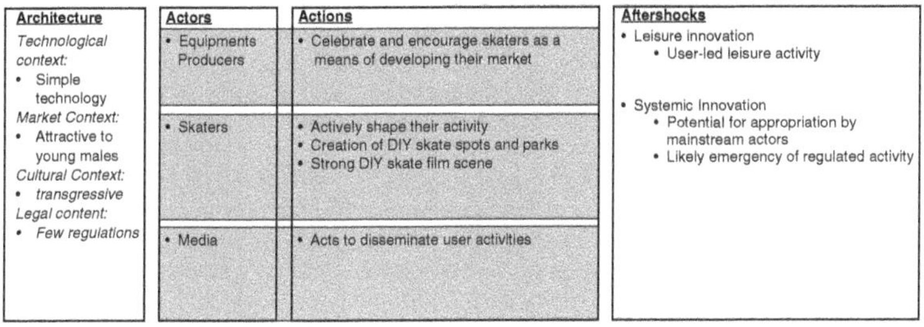

Architecture	Actors	Actions	Aftershocks

Technological context:
 • Simple technology
 Market Context:
 • Attractive to young males
 Cultural Context:
 • *transgressive*
 Legal content:
 • *Few regulations*
	• Equipments Producers	• Celebrate and encourage skaters as a means of developing their market	• Leisure innovation
			   • User-led leisure activity
			
			 • Systemic Innovation
			   • Potential for appropriation by mainstream actors
			   • Likely emergency of regulated activity

	• Skaters	• Actively shape their activity • Creation of DIY skate spots and parks • Strong DIY skate film scene	
	• Media	• Acts to disseminate user activities	

Figure 4.2   Innovation Opportunity Space – DIY skate parks

BOX 4.2   A MEN'S HAIRDRESSER IN THE UK: INCREMENTAL INNOVATION WITHIN A STABLE INNOVATION OPPORTUNITY SPACE

This is an example of an incremental innovation within a Stable Innovation Space in a mature industry. Men's hairdressers in the UK tend to have a very traditional business model and are part of a sector that is characterised by small-scale ventures, low costs of entry, and low use of ICT. In this sector business practices evolve slowly over time and regulations, norms and practices tend to be very stable. Put simply, going to a barber in the UK today is not so different from 50 years ago.

One of the accepted norms in this sector is that men's hairdressers in the UK tend not to operate according to a booking system – if you want a haircut you simply have to turn up and join the queue. Indeed, queueing is such a part of this sector that it is widely accepted and tends not to be questioned or challenged, it is just part of the overall service experience. Solutions to deal with this issue have been widely available for many years but such are the strength of the accepted norms and practices that they tend not to have been widely adopted. Men's hairdressers operate in much the same way as they have always done and customers still have to queue to get their hair cut.

It is clear that male hairdressing (despite being much cited by the service and innovation literatures) is a sector in which there has been little service innovation. The long-established norms and practices within this sector are so strong that there is little need or impetus to innovate and customers are largely happy to comply. Arguably, male hairdressing in the UK operates within a highly stable Innovation Opportunity Space in which it may be expected that innovations would occur only slowly. Enter the webcam.

In an incremental innovation that was so obvious (as all good innovations usually are) one tiny men's hairdressers in a small town in the UK allows potential customers to check the size of the queue before they go to the shop. Starting in 2013 the barber shop[1] began to show the waiting area on the web, enabling potential customers to see the size of the queue, estimate the time they have to wait, and enable them to manage their visit more efficiently. In an age of near-ubiquitous wifi and widespread use of smartphones this innovation has been widely welcomed by customers.

From an Innovation Opportunity Space perspective it is likely that this small-scale, albeit highly significant, innovation has been successful largely because it was incremental and did not conflict with existing norms and practices. The Architecture of the Opportunity Space remains largely unchanged, as do the Actors, with the Actions and Aftershocks being quite minor in scale (Figure 4.3). The webcam was replaced by a specialist queuing app in 2016.

Architecture	Actors	Actions	Aftershocks
Technological context: • Very Simple technology • Low ICT usage *Market context:* • Very stable • Small Firms *Cultural context:* • Queuing expected *Legal context:* • Few regulations	• Barbers • Customers	• Little imitative activity • Welcome change • Largely passive	• Service innovation • Queue now visible

Figure 4.3   Innovation Opportunity Space – men's hairdressers

BOX 4.3   UBER: REFRAMING AND CONFLICT WITHIN A STABLE INNOVATION OPPORTUNITY SPACE

This is an example of an Emerging Innovation Space within a mature industry. Uber is an app-based transport system that directly competes with traditional taxi services. Established in 2009 in San Francisco and supported by significant external funding, Uber disrupted the highly regulated and largely stable taxi Innovation Opportunity Space, something that has been highly controversial and led to many protests around the world.

Taxis, sometimes called 'taxi cabs' or simply 'cabs', are vehicles that take passengers from one place to another on demand. Key differentiators for taxis is they may be hired on the street, fares are calculated by taximeters (originally introduced in the 19th century), and they are subject to rigorous licensing procedures. For example, the famous London Black Cab (technically a Hackney Carriage) is a licensed vehicle whose drivers have to pass a test (called The Knowledge) that demonstrates their detailed knowledge and understanding of routes across London. In order to pass the test drivers must be able to plan a route across London without any assistance (for example, without referring to maps, SatNav or asking directions). Initiated in 1865 this test examines knowledge of 320 routes, plus tourist sites, hospitals, theatres and other locations, with drivers often taking three years and multiple attempts to pass. Trainee drivers can often be seen, warmly dressed, driving a moped with a laminated map pinned onto the clipboard on their handlebars.

Having acquired The Knowledge and being properly licensed drivers of Black Cabs in London are the only vehicles that can be hailed from the street or hired from a taxi rank – private hire vehicles (also called minicabs) are not able to do this and must be booked via a central despatcher. As a result London's Black Cabs have a monopoly on the ability to pick up paying passengers on the street, something that they very strongly defend. However, technological changes (for example, widespread adoption of wifi, smartphones, GPS, digital mapping) have made this situation increasingly anachronistic and laid the foundation for a wave of potentially disruptive innovations.

Uber is an example of an organisation that combines a range of modern technologies with accepted norms and practices common in social media to reinvent a traditional service. Passengers use the Uber app to identify and summon a car, with passengers and drivers able to rate their experiences, giving each the ability to select according to ratings. Costs are clear in advance and all transactions take place electronically, eliminating the need for drivers to carry a large amount of cash. Drivers make use of GPS and digital mapping and although they are subject to a rigorous checking procedure, they are not required to pass The Knowledge. The launch of Uber in London proved to be highly controversial and led to widespread protests, including mass blockades of traffic by Black Cabs in the city centre.

It is likely that the rise of Uber is simply the beginning of a period of disruptive innovation for London's Black Cabs whose origins lay in the locked down, anachronistic, highly regulated Architecture of their Innovation Opportunity Space. The application of modern technologies to taxi services effectively mean that the Opportunity Space was extended beyond its tightly regulated core and enabled Uber to develop a new service that operated in this new area. In effect, the size of the Innovation Opportunity Space was increased, enabling Uber to operate in this new area and bypass the initial space in which innovation had largely been locked down for many decades. Despite changes that have happened so far, this is likely to be the beginning of a long period of disruptive innovation in which the Architecture of the Innovation Opportunity Space changes as regulations are revised, new Actors emerge, legal, regulatory and PR battles take place, and the Aftershocks impact all those involved (Figure 4.4).

Architecture	Actors	Actions	Aftershocks

Technological context:
• Simple technology
• Low ICT usage
Market context:
• Stable
Legal context:
 	
• Highly regulated
	• Taxi drivers	• Low innovation
		• Backward-looking
		• Resistant to change
			• Service innovation
			  • Technology enabled
			  • Technology enhanced
			  • Undermines trational taxi service
			  • Improves service experience

	• Regulators	• Working within a dated framework
		• Resistant to change
			• Regulatory
			  • The Knowledge bypassed
			  • Regulator bypassed
			  • Notion of 'employee' redefined

	• Customers	• Technology enabled
		• Welcome service innovation
			• Business structures
			  • Upends stable market
			  • Opens up a range of new business models
			  • Potentially opens up new marketst

Figure 4.4   Innovation Opportunity Space – hired local transportation

BOX 4.4   GIFFGAFF: REDEFINING AN INNOVATION
OPPORTUNITY SPACE

This is an example of an Emerging Innovation Space within a mature industry. Giffgaff is a UK-based mobile phone firm that has pioneered a new operating model that makes use of its users to provide many of what would traditionally be viewed as core operational functions. Launched in 2009 giffgaff (the name is a Scottish word for mutual giving) makes use of the O2 technical network to provide its mobile phone service, and (at the time of writing) is owned by Telefónica. The tag-line used by giffgaff – 'The company run by you' – is very telling since they have built a commercial operation around the 'work' of large numbers of users who perform tasks concerned with sales, marketing, customer support and R&D. In undertaking this 'work' users perform many tasks that were once performed by the mobile phone firms themselves, or by other firms in out-sourced relationships. Essentially, giffgaff has developed a new form of outsourcing: user-sourcing.

Mobile telecommunications tends to be dominated by a small number of large firms that tend to conform to the similar operational structures and offer complex charging structures. In the UK many firms provide handsets as part of complex contracts that lock the user into long-term deals. Mobile phones may be locked to a particular network and new handsets tend to command high prices, with older handsets being associated with cheaper deals. Within this market the latest handsets tend to be associated with expensive contracts and norms around high-cost mobile phone contracts are widely accepted. Giffgaff launched into this market offering low-cost sim-only deals and incentives for existing subscribers to recruit new users. In order to get around mobiles that were locked to another network giffgaff created Unlockapedia, a user-generated Wiki containing detailed instructions for freeing mobile phones that were locked to competing networks. Users were also encouraged to submit new service ideas and create funny adverts and promotional videos, but the bulk of user contributions revolved around customer support and the recruitment and retention of new users. Users can 'earn' significant rewards for their 'work' but they do not benefit from employment protection regulations and issues like declaring the income 'earned' for tax purposes are left to the users themselves.

Within giffgaff's operational model users receive points for their contributions to its operations – for example, technical support, recruitment of a new user – which may be converted into call credits or paid in cash. Inspired by the emergence and growth of online communities and the observation that individuals within such communities can perform complex and challenging tasks, giffgaff has created an operational structure that is dependent on its own users in order to develop a low-cost business model. Giffgaff is the first firm in the UK, possibly the first in the world, to attempt to build a complex commercial enterprise of this sort that depends so heavily on volunteer labour. As a result giffgaff has had to develop a set of internal capabilities, structures and processes they require in order to deliver a high-quality customer service in a competitive market using the largely volunteer labour of their own user base. In so doing giffgaff are attempting to reinvent the operational form of such a service firm and redefine the role of service users in service provision.

From an Innovation Opportunity Perspective it is clear that giffgaff has sought to redefine the Architecture of the Innovation Opportunity Space in which they operate (Figure 4.5). Launching into a largely mature context in which the regulations and the accepted norms and practices left little space for innovation, giffgaff moved into uncharted territory, expanding the Innovation Opportunity Space in the process. Given the novelty of their goal (running a successful service firm using largely volunteer labour) and the lack of easily accessible organisational resources in this area (they have had to build many of their internal capabilities in this area from the ground up) other actors in the market can only react by employing traditional means (for example, price competition) in the short term. However, if giffgaff can build a sustainable business around their operational model the Aftershocks are likely to be significant as the model diffuses to other service firms, and regulation develops to deal with the protection of volunteer labour.

Architecture	Actors	Actions	Aftershocks

Technological context:
• Complex
• Technology
• High ICT usage
Market context:
• Largely stable
Cultural context:
• Passive users
Legal content:
• High technical regulation
• Little 'user' regulation
	• giffgaff
	
	• Users
	
	• Competitors
		• Redefines the role of user in Telecoms
		• Creation of new operating model
		• Development of new capability set
		
		• Embraced new roles and opportunities
		• Perform many core operational roles
		• 'Work' for cash, call credits, kudos, etc.
		
		• Little imitation
		• Price competition
			• Service innovation
			  • Technology enabled
			  • Technology enhanced
			  • Redefines traditional service business
			  • Creation of novel business model
			• Regulatory
			  • Notion 'user' redefined
			• Business structures
			  • Marginal impact on stable market
			  • Potentially opens up new business models
			  • Potentially opens up new markets

Figure 4.5   Innovation Opportunity Space – mobile telephony

NOTE

1. In the UK men's hairdressers are also called barbers, a name that goes back to the occupation of Barber-Surgeon, a form of medical practitioner in medieval times. The sign used by many barbers – a pole with alternating red and spiral lines that symbolise a bandaged wound – is a link to that period.

BIBLIOGRAPHY

Akrich, M. and Latour, B. (1992) A summary of convenient vocabulary for the semiotics of human and nonhuman assemblies, shaping technology/building society, in W.E. Bijker and J. Law (eds), *Studies in Sociotechnical Change*, Cambridge, MA and London, UK: The MIT Press, pp. 259–264.
Allen, R.C. (1983) Collective invention, *Journal of Economic Behaviour and Organization*, vol. 4, pp. 1–24.
Braun, V. and Herstatt, C. (2008) The freedom-fighters: how incumbent

corporations are attempting to control user-innovation, *International Journal of Innovation Management*, vol. 12, no. 3, pp. 543–572.

Castells, M. (1996) *The Information Age: Economy, Society and Culture, Volume 1, The Rise of the Network Society*, Cambridge, MA: Blackwell.

Chesbrough, H.W. (2003) The era of open innovation, *MIT Sloan Management Review*, Spring.

Flowers, S. (2008) Harnessing the hackers: the emergence and exploitation of Outlaw Innovation, *Research Policy*, vol. 37, no. 2, pp. 177–193.

Franke, N. and Piller, F. (2004) Toolkits for user innovation and design: an exploration of user interaction and value creation, *Journal of Product Innovation Management*, vol. 21, no. 6, pp. 401–415.

Franke, N. and Shah, S. (2003) How communities support innovative activities: an exploration of assistance and sharing among end-users, *Research Policy*, vol. 32, no. 1, pp. 157–178.

Gardiner, P. and Rothwell, R. (1985) Tough customers: good designs, *Design Studies*, vol. 6, no. 1, pp. 7–17.

Geroski, P.A. (1990) Innovation, technological opportunity, and market structure, *Oxford Economic Papers*, vol. 42, no. 3, pp. 586–602.

Herstatt, C. and von Hippel, E. (1992) From experience: developing new product concepts via the lead user method: a case study in a 'low-tech' field, *Journal of Product Innovation Management*, vol. 9, no. 3, pp. 213–221.

Hienerth, C. (2006) The commercialization of user innovations: the development of the rodeo kayak industry, *R&D Management*, vol. 36, no. 3, pp. 273–294.

Kim, W.C. and Mauborgne, R. (2005) Blue ocean strategy: from theory to practice, *California Management Review*, vol. 47, no. 3, pp. 105–121.

Klevorick, A.K., Levin, R.C., Nelson, R.R. and Winter, S.G. (1995) On the sources and significance of interindustry differences in technological opportunities, *Research Policy*, vol. 24, no. 2, pp. 185–205.

Lakhani, K.R. and von Hippel, E. (2003) How open source software works: 'free' user-to-user assistance, *Research Policy*, vol. *32*, no. 6, pp. 923–943.

Montogomery, T. (2009) The size of the skateboarding industry, retrieved 20 January 2015 from www.shop-eat-surf.com/2009/05/the-state-of-the-skateboarding-industry/.

Oudshoorn, N. and Pinch, T. (2003) How users and non-users matter, in N. Oudshoorn and T. Pinch (eds), *How users Matter. The Co-Construction of Users and Technologies*, Cambridge, MA: The MIT Press, pp. 1–25.

Rothwell, R., Freeman, C., Jervis, P., Horsley, A., Roberston, A.B. and Townsend, J. (1974) SAPPHO-updated: Project SAPPHO phase II, *Research Policy*, vol. 3, no. 3, pp. 258–291.

Sapsed, J., Grantham, A. and DeFillippi, R. (2007) A bridge over troubled waters: bridging organisations and entrepreneurial opportunities in emerging sectors, *Research Policy*, vol. 36, no. 9, pp. 1314–1334.

Sawhney, M., Verona, G. and Prandelli, E. (2005) Collaborating to create: the Internet as a platform for customer engagement in product innovation, *Journal of Interactive Marketing*, vol. *19*, no. 4, pp. 4–17.

Shane, S. (2000) Prior knowledge and the discovery of entrepreneurial opportunities. *Organization Science*, vol. 11, no. 4, pp. 448–469.

von Hippel, E. and Katz, R. (2002) Shifting innovation to users via toolkits, *Management Science*, vol. 48, no. 7 July, pp. 821–833.

von Hippel, E. (2005) *Democratizing Innovation*, Cambridge, MA: The MIT Press.

von Hippel, E. (1986) Lead users: a source of novel product concepts, *Management Science*, vol. 32, no. 7 July, pp. 791–805.

Woolgar, S. (1991) Configuring the user: the case of usability trials, in J. Law (ed.), *A Sociology of Monsters: Essays on Power, Technology and Domination*, London: Routledge, pp. 58–99.

TECHNICAL APPENDIX

Technological opportunity, the new industrial avenues that emerge from research investments, has been extensively explored in the context of issues like R&D intensity and technological advance (for example, Klevorick et al., 1995). The same term has also been a focus in studies on industry concentration and market structure (for example, Geroski, 1990) that have examined the role of monopolies in technological advance and contributed to the debate on competition policy.

In contrast, the notion of entrepreneurial opportunity examines how entrepreneurs exploit technological change to create new processes, products, markets or firm structures. This literature is concerned with issues like the role of prior knowledge in the discovering new opportunities (for example, Shane, 2000) and the role of bridging organisations in facilitating opportunity recognition (for example, Sapsed et al., 2007).

Much of the strategic management literature is also concerned with opportunity recognition and exploitation, but it can be argued that Blue Ocean Strategy is an approach that seeks to help firms identify, and exploit, innovation opportunity spaces that are uncontested (Kim and Mauborgne, 2005).

One major limitation of the terms 'technological opportunity' and 'entrepreneurial opportunity' is that they are both framed in such a manner that they provide a very particular, and partial, perspective on the issues under examination. They both share the widely-held supply-side bias that is inherent within much of the Innovation Studies literature (see below for a brief discussion) and focus on one element of modern economies – producer firms. Whilst this is entirely consistent with what these approaches are designed to do, the lack of a more neutral unit of analysis and subsequent framing is likely to produce analyses that are partial and limited and which do not capture the complexity of modern innovation processes. More importantly, the application of these ideas and conceptual frameworks within wider policy discussions can act to bias analyses with the risk of suboptimal policy outcomes.

The intention behind the Innovation Opportunity Space is to provide a more neutral unit of analysis in which producer firms do not dominate and in which other actors (for example, users, communities) are engaged in the creation and appropriation of value.

Implications for (Re)positioning the Role of New Forms of Innovation

The creation of a neutral unit of analysis offers the potential for creating a less partial approach to understanding processes of knowledge and value creation and appropriation. The IOS approach enables multiple, complementary approaches to the analysis of an innovation opportunity that is not framed around one particular actor or group of actors.

The intention is to provide an approach that enables all actors within an IOS (for example, producers, users, online communities, the crowd, policy) to be considered neutrally from the outset. This small reorientation in our analytical standpoint will be a major shift, as can be seen in the following discussion.

The academic understanding of the role of the user, online communities and the crowd within the processes of innovation tends to be fragmented, with different strands of literature focusing on particular aspects or perspectives. Different strands of literature tend to be framed around a particular story or meta-narrative in which users are perceived as passive 'customers', active 'shapers' or useful 'contributors' to innovation processes. The innovation processes themselves may be located within market-based relationships in which organisations seek to ensure that customers buy their products (thereby becoming 'users'), or they may take place within social or policy contexts in which advocates of an innovation seek to ensure that users 'buy' their ideas.

Users can be both a market for products, services or ideas and a source of ideas, products or services in their own right. Users can also co-create products, services and ideas with firms or with other users. The involvement of users in innovation may be carefully managed, planned and ordered or it may be spontaneous and hard to control, with users creating their own rules of engagement. Certain forms of user innovation can lead to the most fundamental changes for organisations, markets and for public policy. User involvement in innovation is a complex, dynamic and powerful phenomenon.

The Innovation Studies literature has evolved from an initially overwhelmingly supply-side perspective in which users possessed needs (for example, Rothwell et al., 1974), were 'tough customers' (Gardiner and Rothwell, 1985), or 'lead users' (von Hippel, 1986), all of whom may be harnessed to benefit firm innovation processes. This literature has developed to explore many non-traditional sources of innovation, for example communities (Franke and Shah, 2003), hackers (Flowers, 2008), open-source (Lakhani and von Hippel, 2003). It has also explored how firms can actively seek to prevent users from innovating (Braun and Herstatt, 2008). However, the literature has tended to retain its supply-side perspective.

In contrast the Science and Technology Studies (STS) literature tends to adopt a more user-centric perspective, exploring how users actively shape technologies and are, in turn, shaped by them within the processes of innovation and diffusion. These processes are viewed as highly contested, with users, producers, policymakers and intermediary groups providing different meanings and uses to technologies (Oudshoorn and Pinch, 2003). The manner in which design and other activities attempt to define and constrain the ways in which a product can be used have been viewed as an attempt to configure the user (Woolgar 1991). Within this literature, users are seen as having an active role in seeking to shape or re-shape their relationship with technology, developing an agenda or 'antiprogram' that conflicts with the designer, and going outside the scenario of use, or 'script', that is embodied in the product (Akrich and Latour, 1992). Users' lack of compliance with designers and promoters of products and systems, far from being viewed as a deviant activity, is positioned as central to our understanding the processes of innovation and diffusion.

Drawing on both of these bodies of literature, it is clear that users can play a series of important roles in the creation, development, implementation and diffusion of technologies. Arguably, the boundary between producers and consumers of technologies has become less distinct and users play important roles throughout the entire innovation process, potentially developing or extending technologies or applying them in entirely novel and unexpected ways. In this situation the boundary between consumer and producer, or between 'users' and 'doers' (Castells, 1996) becomes harder to discern. Innovation becomes far more open (Chesbrough, 2003), and democratised (von Hippel, 2005), as well as more complex. Users may be drawn into the traditional 'linear' model of innovation, but some forms of user activity may represent the emergence of a parallel or alternative system of innovation that does not share the same goals, drivers and boundaries of mainstream activity. The processes of innovation, diffusion and re-innovation are becoming increasingly complex and potentially contested.

More pragmatic and largely empirical approaches to user involvement in innovation may be found in the Innovation Management literature. This body of work deals with the problems faced by organisations seeking to involve users in some aspect of innovation like design, usability or diffusion. Although this body of literature draws heavily on both Innovation Studies and Science and technology Studies, it is more concerned with the tools, techniques and methods by which users can be beneficially drawn into the processes of innovation. Examples of this literature include methods to enable firms to identify lead users and draw on their ideas (Herstatt and von Hippel, 1992), how firms may shift innovation to users via toolkits (Franke and Piller, 2004), how the Internet can be used to draw users into product innovation (Sawhney et al., 2005) and the role of user communities in the commercialisation of products (Hienerth, 2006).

This body of work is an important contribution towards translating the theoretical and empirical insights made within the Innovation Studies and Science and Technology Studies literatures.

However, one problem with the existing IS, STS etc. literatures is that they exist within an implicit framing that determines what is examined, what issues are important, what data is collected, what methods are employed, the key themes that will be explored, and what counts as a 'contribution'. This implicit framing does two things: it places an invisible boundary around the issues that can be explored and renders invisible issues, approaches or actors that fall outside this boundary. One important contribution that emerges from exploring the notion of the Innovation Opportunity Space is that it surfaces the framings that exist within different literatures and highlights that the contributions within these literatures are partial and limited. But the IOS approach also values these contributions as they provide insights into the wider issues under examination. Intellectual property is not the only thing to think about when trying to understand innovation, but it does provide an important part of the story. Similarly, innovation by users or national rankings of R&D investments are also not things to think about when discussing innovation, but they are also an important part of the story. The IOS approach provides a mechanism to draw on these often competing contributions within a neutral framework.

5. Defending territory: changing forms of intellectual protection

Juha Arrasvuori, Liting Liang, Guo Wen and Jari Kuusisto

5.1 INTRODUCTION

This chapter examines intellectual protection as an Innovation Opportunity Space. Intellectual Property, or 'IP' for short, is a legislative construction for obtaining certain forms of protection to one's intellectual productivity, such as inventiveness or creative output. By obtaining protection to one's invention or artwork through Intellectual Property Rights (IPRs), one can obtain financial gain or some other form of compensation to one's intellectual output, as these rights render an immaterial asset into a property which can be sold or licensed, like a physical asset. In this chapter, we will examine how the global intellectual property rights 'system' has been traditionally exploited by individuals and businesses to obtain profit from their immaterial assets. However, the emergence of new digital technologies and alternative concepts to IPR have challenged the established practices in this area – and have met considerable resistance. This chapter will illustrate how intellectual property is currently a contested space for innovation with many conflicting commercial and creative interests.

5.2 THE IMPORTANCE OF IP IN THE GLOBAL ECONOMY

Before the end of the 20th century, a firm's physical assets were seen to determine the financial health of its business. This view changed by the late 1980s when intellectual property (IP) became the driving force for many firms and the global economy as a whole. An intellectual property is an intangible asset, in other words, an asset other than a monetary asset, which lacks physical substance. Although the value of IP can be complicated to evaluate at a given point in time, intangible property is similar to

---

BOX 5.1   INTELLECTUAL PROPERTY

According to the definition given by WIPO (the World Intellectual Property Organization), 'Intellectual Property' (IP) refers to 'creations of the mind', such as inventions; musical, literary and artistic works; designs; computer software; and symbols, words, phrases and images used in the commerce (WIPO). Basically any novel creation (an artistic work) or invention can be IP. An 'item' of IP can be valuable by itself (for example, a patent that can be sold or licensed), can be used to create a product or service (for example, the IP is a patent describing the working of a product), or can be a part of the content delivered by a service (for example, the IP is a fictional character appearing in videos and games).

BOX 5.2   INTELLECTUAL PROPERTY RIGHTS

Intellectual Property Rights (IPR) are legally recognised exclusive rights to intangible assets. Different types of intellectual property rights include, for example, copyright, trademarks, patents, and industrial design rights, which allow inventors or authors to earn recognition or financial benefit from what they have invented, created, designed or authored. Unpermitted use of an IP by a third party can, by using the legal system, be stopped if the intellectual property owner wants to do so.

---

physical property in the sense that it has ownership that can be recorded and transferred. 'Items' of intellectual property include e.g. patents, copyrighted works, franchises, and trademarks.

The following examples help to appreciate the importance of IP in modern economies. In the early 1990s, IBM decided to begin licensing its IP to other businesses. As consequence, IBM's annual royalties from IP licensing rose from $30 million in 1990 to $1 billion in 1999.[1] Similarly, in 2011, Google acquired for $12.5 billion the struggling Motorola Mobility unit primarily to obtain its 17,000 patents.[2] Three years later, Google sold this business unit to Lenovo for $2.91 billion but kept all but 2,000 of the patents,[3] obtaining fees from other manufacturers for using these patents. Indeed, licensing of IP is an enormous business: for example in 2015, merchandise associated with IP licensed from The Walt Disney Company singlehandedly obtained $52.5 billion in global retail sales.[4]

These examples illustrate the importance for businesses to create new IP, to defend their existing IP and to create maximum value out of their IP. This Opportunity Space is widened by the fact that a lot of things resulting from human creativity can be Intellectual Property, and this IP can be protected by intellectual property rights (IPRs) and monetised in a variety of ways. New technologies enable the creation of new kinds of IP but, as new technologies come into use, also potential new ways of misusing someone else's IP emerge. Next, we will explore how IP is created, and how firms and others often struggle to control and protect it in new technological contexts.

5.2.1 From Established IP to New Kinds of IP

Various types of intellectual property have been recognised by law in different nations for centuries (see Figure 5.1 for some examples). For example, the first patent law was passed by the Republic of Venice in 1474.[5] Although having existed for hundreds of years, artistic works such as literary works and musical compositions became intellectual property when these were recognised in law by authors' rights such as copyright and when there was a technology to reproduce these works in mass (for example, with the introduction of the printing press). National laws on IP were supplemented with the international harmonisation of laws starting with the Paris Convention of 1883 for patents and the Berne Convention of 1886 for copyrights.[6]

Through the centuries, the adaptation of new technologies have led to the introduction of novel kinds of IP, such as photographs, sound recordings, motion pictures, computer software, databases, video games, and most recently, digital 3D objects. It should be noted that photographs, movies and digital 3D object files are simply the medium carrying the IP. Furthermore, a single movie will consist of multiple kinds of IP protected by different IPRs, such as the written screenplay, any original work the screenplay is based on, the soundtrack, possibly certain characters and designs.

When a new technology is launched, a valuable Innovation Opportunity Space can emerge rapidly. This occurred for example with the introduction of the Internet Domain Name System (see Box 5.3). Since the mid-1990s, the boom of the Internet and social media has led to the emergence of new kinds of intellectual property. A web property is a point of presence such as a website used for representing an individual or an organisation on the Internet. A web property can be considered an intellectual property as the ownership of a website can be established through the registration of the domain name, and thus, the domain name becomes a sign of the brand associated with the website.

Three-dimensional objects can also be intellectual property for example as copyrighted or patented designs. At the time of writing, 3D printing (also known as Additive Layer Manufacturing) is making a breakthrough in many areas ranging from home printing to heavy industry applications. For the past 30 years, multiple 3D printing processes have been developed

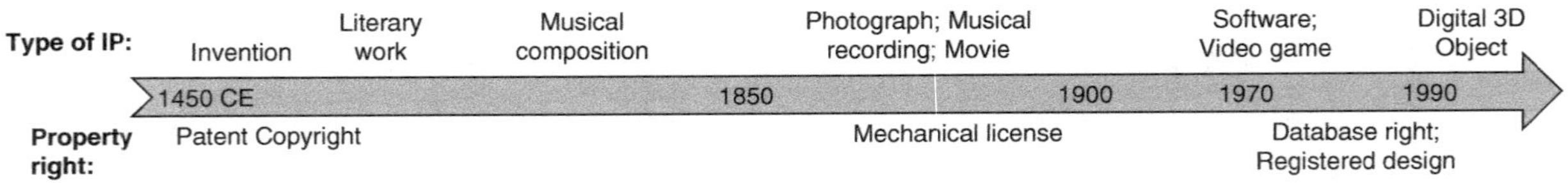

Type of IP:	Invention	Literary work	Musical composition	Photograph; Musical recording; Movie		Software; Video game	Digital 3D Object
	1450 CE		1850		1900	1970	1990
Property right:	Patent Copyright			Mechanical license		Database right; Registered design	

Figure 5.1 *A timeline of the introduction of some types of intellectual property (the years are approximate) and intellectual property rights protecting them. Some types of IP can be protected by several kinds of intellectual property rights*

BOX 5.3   DOMAIN NAMES AS VALUABLE IP

The Internet Domain Name System is an illustrative example of a lucrative Opportunity Space that opened through changes in regulation. A domain name is basically the address of a webpage or an online service. The registrant record of the Internet Domain Name System (DNS) identifies who has the right to use or to hand over a specific domain name. Before the DNS, servers on the Internet were accessed through their numerical Internet Protocol addresses, which were difficult to remember and cumbersome to access. DNS is a solution for mapping human-friendly domain names into Internet Protocol addresses. When domain names became available for registration in the 1990s, some farsighted individuals were quick to register for themselves simple and descriptive domain names for a small fee, with the intention of reselling the domain names for a good profit. At that time, available domain names included essentially all words or phrases that were not trademarks, for example, Jobs.com, Toys.com, and Hotels.com. Some individuals were even able to register domain names that were very similar to existing trademarks and trade names. During the dot.com boom of the late 1990s, some domain names, particularly in the United States, were sold by these individuals to businesses for hundreds of thousands or even millions of US dollars. For example, 'VacationRentals.com' is one of the most expensive domain names ever (re)sold. The domain name was purchased in 2007 by the vacation rental marketplace HomeAway, Inc. for $35 million, in part to prevent a competitor from obtaining the domain name.[7] 'VacationRentals.com' is also protected as a trademark.

---

based on the use of different materials (for example, plastics and metals) and methods for joining together layers of these materials (for example, laser melting, stereolithography, and laser sintering). The 3D printer is controlled by a computer program storing a 3D model file representing a physical object. By changing the 3D model file, different physical objects can be printed. The 3D model files can be created by scanning physical objects with a 3D scanner or by designing the object from scratch with 3D modelling software (for example, CAD application). As such software is readily available even for free, many users have created their own 3D designs and shared these model files on Internet sites such as Thingiverse.

So called '3D scanners' or '3D digitisers' produce copies by making a digital model of a pre-existing physical object. The 'replicated' object is placed in the device and is scanned to produce a three-dimensional model. Next, a 3D printer can then be used to print a physical replica (or a modified version) of the scanned object. With appropriate printing materials, for example spare parts to mechanical devices can conveniently be duplicated. A broken or an outworn component can be 'refurbished' through its 3D model on a computer before printing a spare part copy of it. However, with regard to IPRs, a significant problem is what degree of

BOX 5.4   THINGIVERSE AND 3D OBJECTS AS NEW KIND OF USER-CREATED IP

Thingiverse[8] is a website for sharing user-created 3D model files. Thingiverse was launched in 2008 as a companion site to MakerBot Industries, a firm developing 3D printers. Some of the designs are not simply 3D objects, but functional mechanical apparatuses. Users can publish on Thingiverse their 3D model files through a number of licenses, for example Creative Commons licenses (discussed below). Depending on the used license, a 3D model may subsequently be modified into derivative objects by other users. However, many users are content to simply access from Thingiverse the 3D models they are looking for and manufacture the objects with their 3D printers (Figure 5.2).

In 2012, public concerns that 3D printers could be used to manufacture functional firearms and other weapons led to Thingiverse removing some users' 3D model files of firearm components, justifying this action by referring to its terms of use, which prohibit users' contributions to the creation of weapons, or illegal or otherwise objectionable materials.[9]

Figure 5.2   The emergence of 3D printing technology has brought the struggle of control over IP to the domain of digital 3D objects. Some 3D object files are sold so that a royalty of each sold file is given to the rights owner of the protected design. Many of different models of 3D printers are available even in the 'home printing market'. Shown in the figure is the miniFactory 3D printer. Photo courtesy of miniFactory Oy Ltd

---

BOX 5.5   IQIYI – ACTIVE INVOLVEMENT OF USERS OF A VIDEO PLATFORM

Since its foundation in 2010 by the Chinese Internet service company Baidu, iQIYI has become China's leading online video platform. iQIYI has set up China's first copyrighted video library covering diverse contents including movies, TV drama, variety shows, comedy, documentaries and so on, setting its High-Definition video content as the industry benchmark for quality.

iQIYI involves its users through what is called an active participation model. This model means that users are encouraged to develop new products or services independently for enterprises and deliver them to producers. IQIYI also encourages users to upload and manage videos, and share channels, and it creates competitions to obtain new video content.

To obtain iPPC (Internet Professional Produced Content), iQIYI developed a 'sharing taste' strategy and provided a platform for profit sharing in cooperation with domestic content production companies. The aim of 'sharing taste' is to support and promote content production, and to establish an ecosystem including users, content producers, advertisers and video sites. The core function of 'sharing taste' is a major feature of its business model and is designed to ensure long-term engagement of users, content producers, platform operators and advertisers. The rights and obligations of both parties are clarified through a developer agreement, and the processes from uploading to sharing videos are protected by a user authorisation mechanism.

---

control the designer or producer of the physical object has over producing copies of the object.

Indeed, although 3D printing technology was first introduced in the mid-1980s, 30 years later the regulations related to 3D object files and their IPR management are still being shaped. Businesses raise concerns that consumers may use 3D printing to manufacture copyrighted or patented designs and parts by themselves. As a result, 3D printing has become a battleground between the interests of businesses desiring tight control for their IP and consumers wanting openness and freedom for their activities, with policy trying to strike a balance between these conflicting interests.

5.2.2   New Kinds of IP in the Online Media

Since the 1990s, digital services have challenged the traditional media companies for delivering professionally produced IP such as books, music, television programmes, movies and video games. Record distributors, and radio and television companies have seen their core business been challenged by pioneering digital services such as Napster and YouTube. Even Internet businesses that started as retailers, like Amazon.com, have begun to professionally produce their own media content such as 'television' programmes. Following the example of global access to 'multinational' content that YouTube has established, also some national businesses have set up digital services for delivering IP produced in the country for a national audience, for example iQIYI in China.

In addition to delivering professionally produced IP, digital services deliver content produced by its users. However, by using a digital service such as Facebook or YouTube, a user may give to the service firm some rights of his or her IP such as a photograph or video published in the service. The terms of the online service may specifically define that the service has rights to utilise the user's IP in any way it deems appropriate. Similarly, the terms of using the service may demand that a user must not publish in the service any IP he or she has no rights to. This way, the service firm is not responsible for any unauthorised publishing of IP. In return, the service may have an advertising payment scheme meaning that each view of the IP may be associated with displaying an advertisement, which will generate a micropayment to the user creating and submitting the IP. Millions, potentially even hundreds of millions of views may generate substantial financial compensation for the creator of the IP.

Furthermore, the person creating the IP may build reputational value for himself or herself on the service – in other words, making a brand of his or her public persona. Such value can be built across the Internet, on various services such as YouTube, Instagram, Twitter, blogs and so on. Over time, this reputation may lead to obtaining corporate sponsorships or other forms of monetary value creation, not to mention the enjoyment value from obtaining a potential audience to one's creations. The gamer/ commentator turned comedian PewDiePie (aka Felix Kjellberg) is an example of an Internet personality who is estimated to have more than 45 million followers to his humorous video posts.[10] He has been estimated to earn several million dollars per year from advertising payments based on views of his videos on YouTube.

In addition to establishing new space for novel ways of creating value, the emergence of the Internet, social media and digital technologies like 3D printing have led to a situation where the established global practices towards handling IP have entered into a state of change.

5.3   THE IP 'SYSTEM' IN TRANSITION

Although IP plays a major role in today's global economy, with the emergence of Internet and digital technologies the fundamentals of intellectual property have been challenged by the consumers. For example, in the late 1990s, Napster challenged the music industry by introducing a new approach to distribute digital music files. The music industry responded by attempting to introduce Digital Rights Management technologies first to (largely unsuccessfully) prevent copying music from Compact Discs and subsequently to control the peer-to-peer distribution of digital music files. The music industry also tried to defend itself by litigating against Napster and individual consumers distributing music files.

As is argued throughout this book, with digital technology, any consumer is also a potential producer who can instantly supply to a global audience through the Internet. The Internet has also introduced mechanisms through which consumers-turned-producers can benefit financially from their creativity. For example, the music video 'Gangnam style' was created by the South Korean musician Psy in 2012. Since then, the video has been viewed for free on YouTube more than 2 billion times that have generated advertisement payments (form ads displayed in conjunction with the video) of $2 million to the artist and his record label.[11]

The current situation is an example of the tension between interests of the 'old world' (driven by firms interest to make money by controlling their IP assets to the fullest) and the 'new world' (driven by consumers' interests), as suggested in Figure 5.3.

The 'new world' has emerged in part through changes in technology (in particular the Internet and digital media), and on the other hand, through changes in attitudes towards intellectual property rights, and the conception of creation and artwork. Laws for enforcing IPR are national, while services on the Internet are used effortlessly across national boarders. Besides being a battleground, the tension between the two worlds can make both worlds evolve. For example, Napster as a new method for distributing

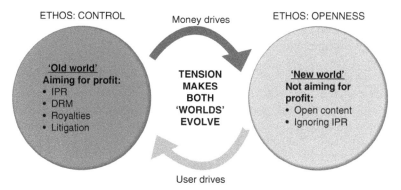

Figure 5.3   Characteristics of the 'old world' and the 'new world' with regard to intellectual property

music was born in the 'new world' basically by ignoring copyright. Napster allowed consumers to share music files with each other for free. The 'old world' responded to Napster by litigation and imposing Digital Rights Management to their products. However, the strongest impact Napster made on the 'old world' was that it led to the development of Spotify, iTunes Store and similar for-profit digital music distribution services. In other words, Napster was a 'rogue' innovation made in the 'new world' that was adapted in a more controlled form in the 'old world'. A major innovation such as Napster could perhaps have never been made within the constraints of the 'old world'. We will now examine intellectual property as an Innovation Opportunity Space, in other words, as a space for creating IP assets, managing these assets, creating value out of these assets, and collaborating between firms and users, online communities and the crowd. This Innovation Opportunity Space is in part driven by the ethos of control (of the 'old world') and the ethos of openness (of the 'new world'). It is likely that the practices and interests of both the 'old world' and the 'new world' will continue to co-exist.

5.4   THE INTELLECTUAL PROPERTY RIGHTS 'SYSTEM' AS AN INNOVATION OPPORTUNITY SPACE

An IP 'item' is an intangible asset that is legally owned by an entity, and thus can be financially exploited by its owner through rights granted in legislation. Thus the focus of examination in this chapter is also more broadly the Intellectual Property Rights 'system' that is a part of the global legal and rights management system (within which, for example, a patent or copyright can be obtained and enforced, and the fees for the use of an IP can be collected). Figure 5.4 presents an abstraction of global IPR 'system' as an Innovation Opportunity Space.

5.4.1   Architecture

The architecture of the global IPR 'system' consists of organisations such as patent, trademark and copyright offices, court and policing organisations, copyright collectives, collecting societies and performing rights organisations. The global IPR 'system' enables firms to obtain profit from their intangible assets, for example from prohibiting others to use the IP assets without permission (by seizing the production, selling or import of such products), collecting licensing fees and royalties from the authorised use, and so on.

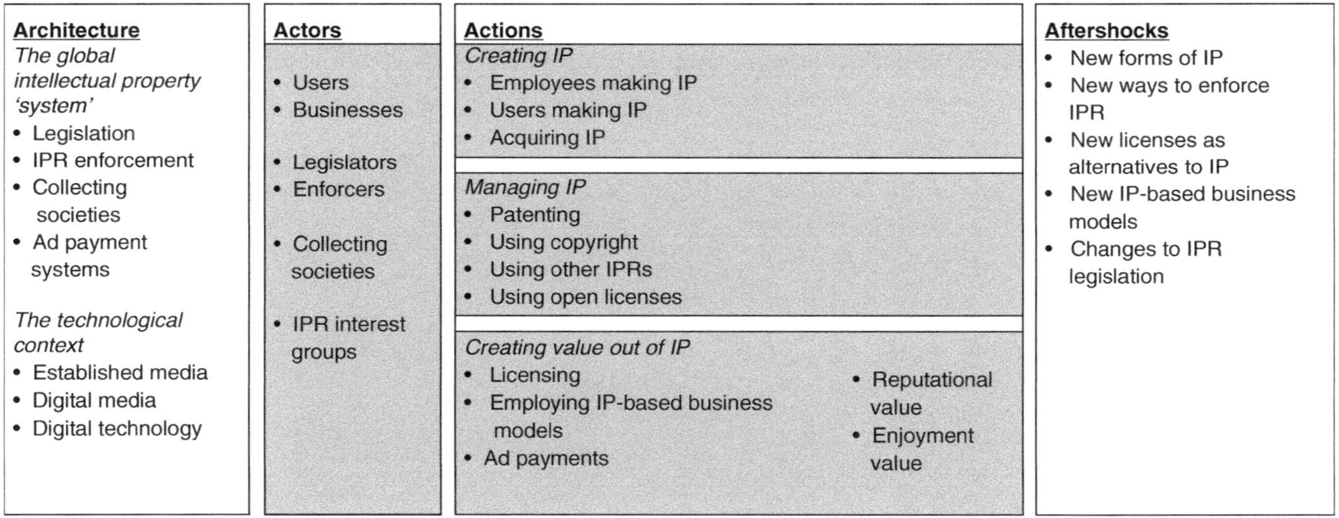

Architecture	Actors	Actions	Aftershocks
The global intellectual property 'system' • Legislation • IPR enforcement • Collecting societies • Ad payment systems *The technological context* • Established media • Digital media • Digital technology	• Users • Businesses • Legislators • Enforcers • Collecting societies • IPR interest groups	*Creating IP* • Employees making IP • Users making IP • Acquiring IP *Managing IP* • Patenting • Using copyright • Using other IPRs • Using open licenses *Creating value out of IP* • Licensing • Employing IP-based business models • Ad payments • Reputational value • Enjoyment value	• New forms of IP • New ways to enforce IPR • New licenses as alternatives to IP • New IP-based business models • Changes to IPR legislation

Figure 5.4 An abstraction of the Innovation Opportunity Space framework's Architecture, Actors, Actions and Aftershocks of the global IPR 'system'

5.4.2   Actors

There are several actors in this Innovation Opportunity Space, including firms and users, but also the people involved in defining the IP-related legislation, enforcement of the law, collecting licensing fees and royalties, arranging licensing deals, providing ad payment systems, and so forth. Innovating in this space involves exploiting these organisations and functions in novel ways, within the limits of the IP law.

5.4.3   Actions

There are three main types of actions in this IOS, namely creating IP, managing IP, and creating value out of IP. Different firms may have radically different approaches to these activities. Creating IP may be done internally by the firms' employees, in collaboration with other firms and users, or in an 'outsourced' manner by the users. IP can also be obtained by a firm through acquisition, licensing or some other form of rights transfer or lease. The actions of managing IP that a firm chooses to employ may also influence the creation and creating value out of IP by that firm. Indeed, these three kinds of actions may take place more or less simultaneously and influence each other. For example, at a given time, there may be a market pull for selling a certain kind of IP, which may heavily guide the short-term IP creation and management activities in an organisation. In other words, the optimal management and value creation out of IP may be considered already while creating the IP.

5.4.4   Aftershocks

The aftershocks from these actions in the IP IOS include new forms of IP, new ways to enforce IPR, new licenses for facilitating sharing and collaborating in the digital environment, new IP-based business models and changes to IPR legislation or interpretation of the legislation. These aftershocks will be discussed throughout the remainder of this chapter.

5.5   THE CHANGING LANDSCAPE OF IP

In this section we examine some approaches to the actions of creating IP, managing IP, and creating value out of IP. We will now examine how firms are engaged in these activities, and in some instances, how they collaborate with consumers.

5.5.1 IP Creation

Until the final decade of the 20th century, intellectual property was typically created internally and in secrecy in firms by employed researchers, engineers, designers and artists. The IP that was created was secured through patents, copyrights, trademarks, trade secrets and various other protection mechanisms. It was monetised primarily by the firm manufacturing physical goods based on the IP (for example, in the case of a patent describing the core functionality of a product) or through physical goods delivering the IP (for example, music on Compact Discs). Indeed, the patenting system was originally developed to support this exploitation of IP through physical manufacturing. Firms held strongly to their IP and defended it aggressively from misappropriation, with IP licensing to other firms (for example, operating in other territories or business areas) a viable alternative approach to create additional value. However, patents are less relevant in the service sector, where IP is protected mainly through copyrights and trademarks,[12] with franchising a typical method that is used in the service sector to create value out of IP by licensing trademarks and methods (for example, a fast food restaurant concept).

As patents have a lifespan of about 20 years at the most, firms must constantly renew their patent portfolios with new inventions. In a digital media service, there is a constant demand for new content in the form of videos, images and music. Opening up the innovation process to users, online communities and the crowd is used by firms to obtain IP such as patents, or artistic and practical creations. Firms will often collaborate with these groups to understand better their needs and provide solutions – potential IP – to these needs. As discussed elsewhere in this book, digital services such as Facebook and Pinterest rely on users publishing their creations – in other words their IP – on the service, with much of the content on these services being user IP. Similar practices have also been applied directly in patent creation. Firms such as Intellectual Ventures, Procter & Gamble and Nokia Corporation have launched programmes that allow any individual to submit unsolicited ideas of potential inventions. The firms evaluate the submitted ideas confidentially and may choose to apply for a patent for them. The firm will be the patent applicant and owner paying the patenting fees (and obtaining the potential future profits), while the inventor will obtain a financial compensation from the firm.

5.5.2 IP Management

The management of intellectual property typically starts with protecting an IP item. There are several approaches to protect an IP item, depending

BOX 5.6   GATHERING IP FROM EXTERNAL SOURCES

In addition to utilising their internal research and development personnel and con-tracted external workforce to generate new IP particularly in the form of patents, companies such as Procter & Gamble (Connect + Develop[13]), Nokia (Invent with Nokia[14]) and Intellectual Ventures have begun to involve their users to obtain new patents. In the following case description we discuss the approach taken by Intellectual Ventures to obtain new IP from outside the company. Furthermore, we discuss how new business has been generated in Finland when certain companies have given away their non-core IP to start-up entrepreneurs.

Intellectual Ventures – 'Outsourcing' IP Creation
Intellectual Ventures is a US-based patent holding, licensing and enforcement company. In addition to buying patents, Intellectual Ventures obtains new IP through the efforts of its internal R&D staff, and also through an extensive external network. The company has essentially outsourced some of the basic work of turning new ideas into patents by establishing a network of 3,000 inventors at more than 400 universities, firms, and research institutions.[15] According to the company's website,[16] any individual can apply for joining the Intellectual Ventures Inventor Network and once they have joined, can submit their potential inventions to the firm for review.

Intellectual Ventures has two programmes for obtaining IP from external inven-tors: the Topic Invention Program and an Open Invention Program. The latter programme offers flexibility to inventors so they can submit invention ideas on any technical field, whereas the topic invention programme targets inventions that solve a particular problem as defined by a 'Request for Invention' specification made by the company.

The invention selection process has three steps: first, there is a pre-screen inven-tion review by local specialists; this is followed by a single invention review by exter-nal experts; with a final review round where an international panel scores inventions and the most promising are selected for patenting. Licensing rewards for the external inventor can exceed $50,000 per invention with ideas not selected for patenting being returned to the inventor, who can then apply for a patent on their own account.

Innovation Mill – Creating Value from Non-core IP
The Innovation Mill is an initiative driven by Nokia Corporation in Finland. While being the leading mobile phone company for a decade, Nokia accumulated many patents, business ideas, technologies and concepts for which business develop-ment had been stopped at some point, even though this IP could hold a significant business potential. In 2009, Nokia launched the Innovation Mill programme for turning several of such unused non-core IPs into commercial products and ser-vices. The idea of the initiative is that Nokia gives away its non-core IP to existing companies or start-ups for developing these inventions and ideas into valuable new products and services. In practice, companies receive free licenses to use IP, with Nokia often obtaining little direct financial benefit and positioning the Innovation Mill programme as a part of its corporate responsibility.[17] Other Finnish companies have joined the Innovation Mill initiative to license their non-core IP and five years after the initiative was launched, more than 80 start-up companies have been formed in Finland with the help of the IP made available.[18]

on the type of the property. For example, IP that is a technical invention may be protected through patenting whilst an artistic work is protected by copyright. In this section, we will describe the most important types of intellectual property rights, namely patent, copyright and trademark and discuss their use in the context of the IPR system. The recognition and definition of these rights vary across legislations in different countries, however, we concentrate on describing the situation mainly in the United States and Europe. In the past decade, alternatives to traditional IPRs have become available in the forms of Copyleft and Creative Commons licenses.

Different Intellectual Property Rights offer different kinds of protection for varying time periods and varying costs are associated with obtaining certain IPRs, patenting being the most expensive method of IP protection. Intellectual property rights are not mutually exclusive and, for example, it may be possible to obtain a design patent to a creation that is also protected by copyright or trademark. As a result, many IP producers attempt to protect their creations as broadly as possible through various complementary IPRs.

The copyright system originates from the era of print media, fixed

---

BOX 5.7 PATENT

A patent is a set of exclusive rights granted by a state to the owner of an invention for an invention for a limited time, typically 20 years. A granted patent provides the patent owner with the right to decide how the invention can be used. A patent also provides the right to *exclude* others from using the invention, for example, to develop products that infringe the invention disclosed in the patent document. Traditionally, a patent was used by its owner to protect the manufacture of a product. When the patent owner observes that a patent is infringed, it can litigate in a court to stop the infringement.

The owner of the patent who has the rights to exploit the patent is not necessarily the inventor of the patented invention. In many cases, the inventor is an employee of the patent owner. In some cases, the inventor has given away his rights to the invention to an entity who has the financial means to pursue a patent for the invention.

An invention can be granted a patent if it has a patentable subject matter, novelty, inventive step or non-obviousness, and utility. A patent has to be applied for in each state separately. A granted patent may later be invalidated by a court ruling, for example, if it can be shown that there was prior art to the claimed invention, in other words, the proposed invention was already known or published.

In addition to patents, some similar IPRs are available for inventors and firms for obtaining protection to their inventions. For example, *business method patents* claim new methods of doing business, for example, new types of e-commerce, insurance, banking and tax compliance. Business method patents can be obtained only in certain jurisdictions, for example, the United States.

BOX 5.8   COPYRIGHT

Copyright describes the rights that creators have over their creations. Works protected by copyright include for example books, music, paintings, sculptures, movies, maps and technical drawings. Authors' rights are a part of copyright law. Here, an 'author' is the person(s) whose creativity led to the protected work being created. Authors' rights include economic rights, which is a property right limited in time and which may be transferred to other people or organisations. These economic rights allow the author or their holder to profit financially from the creation, including the right to authorise any reproduction or adaptation of the work.

Copyright does not have to be applied for. Copyright is secured automatically when a work is created, that is, when a work is fixed in a tangible form. To secure copyright, the work must be independent and original. Copyright protection applies to expressions of ideas, but not to ideas themselves, nor to procedures or methods. The copyright of artistic works varies across jurisdictions but will typically expire several decades after the author has deceased.

---

media (for example, vinyl records), and broadcast media. The rise of computers, digital media and the Internet has motivated some actors to develop alternatives to established IPRs. With a computer, any person can create an artistic work (for example, an image or musical composition) and distribute it through the Internet. That work may then be used by others as the starting point of a new derivative work such as a remix, collage or mash-up. Established IPRs such as copyright may prohibit global distribution, presentation, and re-use of artistic works and other creations, even if the original work's creator does not want to impose such restrictions but the rights owners choose to. Indeed, copyright is typically used by an author or rights owner to prohibit unauthorised distribution and modification of a work, and to stop plagiarism. Importantly, an author has moral rights over his or her creation, and can appeal for a defaming representation of his or her work to be removed.

From the viewpoint of encouraging creativity, the copyright system may have a negative effect as there is the threat that by creating and publishing a work, one can unintentionally break someone else's copyright. In practice this can mean that the rights owner or a rights management agency can claim for damages if someone's published work is considered to violate an earlier copyrighted work. Here we again can see the tension between the 'old world' and the 'new world' and copyright can be seen as a typical control mechanism of the 'old world'. As viable options to copyright, activists of the 'new world' have developed 'open licenses' such as Copyleft and Creative Commons.

Copyleft is an alternative form of licensing using copyright law to offer

*Figure 5.5   The copyleft symbol appears like the copyright symbol mirrored.
Although visually suggesting to be an 'opposite' to copyright,
copyleft actually uses copyright law to give creators a range of
new possibilities to have their works distributed and potentially
adapted by others into new versions or essentially new works*

the right to distribute copies or modified versions of a work on the condition that the same rights are preserved in the modified versions as in the
initial work (Figure 5.5). Copyleft was first proposed by the programmer
Richard Stallman in 1989. People advocating copyleft licensing aim to
build a richer public domain by providing a 'some rights reserved' alternative to the 'all rights reserved' condition of copyright. Copyleft-type
licenses ensure that a work remains available for re-use and define the
rules under which the work can be adapted. So far copyleft-type licenses
have been used for making creative works freely available to be adapted by
others under the condition that all modified versions of the work are also
free. Images, music, written text, computer software and 3D object files
have been published under copyleft-type licenses.

Creative Commons is a non-profit organisation for countering what
are perceived as restrictive permission conditions of established IPRs.
Since its founding in 2001, the Creative Commons organisation has been
acknowledged for its redefinition of the role of the 'commons' in the era of
digital media and the Internet. As any 'creation of the mind' can be an IP,
any 'common' user can be a creator producing new IP. Creative Commons
offers a variety of licenses that have been used by 'commons' but also by
professionals.

For computer software, the GNU General Public License was the first
Copyleft-type license to be used extensively. Currently it is the most used
free software license allowing end users the freedoms to use, examine, share
and modify software and other digital content. By using the GNU General
Public License, a software developer may require that all adaptions of the
original software must be released as source code as well as the executable

BOX 5.9   CREATIVE COMMONS LICENSES

The Creative Commons organisation has released a set of licenses that allow creators to define which rights they reserve when publishing a work, and which rights to their work they give up for the benefit of their audience or other creators (Figure 5.6). Many online services allow users to publish their creations on the service under Creative Commons licenses. For example, by early 2016, more than 315 million photos have been published on Flickr under the Creative Commons licenses.

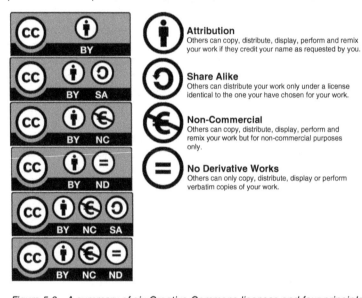

Attribution
Others can copy, distribute, display, perform and remix your work if they credit your name as requested by you.

Share Alike
Others can distribute your work only under a license identical to the one your have chosen for your work.

Non-Commercial
Others can copy, distribute, display, perform and remix your work but for non-commercial purposes only.

No Derivative Works
Others can only copy, distribute, display or perform verbatim copies of your work.

Figure 5.6   A summary of six Creative Commons licenses and four principles they entail in different combinations.[19] In all these licenses, the creator of the original work must be attributed. A work can be licensed for either commercial or for non-commercial purposes such as copying, displaying, or adapting. There are also other Creative Commons licenses, for example 'CC0', which is for waiving all rights over a work, essentially submitting it to the public domain. License Buttons and Icons by Creative Commons

application. This approach can stimulate the redevelopment of a software application or the re-use of some of its components in another application.

Closed IP versus open IP
In the context of an opening out of innovation, the broader challenge firms face in managing their IP is what property to keep closed (that is, protected) and what IP to keep open as an input to open and user innovation or

creation. The established practice towards managing intellectual property has been that firms should aim to keep their IP as closed as possible, in other words, tightly protected by IPRs such as patents, copyright and trademarks. This practice has made sense in the manufacturing context, when firms manufacture physical goods on the basis of the IP. Furthermore, the business may have obtained additional revenue by selectively licensing its IP to other manufacturers. This established practice might no longer be optimal in the context of services and new digital products. As discussed throughout this book firms may collaborate with external groups to create innovations or a firm may open some of its intellectual property to stimulate innovation by users and others in order to benefit the firm's products and services.

A firm may also 'open' its IP by choosing not to prohibit use of its IP for non-commercial purposes. For example, Lucasfilm Ltd, the owners of intellectual property related to the Star Wars universe have allowed fans to create their own movies that use copyrighted designs from the Star Wars movies, like characters, costumes, spaceship designs, sound effects and music, as long as these fan films were not distributed for profit. Lucasfilm has even supported competitions for Star Wars fan films. Making and viewing fan films does not cut Lucasfilm's (since 2012 a part of The Walt Disney Corporation) businesses offering of movies and TV shows, and licensing the Star Wars IP to video game developers and merchandise manufacturers.

Smart management of a firm's IP assets involves combining the closed and open approaches, for example, by patenting some parts of a technology and offering free access for users and others to utilise other parts of the technology. For example, a firm offering digital content may give partial open access for application developers to some of its IP (for example, the contents of a database) through a software interface (API) with features controlled by the firm. Through the API, the firm owning the IP can obtain information on how the accessed data is used through the various applications made by third parties and thus obtain information on users' behaviour towards the IP.

In other industries leading companies like Toyota and Ford have shared their patents with the other parties in this area essentially for free in order to boost the industry and technology development as a whole.[20] Organisations such as Global Innovation Commons and Open Invention Network (discussed below) assist small players to utilise existing IP without fearing patent infringement litigation.

5.5.3 Creating Value Out of IP

The traditional approach to create value out of IP has been to manufacture and sell goods based on the IP. We call this the Old Form Innovation

BOX 5.10   ROVIO AND ANGRY BIRDS: CONVERTING 'IP PIRATES' INTO PARTNERS

Unlicensed use of its IP in the form of 'pirated' products is a major problem for many companies. The typical response has been to try to litigate to get the pirated products removed from the market. An example of a company which has adopted an unusual approach towards unauthorised use of its IP is the Finnish company Rovio Entertainment Ltd, famous for its Angry Birds game and related IP. Immediately after the first Angry Birds game became a global hit in 2010, Rovio became a merchandising giant by working with firms from different sectors through licensing. Within just two years, by the end of 2012, the company had nearly 40 per cent of its roughly $200 million in revenues coming from its licensing operations. The company has built Angry Birds into an international prominent brand rather than focusing on developing new games exclusively (Figure 5.7). Rovio has been involved in everything from plush toys to theme parks and even a new game franchise by creatively blending its Angry Birds IP with the Star Wars IP. It has been very unusual for a mobile game developer to take one piece of original mobile game IP, make it successful and then turn the success into the foundation for developing itself as a global entertainment company. However, Rovio has arguably been one of the most recognisable entertainment properties in the global market during the early 2010s.

Rovio surprised the public when an unlicensed Angry Birds theme park was opened in China. Rather than responding with a lawsuit, as has been the 'old world' approach in IP infringement cases, Rovio decided to attempt to collaborate with the theme park's operators. Likewise, following the popularity of the Angry Birds game, there were a host of Angry Birds products produced by companies that are not official licensees. Rovio is taking a mixed approach in dealing with this issue – on the one hand, it waves a legal stick at some pirates; on the other hand, it seeks to turn most pirates into partners. In order to collaborate with these pirates, Rovio has employed a set of tactics such as recruiting some IP infringers to be partners, and even providing some of them free advertising space in its Angry Birds games. If there are sound ideas, Rovio adopts them, calling this approach 'pirating the pirates'.

Rovio's IP strategy has broken business routines regarding IP in this area as established companies usually see pirates as enemies rather than partners. Rovio's way of dealing with piracy is based on the lessons of the mostly failed attempts of the music industry trying to fight piracy. Based on the lessons, Rovio decided that instead of treating the customers as users, it would prefer to see them as fans. The company believes that the most important thing for its business to grow is to keep expanding its fan base. Therefore, it is reasonable to believe that Rovio actually welcomes piracy as it could help the company get a broader fan base. After having established a global fan base, the company may protect more aggressively it's core business against IP infringement, for example, it may choose to fight in court against pirated versions of games and videos.

Figure 5.7 *Angry Birds IP has been used in more or less everywhere from video games to animated films, and from plush toys to soft drink cans. Image © Rovio Entertainment Ltd*

that was shaped during the Industrial Revolution of the 19th century and continues into the present day as the 'old world' mindset. However, alternatives to this approach have begun to emerge. In this section we examine some alternative approaches of financially profiting from intellectual property. We look at established and emerging IP-based business models including IP licensing and enforcement, brokering and auctioneering, and defensive patent pools as a counterforce to IP-based business models.

IP licensing

Licensing means obtaining permission to use someone's IP. Most kinds of IP can be licensed. Licensing is done under contract between the licensor (IP owner) and the licensee who wants to use the IP in association with a product or service. Typically, the licensor operates in a different business area than the licensee, so they are not direct competitors. When manufacturing products that use common technology and are based on standards, firms must license IP from firms owning patents related to these technologies and standards. A convenient way for such a firm is to license all the necessary IP for a product by signing a single contract with an IP pool. Obtaining a license spares the licensee from possible claims of IP infringement brought by the licensor. Contractual terms for licenses include, for example, a specific time period and market area, and renewal and invalidation conditions.

Brand licensing is used by brand owners to extend an IP such as a trademark or copyrighted character into products of a different nature

---

BOX 5.11   GLOBAL INNOVATION COMMONS – FREE LICENSING OF 'DISCARDED' IP

Global Innovation Commons is an undertaking by the intangible asset management firm M-CAM (Mosaic Collateral Asset Management) aiming to stimulate innovation all over the world. Global Innovation Commons has assembled hundreds of thousands of IP items, mostly patents that are either expired, no longer maintained, disallowed, or unprotected in at least some market areas. Global Innovation Commons shares these patents under a license requiring licensees to share with everyone else what they have done based on the licensed IP. Also, the Global Innovation Commons must be referenced. On the Global Innovation Commons website,[21] the available IP is grouped into four main categories: Agriculture, Clean energy, Water, and World Health. Through the website, it is possible for a budding entrepreneur to see, for example, which patents are in the public domain in a certain country and in which countries the patent in question may still be enforced.

---

manufactured and marketed by another firm. To name an example, the Angry Birds IP started as a mobile game but was rapidly licensed by its owner Rovio Entertainment to diverse products such as toys, clothes and foodstuff, and even to services like activity parks. Brand licensing is an enormous worldwide business: in 2015 merchandise associated with IP licensed from The Walt Disney Company obtained $52.5 billion in global retail sales, making Disney the top licensor.[22]

Licensing patents is a major approach to create value out of IP. As discussed earlier, before the 1980s firms tended to keep most of their IP for themselves whether or not they used them in their products. Over the years, firms investing heavily in R&D had created lots of IPs such as patents that they have not used in any way. Starting in the late 1980s, some of these firms began to sell or license these IPs to other firms. IBM was one firm leading this trend: the firm's royalties from licensed IP increased from $30 million in 1990 to more than $1 billion in 1999. Following the success of IBM, many other firms began to systematically license their IP.[23]

IP brokering and auctioneering
IP brokering and auctioneering firms seek to assist IP owners in finding buyers rather than licensees for their IP. Selling IP may be implemented through auctions, such as those organised by Ocean Tomo. Unlike IP licensing firms, IP brokers operate both with sellers and buyers. They may also offer consulting services to clients for acquiring patents, for example for defensive purposes. Some IP brokers may have the resources to obtain IP for themselves, and aggregate IPs from different sources into portfolios that they resell for profit.

BOX 5.12   SISVEL – THE BUSINESS MODELS OF A PATENT LICENSER

Sisvel is a patent management and licensing company founded in Italy in 1982 to acquire and maximise the value of an Italian television set manufacturers' portfolio of patents related to television technology. The firm rapidly became a global player in the IP licensing community. The company added Sisvel Technology as a subsidiary to obtain research and development capabilities to create new IP.

Sisvel targets the entertainment industry and holds a portfolio of nearly 500 patents. Sisvel assists firms to identify, value, and market IP to generate new income streams derived from licensing programmes, and to collect and distribute the royalties. Sisvel offers licenses to single patents or to patent pools. The single licensed IP either belongs to Sisvel or has been acquired from third parties based on a valuation by the firm. Sisvel then acts on behalf of the owner of the license to deal with any issues related with the patent including legal conflicts.

Sisvel also puts together patent pools that are essential to a particular technology and then grants licenses to third parties at a fee less than the total cost of individual licenses. The royalties derived from sub-granting the patent pool may be shared between the owners of the licenses and Sisvel as the administrator of the patent pool. The licensors belonging to the patent pool, which are at the same time producers of the technology, will act as normal licensees when it comes to acquiring a license to the patent pool. This generates a flow of royalties also among the members of the patent pool.

IP enforcement

IP enforcement describes the business model of firms owning patents or other IP assets that attempt to license their IP by contacting firms operating in the field related to the IP, and then file infringement suits against firms refusing licensing the IP. Some of these firms are called non-practicing entities (NPE) because they do not use their IP to manufacture products or provide services. These firms are sometimes derogatively called 'patent trolls'.

Defensive patent pools

Organisations providing defensive patent pools seek to acquire patent portfolios for defensive reasons. These may be formed by multiple firms who join forces in response to litigation threats from patent enforcement companies. Defensive pools may be formed when each joining firm brings (some of) its patents to the pool for the other pool members' use. The pool members may also collect funds when attempting to purchase the relevant patents in their area of business before the enforcers obtain them.

BOX 5.13   OCEAN TOMO – THE BUSINESS MODEL OF A IP BROKER AND AUCTIONEER

Ocean Tomo is an US-based IP merchant bank offering financial products and services related to IP, including expert services, valuation, research, ratings, investments, risk management, and transactions. Ocean Tomo not only obtains patents and offers legal services but also provides customers with various ways of IP transactions and financial products.

Acting as a patent broker is the basic IP-based business model of Ocean Tomo. Like many other patent brokers, the company aims to help patent owners in finding buyers rather than licensees. As a patent buyer, Ocean Tomo assists technology companies in acquiring patents and helps them develop IP strategies. By offering IP management advice to patent owners and buyers, Ocean Tomo has been able to continue its engagement with these patent owners even after patents or portfolios are sold.

Ocean Tomo has also pioneered live IP auctions. It introduced the world's first public auction of patents, trademarks and copyrights in 2006. The auctions have included patents, business method patents and, for example, the rights to Jimi Hendrix's music recordings. These IP live auctions functioned like any other live auctions, similarly to, for example, art at Christie's. Prior to the event, an information kit was sent to the potential buyers containing non-confidential information on title clearance, market potential value, technology and patent description, and other details on the lot. The lots were sold to the highest bidder on condition that the highest bid exceeded the seller's reserve price. Ocean Tomo collected fees from both sellers and buyers: sellers paid a listing fee, bidders paid registration fees. Ocean Tomo sold this auction business in 2009, but launched in 2014 a next generation live IP auction operation in response to demand from the patent acquisition community.

5.6   FUTURE POSSIBILITIES FOR IP

As discussed earlier in this chapter, although the global IPR system gives ample opportunities to obtain financial and other forms value from inventions or creations, there are also tensions between 'old world' and the 'new world' approaches to IP. The current situation can be understood as a continuum on the potential attitudes towards IP, as suggested in Figure 5.8. As the figure suggests, on one end, there is the 'old world' view of IP, whilst at the other end, there is a quite different approach. New approaches to IP like the Creative Commons and Copyleft act as a link between the interests at the opposite ends of the continuum, and different actors can move their attitudes towards IP along the continuum based on their interests and resources. Firms can also seem to attract users and others towards the traditional end of the continuum by offering compensations (for example, ad view payments or inventor fees for patents). Perhaps most significantly,

BOX 5.14   INTELLECTUAL VENTURES

Intellectual Ventures is a US-based patent holding, licensing and enforcement company. It licenses patents through patent portfolios put together within a broad range of 50 technology areas. Intellectual Ventures was founded in 2000 and has obtained capital to buy patents through investors including Google, Microsoft, Nokia, eBay, Amazon.com, Yahoo, and Sony.

Intellectual Ventures acquires patents from different owners and aggregates similar patents into portfolios in order to license these portfolios to third parties, or to litigate firms claimed to infringe these patents. The result of the litigation may be income in the form of licensing fees. The company reports having 70,000 'IP assets' (that can be, for example, granted patents and patent applications) out of which 40,000 are in 'active monetisation programmes'. The company is estimated to own 30,000 granted patents, thus making it one of the largest patent holders worldwide.[24]

Although the company develops some products from its patents through its unit Intellectual Ventures Lab, some commentators argue that Intellectual Ventures is nevertheless a non-practicing entity because its products don't reach commercial use and this situation gives them an advantage for counter-claims of patent infringement; as the company doesn't make products, it cannot infringe other companies' patents.[25]

BOX 5.15   OPEN INVENTION NETWORK – PROVIDING DEFENCE AGAINST PATENT ENFORCERS

Open Invention Network is a company that acquires patents and licenses them royalty free to entities who agree not to assert their own patents against Linux-related systems and applications. It has more than 650 licensees. Open Invention Network holds more than 850 patents and patent applications, for example, patents that cover fundamental aspects of business-to-business e-commerce. Open Invention Network is financially backed up by its members including Google, IBM, NEC, Philips, Red Hat, and Sony.

Additionally, Open Invention Network drives a 'Linux defenders'[26] programme involving the open source community. The aim of this programme is to eradicate what it considers 'poor quality' patents, which patent enforcement companies may apply for and use in litigation. 'Linux defenders' produces 'defensive publications' that disclose solutions and inventions, which are known by practitioners, but so far have not been patented. The aim of these publications is to make such inventions known to patent examiners, thus preventing them from granting patents to applications claiming such inventions. 'Linux defenders' also asks for prior art contributions from the open source community to ensure that patent examiners become aware of prior art relevant to patent applications that are being examined. Additionally, prior art relevant to issued patents is requested from the open source community in order to permit invalidation of patents that were granted because of the patent examiners' unawareness of the prior art.

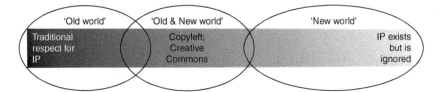

Figure 5.8   *The 'continuum' of IP has traits of both the 'old world' and the 'new world'*

major innovations made in the 'new world' can be adapted in a more manageable form by the 'old world'.

The potential benefits of following the practices of the 'old world' have been established for a much longer period and, as a result, are easier to grasp and describe than the potential gains to be obtained from the 'new world'. Different IPR laws protect the interests of, for example, an author or an inventor. The two primary approaches of protecting IP discussed in this chapter have been copyright and patenting. These two main 'paths' for obtaining value from one's inventiveness and creativity, that is, patenting and copyright, are summarised as simplified process charts in Figure 5.9.

For obtaining protection to several kinds of IP, copyright can be a viable option to use. Copyright does not have to be applied for. However, there may be advantages of registering the work at a national Copyright Office, and as such obtaining a stronger position to take legal action for infringement. Through copyright, the creator of a work can ensure that for example the ad view payments to one of his videos are directed to him and unauthorised duplicates of the video are removed. Copyright protects computer software. Not all creative people are motivated by pursuing financial gain from their creative activities. Copyleft is an approach of giving away in a controlled manner certain of one's rights towards a creation. Various licenses, for example, those provided by Creative Commons can be used for this purpose.

Patenting requires funds for authoring a patent application usually with the help of a patent agent or lawyer and for the costs for pursuing for a patent and periodically maintaining a granted patent in each state the patented invention is to be exploited. A granted patent may be monetised by an individual through manufacturing a product based on the patent, or by licensing or selling the patent to firms creating patent pools such as Intellectual Ventures or firms welcoming the efforts of external inventors like Procter & Gamble and Nokia.

As illustrated in this chapter, the global IPR 'system' is a vast Innovation Opportunity Space that evolves from the tension between the control- and

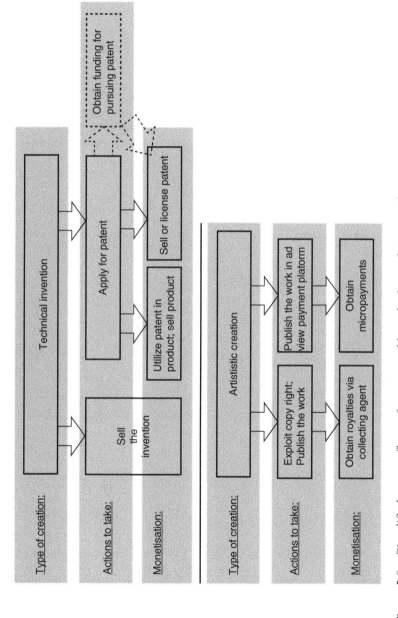

Figure 5.9 Simplified process flows of some possible paths for exploiting one's IP

monetisation-driven interests of the 'old world' and the 'information must be free'-ethos of the 'new world'. This Opportunity Space has plenty of room for both innovative and artistic minds to operate in.

NOTES

1. Rivette and Kline (2000).
2. http://money.cnn.com/2012/05/22/technology/google-motorola/ (accessed 8 February 2017).
3. https://investor.google.com/releases/2014/0129.html (accessed 8 February 2017).
4. http://www.licensemag.com/license-global/top-150-global-licensors-2 (accessed 23 March 2017).
5. Kaufer (1980), pp. 5–6.
6. Granstrand (2005).
7. http://www.techworm.net/2015/07/20-most-expensive-domain-names-of-all-time.html (accessed 8 February 2017).
8. https://www.thingiverse.com.
9. http://www.forbes.com/sites/andygreenberg/2012/12/19/3d-printing-startup-makerbot-cracks-down-on-printable-gun-designs/ (accessed 8 February 2017).
10. http://www.techtimes.com/articles/99097/20151024/how-pewdiepie-gained-40-million-followers-and-became-emperor-of-the-internet.htm (accessed 8 February 2017).
11. http://www.forbes.com/sites/hughmcintyre/2014/06/16/at-2-billion-views-gangnam-style-has-made-psy-a-very-rich-man/ (accessed 8 February 2017).
12. Blind, Evangelista and Howells (2010).
13. http://www.pgconnectdevelop.com/.
14. https://inventwithnokia.nokia.com/.
15. Kersetter and Lowensohn (2012).
16. https://ivin.intven.com/.
17. Hossain (2012).
18. http://www.spinverse.com/accelerating-innovation/results/ (accessed 8 February 2017).
19. https://creativecommons.org.
20. http://www.forbes.com/sites/matthewdepaula/2015/05/31/ford-follows-tesla-and-toyota-in-releasing-ev-patents/ (accessed 8 February 2017).
21. http://www.globalinnovationcommons.org.
22. http://www.licensemag.com/license-global/top-150-global-licensors-2 (accessed 23 March 2017).
23. Rivette and Kline (2000).
24. Kersetter and Lowensohn (2012).
25. Kersetter and Lowensohn (2012).
26. http://www.linuxdefenders.org/.

BIBLIOGRAPHY

Barton, J.H. (1993) Adapting the intellectual property system to new technologies, in M.B. Wallerstein, R.A. Schoen and M.E. Mogee (eds), *Global Dimensions of Intellectual Property Rights in Science and Technology*, Washington, DC: National Academy Press, pp. 256–283.
Blind, K., Cremers, K. and Mueller, E. (2009) The influence of strategic patenting on companies' patent portfolios, *Research Policy*, vol. 38, pp. 428–436.

Blind, K., Evangelista, R. and Howells, J. (2010) Knowledge regimes and intellectual property protection in services: a conceptual model and empirical testing, in Faïz Gallouj and Faridah Djellal (eds), *The Handbook of Innovation and Services: A Multi-disciplinary Perspective*, Cheltenham, UK and Northampton, MA, USA: Edward Elgar Publishing, pp. 342–366.

Cornish, W.R. (1999) *Intellectual Property: Patents, Copyright, Trade Marks and Allied Rights*, London: Sweet and Maxwell.

Crouch, Dennis (2012). Intellectual ventures. Accessed on 8 February 2017 from http://www.patentlyo.com/patent/2012/09/intellectual-ventures.html.

de Laat, Paul B. (2005) Copyright or copyleft?: an analysis of property regimes for software development, *Research Policy*, vol. 34, no. 10, pp. 1511–1532.

Granstrand, Ove (2005) Innovation and intellectual property rights, in Jan Fagerberg, David C. Mowery and Richard R. Nelson (eds), *The Oxford Handbook of Innovation*, Oxford: Oxford University Press, pp. 266–290.

Hossain, Mokter (2012) Open innovation mill: utilization of Nokia's non-core ideas, *Procedia – Social and Behavioral Sciences*, 12 October 2012 (vol. 58), pp. 765–773.

Kaufer, E. (1980) *The Economics of the Patent System*, London: Harwood Academic Publishers.

Kersetter, Jim and Lowensohn, Josh (2012) Inside intellectual ventures, the most hated company in tech, accessed on 8 February 2017 from http://news.cnet.com/8301-13578_3-57496641-38/inside-intellectual-ventures-the-most-hated-company-in-tech/.

Neuhäusler, P. (2012) The use of patents and informal appropriation methods – differences between sectors and among companies, *Technovation*, vol. 32, pp. 681–693.

Päällysaho, S. and Kuusisto, J. (2008) Intellectual property protection as a key driver of service innovation: an analysis of innovative KIBS businesses in Finland and the UK, *International Journal of Services Technology and Management*, vol. 9, no. 3/4, pp. 268–284.

Risch, Michael (2014) Functionality and Graphical User Interface Design Patents. Villanova University School of Law, Paper 189, accessed on 8 February 2017 from http://digitalcommons.law.villanova.edu/cgi/viewcontent.cgi?params=/context/wps/article/1198/&path_info=.

Rivette, Kevin G. and Kline, David (2000) *Rembrandts in the Attic: Unlocking the Hidden Value of Patents*, Boston, MA: Harvard Business School Press.

Rosoff, Matt (2011) Who does patent-trading firm intellectual ventures work for, anyway? Accessed on 8 February 2017 from http://www.businessinsider.com/intellectual-ventures-2011-7.

Teece, D.J. (2000) Strategies for managing knowledge assets: the role of firm structure and industrial context, *Long Range Planning*, vol. 33, no. 1, pp. 35–54.

WIPO (2004) *Intellectual Property Handbook: Policy, Law and Use*. Accessed on 8 February 2017 from http://www.wipo.int/about-ip/en/iprm/.

WIPO (n.d.) What is Intellectual Property? WIPO Publication No. 450(E). Accessed on 8 February 2017 from http://www.wipo.int/edocs/pubdocs/en/intproperty/450/wipo_pub_450.pdf.

TECHNICAL APPENDIX

As most broadly defined in the literature, intellectual property comprises the knowledge, skills and other intangible assets which business can convert into usable resources to generate a competitive advantage.[1] Therefore, IP has a significant role in firms' innovation processes and competitive strategies. Intellectual property is essential to a firm's prosperity. IP can be 'embedded' for instance in individuals (as, for example, human capital, know-how, and experience), products, systems, work routines or services, and it can take various forms.

Intellectual property rights (IPRs) protect knowledge, human capital and the competition advantage acquired by an organisation or an individual. The World Intellectual Property Organization defines the intellectual property right system as a set of legal rights that result from intellectual activity in industrial, scientific, literary and artistic fields.[2] The intellectual property rights offer a way to protect intellectual property from any unauthorised misuse in the form of theft, imitation or modification. In other words, IPRs allow people to claim ownership over their creativity and inventiveness producing intangible property in a similar way that they claim ownership of their physical property.

Intellectual property rights laws specify the items they protect. Intellectual property rights comprise of *copyright* and of *industrial property rights* e.g. patents, utility models, trademarks and registered designs (see Table 5A.1).

From the lawmakers' perspective, intellectual property rights aim to offer a lucrative balance between exclusivity for making invention and creation beneficial activities (for a period of time, a person can obtain financial benefit from the invention or creation), and on the other hand, not to completely block subsequent invention and creativity (after a period of time, other people may further develop or build upon the invention or creation).

Copyright protection is automatic and exists as soon as an independent and original work has been created in a fixed form. Copyright extends only to expressions, but not to ideas, procedures or methods. Copyright belongs to the person who has created the work in question, but for a collective work, all authors have copyright to the work. In such cases the consent to use the work needs to be obtained from all authors or their representatives. Copyright protects literary and artistic works, for example literary works, musical compositions, films, photographic works or other visual art products.[3]

Furthermore, copyright protects computer software,[4] which may put obstacles to software development projects where existing program code is repurposed. Copyleft licenses have been provided as a solution to make

Table 5A.1   Summary of common Intellectual Property Rights

		Type of IPR	Target of protection	Requirements for the protected item	Actions for obtaining protection
Intellectual Property Rights		Copyright	Literary or artistic work	Independent and original	Automatically, provided that the work is independent and original
	Industrial Property Rights	Patent	Product, method	New, differs fundamentally from others and is industrially applicable	By filing for and obtaining a granted patent
		Utility model	Product	New, differs clearly from others and is industrially applicable, but does not necessarily meet patent requirements	By registration
		Trademark	Symbol of product or service: character, work, number, pattern, signal, sound, etc.	Identifying, clearly distinctive, not contrary to good practice	By registration or establishing
		Registered design	Appearance of concrete object made industrially or by hand	Design differs essentially from others	By registration

clearer the possibilities of software code reuse. Paul de Laat[5] presents a comprehensive discussion on the key differences and implications between copyright and copyleft approaches in software development.

A special case is the database right, which prevents unauthorised copying of substantial parts of a database. This IPR protects the information itself, rather than the expression of information as in the case of copyright.

Fair use is a notable exception in copyright law, which varies from country to country. For example in United States copyright law, limited use of copyrighted material is permitted without the need for acquiring permission from rights holders. Some examples of purposes for fair use include commentary, search engines, news reporting, research and parody.

In contrast to copyright, industrial property rights are not created of their own accord, but they are granted through applications after outside inspection and analysis. Maintenance of industrial property rights usually depends on the payment of regular fees and the usage of the rights (for example, if a patent is maintained in one country or in multiple countries).

Patents are one of the first established intellectual property rights. Granstrand[6] suggests that since the late 15th century, a national patent era has been extended to first a multinational and then an international patent era. Finally we have since the late 20th century entered a United States-led pro-patent/pro-IP era characterised by global activism for IP industrialised countries. In the pro-IP era, intellectual capital exceeds physical capital for many organisations.[7]

Patenting can have a number of objectives for a business in addition to the traditional motive of directly profiting from a patented innovation. In fact, it has been estimated that only 2–3 per cent of registered patents are actually used in products sold on the market. Blind and his co-authors[8] note that the patent system is increasingly used for strategic motives such as licensing and defensive or offensive blockade of competitors' efforts. Neuhäusler[9] similarly argues that patents are used for strategic purposes rather than as a protection for imitation. According to Päällysaho and Kuusisto,[10] patenting can be used in building up the reputation of the business. It can also be a way to raise the status and marketability of the new service or product. In addition, patents improve the chances of securing venture capital financing. Patenting is also used as a way to ensure that the company itself is not violating other businesses' IPR. Furthermore, it can prevent competitors from patenting inventions that are essential for the firm's own business.[11] In particular in the US, patents have been granted to software.

Utility models provide patent-like protection for technical ideas and solutions that do not meet the requirements set for granting a patent. Utility models provide protection especially for smaller-scale inventions for which gaining patent protection would be too slow or expensive. Utility model is a practical protection tool in situations where the invention is intended for domestic exploitation only or for a short period of time.

A trademark is any sign that can distinguish the goods and services of one trader from others. A trademark can be gained by registration or establishing, and it grants the trader exclusive rights to use the mark as a symbol of products or services. Besides for protecting purposes, trademarks are used as a marketing tool so that customers can recognise the product of a particular trader.[12]

Registered design protects the appearance of a product (for example, shape and/or pattern. This protection can be granted for the whole or a non-separable part of a product. In addition, multi-part products can also be protected. Design rights and trademarks overlap to a certain extent in that the appearance of a product can also be registered as trademark.

According to Risch,[13] a recent trend is that the graphical user interface (including the look and feel) of, for example, smartphones' operating systems and their applications are increasingly being protected through registered design rights and design patents.

NOTES

1. Teece (2000).
2. WIPO (2004), p. 3.
3. Cornish (1999).
4. Barton (1993).
5. De Laat (2005).
6. Granstrand (2005).
7. Granstrand (2005).
8. Blind et al. (2009).
9. Neuhäusler (2012).
10. Päällysaho and Kuusisto (2008).
11. Päällysaho and Kuusisto (2008).
12. Cornish (1999).
13. Risch (2014).

6. New frontier business models: creating value through innovation

Liting Liang and Arja Kuusisto

6.1 INTRODUCTION

This chapter explores how firms can develop business models by accessing the wide range of resources possessed by users, online communities and the crowd. Gaining access to these resources – resources they do not own or control – has become a key factor in the creation of a series of new businesses, and the implications for firm business models will be examined throughout this chapter.

The importance of business model development has been widely acknowledged, with firms traditionally focusing on the use of internal resources in the development of novel products or services. However, the increasing digitalisation of business and society has enabled firms to access external resources, with resources drawn from users, online communities and the crowd playing an increasing role in the development of new business models. The different forms this may take is amply demonstrated by the examples of giffgaff and Lego: giffgaff, a mobile virtual network operator based in the UK (see more detail on giffgaff in Chapter 7) has developed a business model that depends on the contributions of its online user community. As part of this model its users are encouraged to take major roles in the firm's core business activities, including marketing, sales, technical support and new product/service development. In contrast, Lego, the world's fifth-largest manufacturer of play materials, has integrated users into its New Product Development process in order to make use of the creative potential of Lego's huge fan base. On Lego Design byME, users are able to create their own designs with existing Lego bricks and then freely exchange these designs with each other or commercialise them to their peers. The two cases demonstrate that firms can develop successful business models by engaging users in very different aspects of their core activities.

6.2 THE CHANGING CONTEXT OF BUSINESS MODEL DEVELOPMENT

The gradual coalescence of the physical and digital worlds has fundamentally changed the Innovation Opportunity Space for many businesses. This shift offers unprecedented business opportunities by enabling human participation and interaction in business activities in ways that have not been previously possible. As Paul Krugman, the Nobel Prize winner in Economic Sciences in 2008, has said, 'Bit by bit, everything that can be digitized will be digitized. . . And we'll have to find business and economic models that take this reality into account.'[1] One notable phenomenon is how the digital technologies have enabled the transformation of user behaviour, from passive recipients to potentially active participants in businesses, as illustrated in Figure 6.1.

One noticeable change in behaviour has been in the way consumers acquire product-related information in making their purchase decisions. In the past, consumers have mainly relied on information offered by suppliers. By contrast, many of today's consumers increasingly make their decisions based on price comparisons and reviews by other consumers online. Since the 1990s, many price comparison websites have been set up, offering not only price comparisons but also rating and review services for

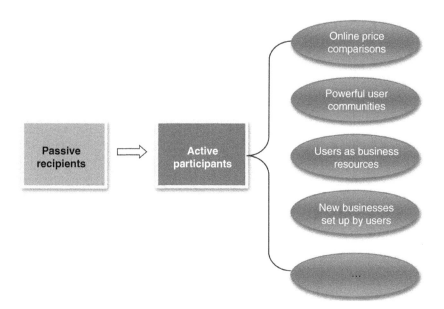

Figure 6.1   Changing user behaviour in the era of digitalisation

online retailers and products. For example, many travellers are now relying on information provided by websites such as ebookers and TripAdvisor to choose their flight tickets and hotels. The increasing transparency enabled by the Internet has increased consumer power and raised consumer expectations of many products and services.[2] In addition, being the world's largest travel site, TripAdvisor members provides more than 465 million reviews and opinions covering more than 7 million forms of accommodation, restaurants, and attractions. With over 390 million monthly visitors of the site, the TripAdvisor online community has gained great power by shaping business operations in the travel industry.

Digital interaction has enabled businesses to generate new types of services by integrating external resources in new ways. A well-known example is the recommendation system of Amazon, which integrates recommendations into many parts of the customers' purchasing process. Based on a number of elements – including previous purchase history, browsing patterns, prior ratings and items other users have bought – the Amazon website customises the browsing/shopping experience for returning customers and provides them with 'Frequently Bought Together' suggestions.[3] By accumulating information of the users' prior interactions, the value of the service increases as a result of each and every interaction. The example further suggests that the digital environment provides new opportunities to all parties who engage in the interactions. This everyday example is a good illustration of the way in which digitalisation can provide the basis for the creation of new kinds of value and partnerships which have not traditionally been either feasible, or were simply unrecognised. As a result, new businesses can be constructed using resources that were inaccessible because they were previously highly distributed.[4] The resources possessed by users, online communities and the crowd can now be at the core of business models.

The shift to digital fundamentally changes the nature of business possibilities within an Innovation Opportunity Space and offers new business opportunities to both new and established firms. For example, the development of the Industrial Internet, the combination of Big Data analytics with the Internet of Things, reshapes the Innovation Opportunity Space for traditional sectors. The Industrial Internet may be positioned as an opportunity to improve operational efficiency by adopting automation and agile production techniques. However, it could also be viewed as a novel tool to create new hybrid business models, with firms like GLAAS KGA mbH, General Electric and Michelin, exploring innovative ways to use the Industrial Internet to create new value for customers.[5]

Once industries become more and more digital, it can be much easier for new firms to enter the industry and compete with established producers.

For example, Google's entry into driverless automobiles has the potential to change the structure of several industries such as car insurance and government licensing. Apple's HealthKit enables the firm to compete with caregivers, insurers and pharmaceuticals in the healthcare data market.[6] These examples illustrate that while the shift to digitalisation can create many opportunities for established firms, a shift in their Innovation Opportunity Space can also challenge them with new competition that may be difficult to predict and counter. The following sections will focus on how firms can adopt a proactive and innovative approach to developing their business models in this new context.

6.3   OPENING UP BUSINESSES TO USERS, ONLINE COMMUNITIES AND THE CROWD

Businesses have traditionally followed an inside-out approach in developing their business models. Accordingly, firms rely on their internal resources and capabilities in developing and conducting their business activities. Simply put, firms produce products and services, which are then consumed by users.[7] However, reliance on internal resources is not enough, as illustrated in the following quote, attributed to Sun Microsystems co-founder Bill Joy: 'No matter who you are, most of the smartest people work for someone else.'[8]

In other words, given the constraints of internal resources, firms may be unable to fully explore business opportunities without integrating knowledge and other resources from external sources. Looking beyond organisational boundaries in seeking resources has become vitally important for firms to gain competitive advantages. In particular, many firms have started to engage users, online communities and the crowd in a wide range of business activities.

Advances in ICT have allowed firms to explore innovation opportunities by placing users, online communities and the crowd at the centre of their innovation processes. Open source software projects provide pioneer examples of the open model of innovation and value creation. The success of the Linux operating system and other open source software (OSS) projects suggests the initial role transition of users, online communities and the crowd in business activities. These OSS projects have been conducted at no financial cost by a virtual community of volunteer computer programmers: the OSS projects are based on distributed innovation systems characterised by decentralised problem solving, volunteer participation, self-organised coordination and collaboration, and free flow of knowledge. Firms like IBM, Sun, Apple and Oracle have welcomed OSS communities by encouraging the participation of their employees, donating their intellectual property to the projects and integrating OSS into their products and services. OSS projects have also been widely conducted by many small firms to compete in the market.[9]

Many innovative companies have now changed the way they generate new ideas by involving a wide range of external actors in their innovation process through a range of different approaches. For example, Procter & Gamble has engaged its customers in their new product development (for example, generating new ideas and testing new products) through its Vocalpoint programme for mothers, its Tremor programme for adolescents and its Living It programme for lead-customers.[10] Similarly, the Ford Motor Company established the OpenXC community to attract top developers to experiment with DIY projects in Ford vehicles and design their own plug and play hardware modules, buttons, knobs and simple displays.[11]

The rapid development of the Internet and social-networking technologies has enabled some companies to go beyond the inclusion of users in new product development and engage them in activities such as marketing and branding. For example, Peugeot, a French car manufacturer, encouraged customers to submit car design online, with a demonstration model of the winning design built and displayed at automotive marketing events. Peugeot also worked with software developers to get the design in a video game. Similarly, Missha, a cosmetic brand in South Korea, took up 40 per cent market share in its segment by involving users in its branding strategy.[12] Although collaborating with users has enabled firms to shorten time to market and obtain high margins, in themselves they may not be sufficient to generate long-term competitive advantages for a firm.

The increasing digitalisation of the business environment has enabled firms in different industries to utilise user resources via digital interaction on the basis of different digital technologies and platforms. In this context, the outside-in approach in business model development, emphasising co-creating value *with* users (rather than *for* users), and fostered by digitalisation, continues to stimulate business model renewal of industry incumbents as well as the creation of entirely new business models. In the following sections, we will examine how firms have adopted novel ways of business model renewal and development through extending and diversifying user roles.

6.4 BUSINESS MODEL RENEWAL USING EXTERNAL RESOURCES

Industry incumbents generally follow the traditional inside-out approach in developing their business models. However, in response to their changing environment – especially in the emergence of new opportunities that have emerged due to digitalisation – firms, such as Telefónica, Coloplast, and Lego, have taken the opportunity to renew their business models. This has been achieved by setting up platforms to access resources possessed by users, online communities and the crowd in their core business activities (for example, design, marketing, sales or R&D) on a regular basis.

As discussed earlier, the toy maker Lego has set up several platforms for involving the many passionate fans in its value creation activities. Apart from encouraging their users to create designs on Lego Design byME, the firm has also encouraged fans to submit their innovative ideas through 'Lego Ideas' and users can propose an idea, or show support for the ideas of others. Based on a set of internal criteria, Lego then selects among user ideas which have received support from at least 10,000 others and develops the selected projects into an official product in collaboration with the project creator. When the new set is launched, the creator receives a reward of 1 per cent of the net sales. The Lego ideas website has over 100,000 registered users, and many thousands of user developed projects are published on the site. By getting users more engaged in the process of new product development, Lego has been able to gain a deeper understanding of what their customers want. In order to obtain early insights into new trends, Lego also scans external websites where Lego fans interact independently of the company. For example, Lego often seeks collaboration with creators of projects based on Lego products on Kickstarter. In pursuit of the same goals, Coloplast, has developed similar mechanisms to gain access to the external resources that users and others possess, albeit in a very different industry. Coloplast, a Danish producer of medical devices, was founded by a nurse in 1957, and it has always had the tradition of involving external groups like customers, users and carers in new product development. Traditionally, Coloplast's main focus was engaging nurses. The invention of the ostomy pouch, which the company was founded on, was made by a nurse based on her practical experiences with patients. Over the past few years, however, the firm has started to seek user and carer insights related to its specific projects by combining quantitative studies and anthropological research on an ongoing basis throughout a development process.

Renewing business models by engaging users seems more difficult in very traditional manufacturing, mostly due to its special procedures for production, the skills and technologies used and stricter industry regulations. However, in the automotive sector manufacturers have made certain efforts to have more digital interaction with their users to extend the value of their products. Ford, for example, has established its OpenXC platform that allows users to not only extend their vehicles with custom applications and pluggable modules but also contribute to develop the applications and modules.[13] Wikispeed, an US manufacturer, has developed a 100 mpg car in just three months based on R&D inputs from volunteers worldwide.[14] Local Motors, another US firm founded in 2007, has taken a step further – the company has defined itself as a next-generation, crowd-powered car manufacturer. The company involves users to create, develop, build and modify vehicles and components.[15] However, although firms in traditional sectors like manufacturing tend to try and connect users, online communities and the crowd into their existing R&D activities, there are many other possibilities available.

Lily Robotics, a short-lived US start-up founded in 2013, provides a good example of how manufacturers can attract external groups to co-create value for their businesses in different ways. The firm developed an autonomous flying video camera and has also generated sufficient financial resources ($1 million seed money) to get its prototype into production. It has also been able to get other resources to develop an advanced flying camera. However, one issue with the camera might hinder its success in the market: the product looks more like a drone than a flying camera that follows its users in several different modes: following from behind, tracking from a set distance in front, circling, or hovering in mid-air as if held by an invisible selfie stick. To make its potential users aware of how Lily is different from a camera carried by a drone, the firm came up with an innovative idea: it marketed Lily as 'the coolest drone camera you can pre-order for $499'.[16] Although at this price, the firm would not be able to make any money (standard retail pricing will be $999), the pre-ordering strategy not only provided financial resources for its production but also allowed the firm to attract early adopters to act as beta testers and marketers for Lily. By engaging its users in its finance, R&D and marketing, the firm can reduce three main business risks for a start-up: financial risks, market risks, and product risks.

In addition, established firms have sought to strengthen their market positions by renewing their business models through an ambidextrous strategy: the firms develop entirely different business models based upon user communities, undertaking tasks that have previously been performed by the firms themselves. Giffgaff, the UK-based mobile phone company, can be seen as a typical example in this regard: the firm was set up by Telefónica, one of the largest mobile network providers in the world. By offering two versions of the same mobile phone service in parallel (the user-community giffgaff and its traditional mobile phone service) Telefónica is able to maintain its core competences while developing new competences in response to changes in its Innovation Opportunity Space.

By integrating users, online communities and the crowd into their core innovation and operational activities firms are able to greatly expand their resource pools, and renew their business models. However, renewing business models in this way can be challenging, which may explain why by drawing on users, online communities and the crowd has not been more widely adopted in traditional industries. Further reasons may be related to the past success of their existing inside-out business models, potentially making it difficult for decision makers to recognise alternatives. Involving users, online communities and the crowd in traditional business activities can also increase the risk of losing control over core processes and potential conflict with existing operational routines. It is likely that potential barriers tend to be related to the logic of conducting businesses in traditional industries, an issue that will be discussed in further detail at the end of this chapter.

6.5 BUSINESS MODEL INNOVATION BASED ON THE RESOURCES OF USERS, ONLINE COMMUNITIES AND THE CROWD

Since 2000, online intermediary platforms matching two or more groups have been set up in many industries. Intermediary platform businesses offer online services and infrastructure enabling various types of direct exchanges between the different participant groups (businesses and individuals). Typically, these intermediary platform businesses make their revenues by collecting fees from multiple user groups, potentially reducing search costs or transaction costs (or both) for all participants. In a short time, some of these firms have assumed privileged positions in their respective industries.[17,18] The firms TripAdvisor and ebookers mentioned earlier are typical examples and have greatly challenged the market position of traditional travel agencies all over the world. The emergence and growth of crowdfunding services have the potential to have a similar impact on traditional financial services.

Crowdfunding services are designed to help individuals or businesses generate funding from members of the public for different purposes. According to a recent report, crowdfunding platforms in all raised $16.2 billion in 2014, a 167 per cent increase over the $6.1 billion raised in 2013.[19] Such businesses can be seen as a particular type of matching platform businesses that is designed to link individuals, often termed a Peer-to-Peer (P2P) business. A typical P2P business model works on the basis of playing matchmaker between individual users with a service/product to offer and others who could use that service/product. P2P businesses enable people to share their images, resources, to make or save money, save time, protect the environment, or even to engage in interaction with others. The following sections in this chapter will explore how the intermediary platform business models have been used to open up major new bodies of external resources in finance, accommodation, transport and clothing.

6.5.1 Unlocking External Resources: Finance

This section will examine two mechanisms that enable financial resources to be obtained from non-traditional groups like users, online communities and the crowd: Crowdfunding and Peer-to-Peer Lending.

Crowdfunding
Crowdfunding refers to a process in which a great number of individuals (crowd) contribute to fund an initiative – for example, a start-up business, a charitable cause, or an arts project. The rise of the crowdfunding industry is based on the ability to communicate and pool resources using the Internet and web applications. As the term crowdfunding implies, the obvious purpose for a project owner or an entrepreneur is to collect money for a particular purpose. However, crowdfunding can also very much be about testing and marketing new ideas, and engaging in interaction with people who may become future customers and ambassadors for the project. Crowdfunding platforms serve as intermediaries between project owners and funders, generating revenues by taking a certain percentage of the money raised via their platform. Besides the money raising goal, these online platforms typically provide a place for lively interaction between the project owners and funders, possibly throughout the project implementation.[20] The following section will examine one of the world's most popular crowdfunding platforms: Kickstarter.

Kickstarter
Kickstarter is an American-based company founded in 2009. It provides a good example of a new type of digital company, which breaks the boundaries of traditional sectors, combining the worlds of creative arts, technology projects and finance. Kickstarter connects two user groups via its online portal: creators of creative projects and people who are willing to fund the projects (donors). Project donors are individuals, whilst project creators may be organisations as well as individuals, and the platform helps creators gather money from donors in order to realise their projects.

Project creators, in addition to raising money for their projects, often get valuable feedback for developing their projects further. Feedback is given by both the Kickstarter staff as well as other site users. The service has also become a popular testing ground for new technology and cultural products and ideas. Project creators also use the site to effectively pre-sell the products or experiences they are developing: in exchange for a certain sum of money, the donor (buyer) is promised to get a particular technological or fashion item. Obviously, project creators will benefit from the finance they raise, with Kickstarter taking a 5 per cent fee when the project successfully raises its intended target. For the donors, the motives for backing the projects vary: Many support the projects to simply see the projects take place. Some want to share the enthusiasm of project creators and by donating, they become a 'small part of the story' themselves. Other backers are donating (or paying) in exchange for a specific reward or product the project creator promises to share with those who back the project.

Kickstarter's business model has generated an interactive space in which the creation and enjoyment of creative 'cool stuff' may be as important as the commercial aspects of funding the projects. For the artists and entrepreneurs, and indeed, anyone with a creative idea independent of their training or prior work background, crowdfunding via the Internet offers new opportunities for accessing financial resources. The financial success of Kickstarter has inspired others to copy the business model, and similar types of crowdfunding platforms for creative projects have been set up in several countries.

Peer-to-Peer lending
Peer-to-Peer (P2P) lending provides another interesting case of a new type of business model in which two groups of people are matched online: some individuals (lenders) lend money to other individuals or businesses (borrowers) via an Internet platform company, which provides the matching service and coordinates things between the parties. The intermediary platform company typically makes its money by charging fees from both the lenders and the borrowers. The key feature of the business model is that loan agreements are directly between lenders and the borrowers, and not the intermediary. The number of online P2P lending platforms and businesses has been growing fast since the pioneering company Zopa was founded in 2005 in the UK[21] and Prosper in 2006 in the USA.[22]

There is a great variety of P2P platforms with different features although a common feature is that lenders and borrowers remain anonymous (in particular, when they are individuals). Some P2P businesses spread the investments over a number of loans in order to reduce the credit risk (see Box 6.1), and some firms allow investors to lend directly to small businesses (Funding Circle, launched in the UK in 2010, was the first platform in which borrowers are small businesses). P2P lending firms can increasingly compete with established financial institutions, with banks increasingly cooperating with P2P businesses and becoming themselves investors (lenders) on the platforms.[23] Box 6.1 illustrates key elements of the business model of a Finnish P2P lending company Fixura.

BOX 6.1   FIXURA

Fixura was founded in 2009 in Finland. It provides P2P lending services by match-ing investors and borrowers (who are mainly private individuals) online. Fixura markets itself as an alternative to the traditional loan market. The innovative feature in the business model is the fact that loan agreements are set up between the two user groups rather than between users and Fixura. A key benefit for the borrowers is the possibility of getting a loan for a lower interest rate than the rates typically charged for unsecured loans, and for the borrowers, the reported average interest rate has been highly competitive in the interest markets. On the platform, both investors and borrowers remain anonymous. The amounts that can be borrowed are between €2,000 and €10,000. The loan applicant chooses the conditions for the loan he or she applies for: interest, amount and loan period. When the applicant is accepted by Fixura (based on income and credit data), he or she gets a credit score. The investors, in turn, choose the risk level they are willing to take, and the investment is then automatically divided between numerous loans (or shares of loans) to manage the risk accordingly. The minimum investment on Fixura platform is €1,000. In addition to providing the platform for matchmaking, Fixura takes care of billing, and gives over to a collections agency, if necessary, when payments have been neglected. The company generates revenues by charging both the investors and the borrowers different types of fees.[24]

From a historical perspective, of course, P2P lending has always been here. The fact that banks have taken over so much of the business from people's social networks is as a matter of fact strange. Possibly, the transparency that was once present in small communities is now regenerated via online platforms: the sophisticated ways to assess and manage risk even when the other party of the contract remains anonymous is a crucial factor. It seems that social aspects, such as the possibility for an investor to directly choose the person/company one is investing his or her money in, also play a role in the popularity of P2P lending. In the aftermath of the financial crisis of 2007–2008, some people are also willing to try out alternatives to conventional banks.

The success of P2P lending platform businesses shows how digital technology helps put user resources to new uses. In so doing, new types of business models are thriving, and very importantly, users are getting unprecedented opportunities to benefit from their resources on their own conditions. In P2P lending both investors and loan seekers may be seen as traders on the digital market, who are connected and whose transactions are supported by the new, easy-to-use digital platforms. P2P lending is a great example of how new 'digital only' newcomers are driving the change in established industries – possibly shaking up the mainstream financial companies along with other online service providers in the financial market. When writing this, we assume that the reshaping of the financial industry is only taking its first steps, and it remains to be seen how the interaction of digital possibilities, entrepreneurial spirit and empowered users will further shake up the financial services industry.

6.5.2 Unlocking External Resources: Accommodation

The sharing economy allows individuals to generate value from their own resources. As a new wave of P2P, access-driven operations, the businesses in this area have effectively opened up a new Innovation Opportunity Space that can potentially impact many established firms. The new type of business models address a transition from a private, closed, owner-ship of resources towards accessibility and sharing across a wide variety of markets. In what is called collaborative consumption, people all over the world are showing a robust appetite for the sharing-based economy, from renting homes, sharing cars, swapping goods, or offering knowledge and skills in exchange for money or other benefits. Advances in ICT have provided the basis for the creation of large-scale sharing system of different resources. Sharing economy companies often also have an eBay-style rating or review system so people on both sides of the transaction can build their credits online and gain trust among their peers. Social media and mobile technology has furthered the rapid expansion of these new business models,[25] all of which are based on the principle of opening up private resources for general use. From a firm perspective this business model has unlocked a new source of external resources that were previously not available in the market and threaten to disrupt existing commercial structures and relationships. The following section will examine the implications of unlocking external accommodation resources.

Airbnb

Airbnb, founded in the US in 2008, is an online platform that allows people to list, discover and book short-term accommodation. Operating in more than 34,000 cities across 190 countries, the company connects two groups of users: private house or apartment owners and renters (who may be leisure or business travellers). Airbnb generates its revenues by taking a commission from both the homeowners and the renters.[26] In 2014, Airbnb had over 800,000 listings worldwide, which means the website had offered more lodging than Hilton Worldwide or InterContinental Hotels Group or any other hotel chain in the world at that time. In 2015, it was reported that the company has been on a shortlist to offer rooms for the 2016 Olympics in Rio de Janeiro.[27] On the supply side, Airbnb attracts listings by defining the site as a place where people can offer their home to welcome travellers to their cities and make them discover properties that are unique rather than simply just run a business for making money. For travellers, Airbnb promotes its listings as properties that could offer them home-like experience despite being away from home and also allow them to have cool and quirky travel experiences. In addition, by attracting people all over the world to sharing their home with others directly, Airbnb is able to offer a wide range of options at lower cost, which no traditional hotels can provide.

Travellers can find three types of spaces on Airbnb to match their different needs: sharing a room with others, a private bedroom, and, an entire home. A key advantage of Airbnb is that it makes financial sense to its users. For homeowners, it is free to create a listing on Airbnb, and for travellers, the overall cost of accommodations is generally 30–80 per cent lower than available hotels in the same city can offer. Once a reservation is confirmed, the host of the place pays a 3 per cent service fee and the guest pays a 6–12 per cent service fee. In addition to offering 24/7 customer service, Airbnb has built up a user community where people share their travel experience all over the world. For many people, being part of the Airbnb community has become a key part of modern travel: exploring the art of uncertainty and the mystery of life.[28] Airbnb has also created the Verified ID process to build trust in its user community and give people more information when they decide who to host or stay with on Airbnb. The process requires guests and hosts to verify their identify by uploading their official ID to confirm their personal details and connecting their Airbnb profile to another online profile such as Facebook, Google and LinkedIn accounts. Its review system and minimal online interviews (for example, why are you visiting?) have also helped enhancing trust among users.[29]

However, Airbnb has also been engaged in a series of battles with regulators in countries in which it operates. Although many cities are welcoming Airbnb, many are issuing new laws and regulations: for instance, to limit homeowners' rights to regularly rent out their properties on short-term lets. Some cities require homeowners who are renting out via Airbnb to register and collect city hotel/tourist taxes.[30] It is clear that sharing economy businesses like Airbnb, that unlock previously closed resources and disrupt established industries, are impacting on established Innovation Opportunity Spaces. They are also affecting institutional environments, which is further illustrated by the transport and clothing cases below.

6.5.3 Unlocking External Resources: Transport

Uber (formerly known as UberCap) is another typical example of a new business based on providing access to previously closed external resources. The American international transportation network company founded in 2009 offers an alternative service to taxi cabs by connecting riders and drivers via its app on users' mobile phones. It offers opportunities to people who wish to make money from their own cars according to their own schedule. Riders can request, ride, and pay via their mobile phones. Starting from a small platform business in San Francisco, Uber operates in more than 400 major cities in over 60 countries around the world.[31]

As part of its growth strategy Uber has systematically addressed problems with traditional taxi services. Timeliness: through the Uber app on their smartphones, riders can be connected by a driver nearby their locations in less than 10 minutes. For peace of mind, riders can also track the car service's progress via the app as they wait for it to arrive. Payment: once the car reaches the destination, the app charges from the credit card or PayPal account riders have preauthorised. Quality: Uber has created a rating system: both drivers and riders give a rating, ranging from one to five stars, after the completion of an Uber ride. An average rating for each driver is set up weekly based on driver ratings. If a driver's rating is below a certain score, Uber may warn that driver of the risk of being kicked off the system through its weekly newsletters. If a rider's rating is too low, that rider may find it difficult to get an Uber ride or even be booted off the service completely.[32] As a result, Uber has completely changed key features of getting private transportation, creating an on-demand car service at similar or even lower cost than traditional taxi services.

When it was launched in San Francisco, Uber targeted people in the technology community as its early adopters as these people are often well-connected and like to share their experiences with friends, tech press, and social media audiences online. To drive awareness among this group, Uber used an event sponsorship strategy, offering free rides to attendees at local tech and venture capital events. As expected, once these early adopters were impressed by Uber services, they shared their Uber experiences with people via social media. Since then, Uber's growth has been driven substantially by word of mouth, and the company has spent little on traditional marketing.[33] Uber has also set up a Refer-a-Friend Program: when an existing Uber user refers a friend as a rider, both parties can receive $20 each in credit on their Uber accounts. Its driver Referral Incentive Program encourages existing drivers to earn $200 in cash for inviting new Uber riders (the new driver needs to complete their first 20 rides). Another aspect of Uber's business model is that drivers use their own cars, fuel and insurance and work as independent contractors, eliminating the need for employee benefits. One analysis of Uber drivers in six major cities in the US revealed that if they were full time employees they should be paid holidays and healthcare benefits worth an average of $5,500 annually, in addition to thousands more dollars in mileage reimbursement.[34]

BOX 6.2   BLABLACAR

BlaBlaCar is a Paris-based ride-sharing platform founded in 2006. It connects car owners and co-travellers to share city-to-city journeys through the largest rideshare service in the world. It has been widely welcomed by Europeans who often use its services for long distance and cross-country trips. People registered as drivers of BlaBlaCar offer rides to passengers in 12 countries (for example, France, Germany, Spain and the UK), at prices that undercut any other methods of transportation. Although BlaBlaCar also competes with traditional transportation with low fares like other ride-sharing businesses, it has policies preventing its drivers from turning their services into a job. In the markets it operates, the company sets a cap on the fare based on government guidelines on driving costs, covering fuel costs, insurance and tax. Hence, drivers cannot make profit from their services and BlaBlaCar can ensure its low fares. Also as BlaBlaCar drivers aren't classed as professional workers, there are no requirements from local governments for special insurance or a special license. BlaBlaCar's business model is designed for long distances and targeting drivers who would like to reduce their travel cost by filling empty seats. Therefore, it does not compete directly with ride-sharing companies like Uber and Lyft and even taxi companies. In 2015, it acquired its German competitor Carpooling.com, as well as Hungary-based competitor AutoHop. Carpooling.com was the second largest ride-sharing platform after BlaBlaCar in Europe. After the acquisitions, BlaBlaCar has 20 million members in 18 markets mostly in Europe. Undoubtedly it now dominates the European market.[35]

There are now many other ride-sharing companies emerging in the transportation sector, including Lyft, a service that offers car sharing in a cheaper and more convenient way than Uber. Although the basic features of its model are similar to Uber, Lyft has differentiated its service from Uber by allowing drivers and riders to agree on the cost per ride themselves, while Lyft only offers some recommendations on the fares. In 2014, just two years after its establishment, Lyft had covered more than 60 markets in the US, competing directly with Uber. In Europe, BlaBlaCar and Carpooling have taken the lead in adopting the ride-sharing business model (see Box 6.2 for more details).

In common with other firms that have unlocked previously closed external resources there have been a series of political and regulatory challenges to their operation. For example, there are ongoing battles concerning Uber and Lyft in the US on rider safety and driver screening, with California officials claiming that Uber does not adequately screen its rapidly expanding pool of tens of thousands of drivers. In Los Angeles, Sacramento and San Francisco, Uber has battled demands that it use law enforcement fingerprint checks to eliminate drivers who have recent records of violence or crime from offering riding services. A range of other issues including employee benefits, insurance coverage and liability have also been raised concerning ride-sharing businesses.[36] On the whole, such new businesses have been associated with controversy in many jurisdictions around the world. For example, Japan and South Korea have made it clear that such ride-sharing businesses may not be able to easily enter their markets due to regulatory issues.[37]

6.5.4 Unlocking External Resources: Clothing

Unlike the many challenges facing ride-sharing businesses in the transportation industry, P2P sharing of clothing has not been disruptive in the fashion industry, and there are now many services that enable individuals to swap, sell and donate clothing items.

Swapstyle
Swapstyle is an Australia-based online marketplace for women all over the world to swap, sell and buy fashion items with others directly. Set up in 2003, it is the world's first and longest running fashion swap site. To start a transaction, members need to post pictures of their items they want to swap and can also set a price for each item for those who wish to buy them. All services provided by the site are completely free and members can swap/sell unlimited items. In common with many online services, the service offers a basic rating system in which members can give either a positive or negative 'token' to someone whom they have done a transaction with. To further build trust among members, Swapstyle suggests that all users should complete an 'address verification' process. Users can pay a $10 fee through PayPal to receive a letter in the mail with a personal verification code – users who have verified their addresses will then be shown as 'address verified' on the site. Swapstyle has also created a thriving online community: the site encourages members to communicate with each other directly in forums, create their personal profile pages and make friends. With increasing economic and environmental concern in the past decade, Swapstyle has grown to become the largest clothing swapping community online. The business models of other P2P fashion-sharing platforms, such as Swishing, Vinted, thredUP and Closet Infinite, are very similar to Swapstyle and there are now fashion libraries[38] in many parts of the world, including the Nordic cities of Stockholm, Copenhagen, Malmö, Umeå, Gothenburg, Lund and Helsinki.

The phenomenon of fashion-sharing is a good example of how changes in norms and practices can act to change an Innovation Opportunity Space. The economic, social and environmental value of the fashion-sharing businesses can also well explain their growth. For example, the impact of the financial crisis in 2008 forced many women to cut their budget for fashion shopping, leading to one of the most mentioned recessionista fashion tips on social media to be concerned with swapping fashion items with others. More importantly perhaps, the financial crisis has driven the increasing concern over the social and environmental costs of fast fashion, which in turn has promoted a widespread interest in sustainable fashion practices.

The opportunity to access the previously closed resources held by individuals has been applied to many areas. The following lists additional examples of available P2P intermediary platforms:

> *TaskRabbit* (formerly RunMyErrand) was set up in 2008 in the US based upon the idea of 'neighbours helping neighbours'. The website connects people who need chores done with people willing to complete them.[39]

> *Zaarly* is another similar US website established in 2011. It helps people find local providers for home services, from housecleaners to handymen, from landscape architects to electricians.[40]

> *Skilio* was set up in 2011 as an online marketplace that connects members seeking to learn with its community of skill sharers. It allows people to teach and learn anything via live webcam.

> *Wyzant*, a US-based platform launched in 2005, bridges qualified experts with students in need of private tutoring.

According to the type of value firms create for their users, we could divide these innovative business models we have discussed into two categories: transaction facilitator and resource redistributor. Transaction facilitator businesses create value by supporting business transactions between two groups of users. In this kind of business, one group of users actually act as micro-entrepreneurs who profit from providing goods or services to another group of users who demand the products or services. Resource redistributor businesses create value by simply enabling direct resource exchange between users. The purpose of users involved in the exchange activities is mainly to gain non-economic benefits. Of course, the two types of value creation might overlap in some cases. Accordingly, Table 6.1 below summarises the cases discussed:

The cases demonstrate that the Innovation Opportunity Space for many existing industries has been impacted by the opening up of previously closed resources that may now be made available using P2P platform services. The opening up of this new reservoir of external resources is something quite novel and has resulted in the creation of new and innovative business models. The key element in these businesses (in comparison with

Table 6.1 Business model innovations based on external resources

Types of value creation	Industries					
	Finance	Hotel	Transportation	Fashion	Home-services	Education & Training
Transaction facilitator	Zopa Prosper FundingCircle Fixura	Airbnb	Uber Lyft		TaskRabbit Zaarly	Wyzant
Resource redistributor	Kickstarter		BlaBlaCar	SwapStyle Swishing Vinted thredUP Closet Infinite		Skilio

their industry incumbents), is that they have changed how resources are provided: instead of the firm offering the key resource (for example, room or apartment for temporary accommodation, finance, cars or fashion items), these businesses connect the supply and demand of different user groups. In other words, these new business models are based on a new way of accessing resources: there is a change in how and with whom the core service is co-produced, and consequently, how the revenue for the firm is created.[41]

In fact, the critical features of the innovative business models are all designed around facilitating the interactions of users and eventually maximising the utilisation of third-party resources. Building transparency, trust and authenticity via various means during the interaction and utilisation is the key to the success of the business model innovations. For example, with the new connectivity enabled by the Internet, the transparency of transactions in the businesses is enhanced via the review and rating functionalities (as in Airbnb) or via direct background checks and guarantees provided by the platform provider firm (as in Uber). As the number of ratings accumulates, the information is also becoming one of the most important resources for users to understand the credibility of each other and hence help them make their decisions for service transactions. Hence, the novel way of combining resources via digital means can also create entirely new resources, which further the growth of the business.

6.6   CONCLUSION

User engagement in business activities is not new but user roles in the activities remain rather limited and provisional. In traditional business models, value is created for users based upon internal resources and competences. Business model development with users suggests a holistic and systematic way of value co-creation with users, which is enabled by digitalisation. As suggested by Professor Ezio Manzini (one of the world's leading experts on sustainable design), in the network society, businesses should:

> [C]onsider human beings neither as consumers not as passive users, but as active subjects, endowed with resources . . . (and) look at them for the opportunities they offer, rather than their problems, and their capabilities rather than their needs.[42]

The innovative approach demonstrated in this chapter suggests an open and dynamic innovation system where new services or products are developed based upon novel ways of accessing and generating resources from/with users.

Overall, in these novel business model development activities, firms do not simply create value 'for users', but creatively make users become part of the value creation process. Firms may ask themselves: what resources or capabilities do users have? And how can we motivate and facilitate users to share, to make use of, to develop their resources and capabilities for solving their own problems as well as other users' problems? Fundamentally, novel ways of combining resources from users and the subsequent co-creation of new resources with them for value creation is at the heart of this form of business model development.

The obtaining of resources from users, online communities and the crowd is highly effective in the digital world. As we have discussed, these new business models have been disruptive to several industries, and as such, have often resulted in regulatory controversy. Unlocking of user resources, and making use of the power of digital connectivity with new business models continue to produce fundamental changes in Innovation Opportunity Space across sectors; that is, in the way in which products and services are created and offered to the world.

NOTES

1. Krugman (2008).
2. Accessed 20 February 2015 from http://techtrends.accenture.com/us-en/downloads/ Accenture_Technology_Vision_2015.pdf.
3. Mangalindan (2012).
4. Manzini and Coad (2015).
5. Accessed 20 April 2015 from http://www.accenture.com/SiteCollectionDocuments/ PDF/Accenture-Driving-Unconventional-Growth-through-IIoT.pdf.
6. Accessed 20 February 2015 from http://www.mckinsey.com/insights/strategy/strategic_ principles_for_competing_in_the_digital_age.
7. Hamel (1998); Prahalad and Ramaswamy (2004).
8. Lakhani and Panetta (2007).
9. Chesbrough and Crowther (2006); Bughin et al. (2008).
10. Accessed 25 February 2015 from http://news.pg.com/press-release/pg-corporate-announce ments/pg-connectdevelop-launches-new-open-innovation-website.
11. Accessed 25 February 2015 from https://developer.ford.com/pages/openxc.
12. Bughin et al. (2008); Laursen and Salter (2006).
13. Accessed 25 February 2015 from http://openxcplatform.com/contributors/guide. html.
14. Accessed 20 March 2015 from http://www.forbes.com/sites/stevedenning/2012/05/10/ wikispeed-how-a-100-mpg-car-was-developed-in-3-months/.
15. Accessed 11 February 2015 from https://localmotors.com/.
16. Accessed 27 July 2015 from https://www.lily.camera/; accessed July 30 2015 from http:// www.accountingweb.com/community-voice/blogs/admin/what-does-a-marketing- person-do; accessed 27 July 2015 from http://www.wired.com/2015/05/lily-robotics- drone/.
17. Accessed 8 February 2017 from http://sloanreview.mit.edu/article/strategic-decisions- for-multisided-platforms/.
18. Accessed 20 May 2015 from https://hbr.org/2006/10/strategies-for-two-sided-markets.

19. Accessed 1 August 2015 from http://www.marketwired.com/press-release/crowdfunding-market-grows-167-2014-crowdfunding-platforms-raise-162-billion-finds-research-2005 299.htm; http://fortune.com/2014/04/17/why-investors-are-pouring-millions-into-crowd funding/.
20. De Buysere et al. (2012).
21. Accessed 6 December 2013 from http://en.wikipedia.org/wiki/Peer-to-peerlending.
22. Accessed 29 January 2014 from https://www.conpuscan.co.za/will-peer-to-peer-lending-revolutionise-the-credit-industry/.
23. Alloway (2013).
24. Accessed 19 August 2015 from www.fixura.com.
25. Accessed 8 February 2017 from http://www.pwc.com/en_US/us/technology/publications/assets/pwc-consumer-intelligence-series-the-sharing-economy.pdf; http://www.forbes.com/pictures/eeji45emgkh/airbnb-snapgoods-and-12-more-pioneers-of-the-share-economy/.
26. Accessed 10 June 2015 from https://www.airbnb.com/about/about-us.
27. Accessed 1 June 2015 from http://fortune.com/2015/02/25/airbnb-olympics-rio/.
28. Accessed 17 August 2015 from https://www.airbnb.com/.
29. Accessed 17 August 2015 from https://www.airbnb.com/.
30. Uber, Airbnb and consequences of the sharing economy: research roundup. Accessed 21 August 2015 from http://journalistsresource. Updated 13 July 2015.
31. Accessed 8 February 2017 from https://www.uber.com/; http://www.wsj.com/articles/uber-valued-at-more-than-50-billion-1438367457.
32. Accessed 5 August 2015 from https://www.uber.com/.
33. Accessed 5 August 2015 from https://growthhackers.com/growth-studies/uber.
34. Accessed 8 August 2015 from http://fortune.com/2015/08/11/uber-drivers-fulltime/.
35. Accessed 18 August 2015 from http://www.bloomberg.com/news/articles/2014-08-15/the-anti-uber-way-of-disrupting-transportation-politely; http://techcrunch.com/2015/04/15/blablacar-acquires-its-biggest-competitor-carpooling-com-to-dominate-european-market/#.7gkh41:38Ze.
36. Accessed 19 August 2015 from http://www.latimes.com/local/cityhall/la-me-uber-criminal-drivers-20150821-story.html.
37. Accessed 19 August 2015 from http://circanews.com/news/regulatory-issues-with-uber.
38. A fashion library often refers to a shop that allows its members to borrow fashions of their choice like borrow books in order to create more sustainable fashion practices. The specific business model of different fashion libraries may vary. In Lena, a fashion library in Amsterdam, people with a membership can get access to the library's full closet of vintage and designer clothes. Once customers decide to rent an item, they swipe their library cards instead of paying any cash. Each item is assigned a specific amount of points. Members have different amount of points in their librarycards according to the subscriptions they choose when signing up as a member. For more information about fashion libraries, see http://www.fastcoexist.com/3045366/change-generation/at-this-fashion-library-you-check-out-clothes-instead-of-buying-them#5; http://openarchive.cbs.dk/bitstream/handle/10398/8819/Netter_Pedersen.pdf?sequence=1 (accessed 19 August 2015).
39. Accessed 1 June 2015 from https://www.taskrabbit.com/how-it-works.
40. Accessed 17 August 2015 from http://about.zaarly.com/.
41. Lusch and Vargo (2014).
42. Manzini and Coad (2015).

REFERENCES

Alloway, Tracy (2013) Big banks muscle in on peer-to-peer lending, *Financial Times*, 28 October, accessed 29 January 2014 from http://www.ft.com/intl/

cms/s/0/b0696414-3f3f-11e3-9657-00144feabdc0.html?siteedition=intl#axzz2rn
TzRm6Q.

Amit, R. and Zott, C. (2012) Creating value through business model innovation, *Sloan Management Review*, vol. 53, no. 3, pp. 41–49.

Bughin, J., Chui, M. and Johnson, B. (2008) The next step in open innovation, *The McKinsey Quarterly*, vol. 4, no. 6, pp. 1–8.

Casadesus-Masanell, R. and Ricart, J.E. (2010) From strategy to business models and onto tactics, *Long Range Planning*, vol. 43, no. 2–3, pp. 195–215.

Chesbrough, H. and Crowther, A.K. (2006) Beyond high tech: early adopters of open innovation in other industries, *R&D Management*, vol. 36, no. 3, pp. 229–236.

Coviello, N.E. and Joseph, R.M. (2012) Creating major innovations with customers: insights from small and young technology firms, *Journal of Marketing*, vol. 76, November, pp. 87–104.

De Buysere, K., Gajda, O., Kleverlaan, R., Marom, D. and Klaes, M. (2012) A framework for European crowdfunding, *European Crowdfunding Network*.

Grönroos, C. (2011) Value co-creation in service logic: a critical analysis, *Marketing Theory*, vol. 11, no. 3, pp. 279–301.

Gray, D. and Vander Wal, T. (2012) *The Connected Company*, Austin, TX: Dachis Group.

Hamel, G. (1998) Strategy innovation and the quest for value, *Sloan Management Review*, vol. 39, no. 2, p. 7.

Johansson, F. (2012) *The Click Moment: Seizing Opportunity in an Unpredictable World*, New York: Penguin Group.

Kelly, T. and Kelly, D. (2013) *Creative Confidence: Unleashing the Creative Potential Within Us All*, New York: Random House.

King, A. and Lakhani, K. (2013) Using open innovation to identify the best ideas, *MIT Sloan Management Review*, vol. 55, no. 1, pp. 41–48.

Krugman, Paul (2008) Bits, bands and books, *New York Times* Column, 6 June.

Lakhani, K.R. and Panetta, J.A. (2007) *The Principles of Distributed Innovation*, Cambridge, MA: MIT Press.

Laursen, K. and Salter, A. (2006) Open for innovation: the role of openness in explaining innovation performance among UK manufacturing firms, *Strategic Management Journal*, vol. 27, no. 2, pp. 131–150.

Lusch, R.F. and Vargo, S.L. (2014) *The Service-dominant Logic of Marketing: Dialog, Debate, and Directions*, London: Routledge.

Mangalindan, J.P. (2012) Amazon's recommendation secret, *Fortune*, 30 July.

Manzini, E. and Coad, R. (2015) *Design, When Everybody Designs: An Introduction to Design for Social Innovation*, Boston: MIT Press.

Markides, C. (2006) Disruptive innovation: in need of better theory, *Journal of Product Innovation Management*, vol. 23, no. 1, pp. 19–25.

Mintzberg, H. and Waters, J.A. (1985) Of strategies, deliberate and emergent, *Strategic Management Journal*, vol. 6, pp. 257–272.

Prahalad, C.K. and Ramaswamy, V. (2004) Co-creating unique value with customers, *Strategy & Leadership*, vol. 32, no. 3, pp. 4–9.

Read, S. and Sarasvathy, S.D. (2005) Knowing what to do and doing what you know: effectuation as a form of entrepreneurial expertise, *Journal of Private Equity*, vol. 9, no. 1, pp. 45–62.

Read, S., Dew, N., Sarasvathy, S.D., Song, M. and Wiltbank, R. (2009) Marketing under uncertainty: the logic of effectual approach, *Journal of Marketing*, vol. 73, May, pp. 1–18.

Sarasvathy, S.D. (2001) Effectual reasoning in entrepreneurial decision making: existence and bounds, *Academy of Management Best Paper Proceedings*.

Sarasvathy, S.D. and Dew, N. (2005) Entrepreneurial logics for a technology of foolishness, *Scandinavian Journal of Management*, vol. 21, pp. 385–406.

Vargo, S.L. and Lusch, R.F. (2004) Evolving to a new dominant logic for marketing, *Journal of Marketing*, vol. 68, no. 1, pp. 1–17.

Vargo, S.L. and Lusch, R.F. (2008) From goods to service(s): Divergences and convergences of logics, *Industrial Marketing Management*, vol. 37, no. 3, pp. 254–259.

TECHNICAL APPENDIX

A business model articulates a firm's logic of value creation and value capture based upon a system of interconnected and interdependent activities. Innovation in business models is an alternative for firms to create new value in times of economic change[1] A global survey of more than 4,000 senior managers by the Economist Intelligence Unit suggests that the majority (54 per cent) considered new business models over new products and services as a source of future competitive advantage.[2]

Traditionally, business model development has looked at how firms can allocate internal resources and capacities to create a leap in value creation for their users.[3] This suggests a closed value creation system where users are seen as passive recipients of products or services. The increasing digitalisation of today's businesses and society has greatly empowered users in business activities. Value co-creation with users has now been considered as the most effective way for industry incumbents to maintain their market position and new comers to establish themselves in the market.[4] The digital world is offering a great number of opportunities to harness underutilised user assets, and put them into use via smart digital platforms. More specifically, business model innovation opportunities present themselves as novel ways to co-create value in networks of actors: novel ways of integrating resources will lead to the creation of new resources, and possibly, to unexpected possibilities and outcomes. This line of thinking has been strongly advanced by Robert Lusch and Stephen Vargo;[5] according to them, all actors – producers, individual and organisational users, user communities – may be characterised in terms of resource integrating, transforming and exchanging actors, opening eyes for seeking and perceiving new innovation opportunities.

The novel ways of business model development often follows a different logic than the traditional strategic planning approach recommends. Traditionally, firms rely on a process that begins with market analysis and opportunity identification, followed by the development of a business plan and the acquisition of resources needed to implement the plan. Business model development with users requires entrepreneurs to simply start doing what they can with the means available to them, and see what opportunities and new goals emerge through courses of action. This type of means-oriented action logic has been identified and conceptually developed by Sarasvathy and her co-workers in the context of entrepreneurial decision making.[6] Sarasvathy has named this means-oriented action logic as effectual logic (of entrepreneurial expertise).

Effectual logic is fundamentally different from the prevailing logic of predictive rationality: Predictive rationality involves the idea that even though future consequences of our actions are often uncertain, we typically know what consequences we prefer (strategic management literature is very much based on predictive rationality). In contrast, effectual reasoning holds that our preferences are uncertain as well: our future preferences and goals are unstable, ambiguous, inconsistent, even conflicting.[7] Sarasvathy and Dew[8] stress that ambiguous and conflicting preferences are necessary for the creation of entrepreneurial novelty. Hence, the view of future in effectual thinking is creative: The future is co-created (at least in part) by wilful agents, and, the direction of action is contingent on 'who comes on board and the actions and goals they enable and constrain'.[9]

The means-oriented logic of action is not totally new in management and business studies. In particular, similar ideas are evident in Henry Mintzberg's influential work on emergent strategies.[10] Though the concept of emergent strategy is still more reactive (learning from the unstable reality by taking one action at a time) than creative (creating the reality by one's own actions), it stresses openness to act before things are fully understood and the role of empirical discovery.

Overall, effectual approach emphasises many principles which seem to be important for business development in the digital world: experimentation and testing in small scale, partnerships, and generally, a bottom-up co-creative process in which people and resources connect and shape the future opportunity in a peer-to-peer way.[11] These principles are consistent with and reinforce some of the ideas that currently inspire leading innovation thinkers: that diversity breeds creativity;[12] that a number of small-scale experiments (bets) are needed to succeed;[13] that ability to face failure is an essential part of creative process;[14] that freedom to self-organise based on individuals' interests and passions is key to creating new opportunities in organisations;[15] and, that success cannot be planned, but its chances may be nurtured by our actions.[16]

NOTES

1. Hamel (1998); Markides (2006).
2. Amit and Zott (2012).
3. For example, Casadesus-Masanell and Ricart (2010); Hamel (1998).
4. Grönroos (2011); Vargo and Lusch (2004, 2008).
5. Lusch and Vargo (2014).
6. Sarasvathy (2001); Sarasvathy and Dew (2005); Read and Sarasvathy (2005).
7. Sarasvathy and Dew (2005).
8. Sarasvathy and Dew (2005, p. 387).
9. Read et al. (2009, pp. 3–4).
10. Mintzberg and Waters (1985); Gray and Vander Wal (2012).

11. Read et al. (2009); Sarasvathy and Dew (2005); Coviello and Joseph (2012).
12. King and Lakhani (2013); Gray and Vander Wal (2012).
13. Johansson (2012); Kelly and Kelly (2013).
14. Kelly and Kelly (2013).
15. Kelly and Kelly (2013); Gray and Vander Wal (2012).
16. Johansson (2012).

7. Emerging business models in settled contexts

Pirjo Yli-Viitala, Sami Berghäll, Jari Kuusisto and Stephen Flowers

7.1 INTRODUCTION

This chapter gives two examples of Innovation Opportunity Spaces within mature industries in Finland and the UK. The first of them, the forest sector in Finland, has had a critical role in the development of the national economy for more than one hundred years. Traditionally, firms in the sector have adopted an extractive approach where products are produced based upon natural resources of the sector (for example, wood, fibres and so on), with a bulk-product approach and a focus on technical process efficiency. This has led to all innovations being highly incremental in nature. The second of the case studies is drawn from the mobile telecommunication sector in the UK. This is a mature industry that is typically dominated by a small number of large firms that conform to similar operational structures and offer complex charging regimes. Firms tend to provide handsets as part of complex contracts that lock users into long-term deals. This sector has also become associated with incremental innovation.

The following sections describe how the Innovation Opportunity Space is structured to facilitate or prevent innovation activity with these two examples. The main actors in the Innovation Opportunity Space are outlined in each case and their actions are considered. Each case concludes with an analysis of the activity within the Space, providing pointers to the direction of potential future innovations.

7.2 RETHINKING 'USE': FORESTS IN FINLAND

This case is an examination of the disconnect that can occur between industries that operate in a stable Innovation Opportunity Space and its context when the tectonic plates of technical and social change start to move. The case will explore how the potential innovation pathways of an established industry can be reimagined and entirely new uses for traditional resources can be created.

7.2.1   Forests in Finland: Setting the Scene

As outlined in Chapter 4, an Innovation Opportunity Space (IOS) may emerge due to a technological or other type of a change, it may be latent but unrecognised and have only emerged due to a reframing of the business surroundings. It may also arise due to a shift in the economic and social norms and requirements that are applied to many other things, for instance, to the use of natural resources. At the same time an IOS may be recognised but be effectively closed due to regulation, market structure, inadequate technology, or a lack of market readiness. The incumbents might also act in ways to effectively hinder new entrants from capturing a slice in the emerging possibilities (see Figure 7.1). Thus, this effectively locks the sector into its backward-looking view of innovation. The work of Professor Steven Vargo[1] supports this view but also proposes that radical innovations require a change in the social systems via the change in related norms and behavioural patterns. Drawing on this approach, if barriers to innovation activity are considered more closely, it can be argued that barriers are systemic in the sense that they exist on the vastly different levels of economy, culture, regulation and policy (for example, see Figure 7.2). This case study is based on a series of interviews among visionary forest experts who have outlined the barriers that prevent a reshaping of the business model that underpins the Finnish forest sector. The barriers identified block the innovation activity of the whole sector making movement towards reshaping the Innovation Space difficult. As a result, the barriers are presented and analysed in order to throw new light onto the challenges faced in identifying new opportunities and reframing and reformulating the core business model of this sector. For this reason, analysis of the barriers are discussed through the concept of 'Dominant Logic'[2] that is widely seen as preventing an industry sector as reaching its full innovation potential.

Firms in the Finnish forest sector have primarily adopted a Goods-Dominant (G-D) logic where products are produced from the natural resources of the forest sector but with a heavy emphasis on the technical nature of the production process itself. G-D logic refers to the traditional industrial production logic of tangible goods by employing a process-focused high division of labour in the mills, separating the production process of the mill from the customer, and a concentration on refining the economic efficiency of the supply chain, material management, machinery usage, and capital usage in the broad sense. This results in a

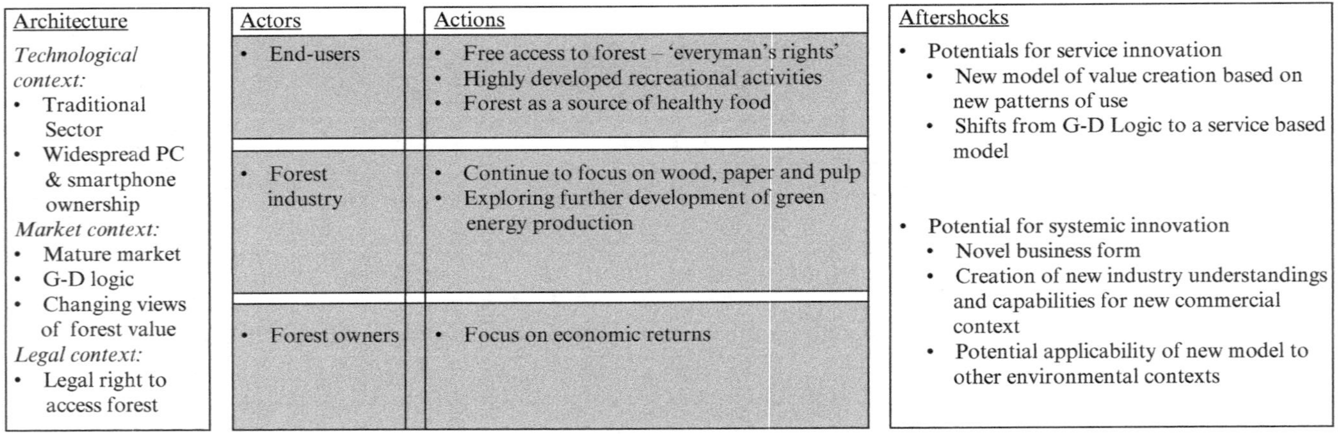

Architecture	Actors	Actions
Technological context: • Traditional Sector • Widespread PC & smartphone ownership *Market context:* • Mature market • G-D logic • Changing views of forest value *Legal context:* • Legal right to access forest	• End-users	• Free access to forest – 'everyman's rights' • Highly developed recreational activities • Forest as a source of healthy food
	• Forest industry	• Continue to focus on wood, paper and pulp • Exploring further development of green energy production
	• Forest owners	• Focus on economic returns

Aftershocks

• Potentials for service innovation
  • New model of value creation based on new patterns of use
  • Shifts from G-D Logic to a service based model

• Potential for systemic innovation
  • Novel business form
  • Creation of new industry understandings and capabilities for new commercial context
  • Potential applicability of new model to other environmental contexts

Figure 7.1 Forests in Finland: the architecture of the innovation opportunity space

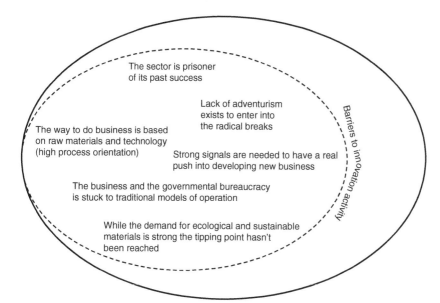

*Figure 7.2   Barriers to innovation activity exist on the different levels of
economy, operational culture, regulation and policy effectively
closing the Finnish Forest IOS*

technical view on the produce where the customer is seen as being the next industrial producer of the mill output and the final end-user at the end of the line is of minimal interest. Thus, the importance of tangible goods and tangible value of the forests is something that represents one of the descriptive dimensions of the present Dominant Logic existing in the sector. The focus being on the tangible dimensions of the production results in an inability to see a new Innovation Opportunity Space (IOS) emerging by shifts in market demand or by shifts in technology that open up new possibilities. In this context a new and emerging IOS will likely go un-noticed by the incumbents since they still control the industry and (by accident or design) limit the developing opportunities to utilise the full potential of the forest sector.

In line with G-D logic, the forest sector business model can also be described as having followed a supplier-driven approach to value creation. In this view firms conduct value chain activities based upon their internal resources to create value for their customers (see Chapter 6). Customers are seen as passive recipients of the firm's products or services, and marketing (or more strictly selling) pushes the produce to the end-user via industrial customers. As a result, a similar supplier-driven value creation approach exists within many forest sector businesses: firms produce value, which is then consumed by end-users, making a distinct separation between value creation (forest firms) and value consumption (end-users). Thus, the traditional supplier-driven approach to value creation in this sector echoes its long-established historical ties to a G-D logic where value is seen as something that the supplier firm plans, manages, creates and delivers.

Although the regeneration challenges of the Finnish forest sector are typical of many traditional industries the forest industry seems to be quite extreme in holding onto conservative, path dependent and mature modes of operation.[3] The Dominant Logic is embedded in standard operating procedures, shaping not only how the individuals in the industry act but also how they think.[4] Because the operating model is the source of the sector's past success, it becomes the lens through which managers see all emerging opportunities.[5] This makes it hard for firms in the sector to recognise new and different opportunities, or to embrace a different approach to competition and value creation. However, barriers to progressive thinking in the forest sector are not limited to companies or governmental organisations. On an individual level barriers to progressive thinking include forest sector professionals and their occupational rewards. For instance, in conducting their job people tend to rely on a professional code of practice developed over time. As a result, they often pay more attention to peer judgement than judgement by the customers and their changing needs.[6]

7.2.2 Forests in Finland: Main Actors in the Innovation Opportunity Space

The attributes of forest usage can vary a lot between different actors and different uses of forest resources. The exploitation of an IOS may require many complementary forms of knowledge that reside within a range of actors including industry, users, and so on, each of which may focus on different forms of value (for example, economic value, value-in-use, existence value). In the context of a natural resource like a forest a multitude of user groups can be identified, each of which is associated with a varying array of uses from forest owners to those working in forestry, business operations (the forest industries) and, more broadly, the general population (forest end-users and consumers).[7] As a result, the *user* in the case of 'forest' is not restricted to the roles of 'customer' or 'end-user' as traditionally defined by forest sector manufacturing firms and there are many stakeholders, each of whom will have a particular interest, perspective and understanding of concepts like use and value.

Typically, users can belong to several overlapping groups (Figure 7.3). For instance, a forest owner assumes the social role of owner, yet in many cases he/she at the same time also fishes, hunts, picks berries and

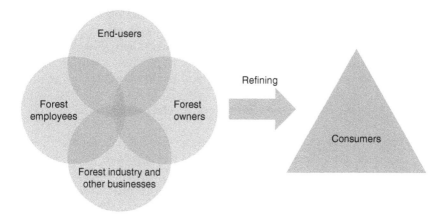

Figure 7.3   Forest user roles are partly overlapping

mushrooms, is a conservationist or hiker,[8] that is, is an end-user of the forests as such, and possibly also a consumer of the forest based produce. This is significant as Finland is one of the world's most forest-rich countries with 75 per cent of the land area covered by forests and nearly 12 per cent of the population being forest owners.[9]

It can be argued that the forest sector may serve as a key enabling platform of the distinct groups of users who interact with each other in some way. For instance, the Finnish forest industry needs the forest owners as a raw material supplier in order to manufacture goods from timber grown in the forests. Similarly, the factor most important for the current profitability of the Finnish forest owners is a continuous industrial demand for each timber grade,[10] even if the dependence on income from wood sales is decreasing.[11] While the forest industry considers it more sensible to refine wood into paper, construction and furniture first, and only then to recycle the products (with the last stage being burning the timber) Finnish forest owners consider that they have the right to sell their wood to whoever pays the best price.[12] Thus, forest owners feel that one should be able to sell the wood to energy production, if the forest industry is not able to purchase it. At the same time, on the basis of the Finnish 'everyman's rights',[13] all Finns have a right to roam over the land and can enjoy forest-related leisure pursuits in any Finnish forest. While the free access to forest land (*everyman's right*) results in a vast number of people enjoying the forests the law can also have a hampering effect on the recognition of new Innovation Opportunities as forest owners do not have an incentive to take care of other forest resources apart from timber. For example, potential areas like nature tourism are not developed as the benefit to the forest owner is unclear. As a result, forests provide an environment that multiple groups can use, albeit with varying degrees of overlap, and the multitude of common interests are only weakly mapped or described. Given this context, it is important to study how forest user groups are using forests as different types of forest use will provide clear pointers to a range of different Innovation Opportunities.

7.2.3   Actions in the Forest Sector Innovation Opportunity Space

The present case focuses on two main actors: the Traditional Forest Industry and End-Users and Consumers. The core feature of the existing Innovation Opportunity Space is the tension inherent in the Dominant Logic that is applied: the traditional forest industry is product-focused and R&D driven, whilst end-users are more focused on intangible values. These two are not necessarily in open conflict but the present modes of operation and commercial approaches applied are likely to be a strong drag on the recognition and development of new Innovation Opportunities.

Actions: traditional forest industries
Forest industries are a branch of manufacturing industry, producing commercial goods from timber grown in forest estates. Forest industries are divided into the pulp and paper industries and the wood products industry.[14] The pulp and paper industries include the production of chemical and mechanical pulp and their further processing into paper and paperboard. The wood products industry includes the production of sawn goods, plywood and other timber boards and their processing into windows, construction components and items like furniture. Sawmills also produce wood chips and sawdust as by-products. Wood chips are used to make pulp, and sawdust is used in the manufacturing of particleboards and pellets which are used to generate energy. The commercial value of the forests is realised through existing products and services, including mass produced paper, pulp and wood products.

This is a stable industry and, according to the Finnish Forest Industry Federation, refining wood, grown in the forests, into paper, pulp and construction is the most 'sensible' way to use Finnish forests. Furthermore, existing industry products will still form a core of business for quite some time, as paper, packaging and wood products are constantly being developed by new generations.[15] Thus, products made of wood and fibre will play a significant role also in the low-carbon 'bioeconomy' of the future. To sum up, the focus of many innovations in the sector is still on incremental development of existing technologies and on tangible goods. Thus, the forest sector's research and development efforts support the goods-dominant logic that remains the key focus of existing operations.

7.2.4   Emerging Innovation Opportunities in the Forest Sector

Global trends show that people are changing the way they work, communicate and spend their leisure time. For instance, consumer behaviour is rapidly changing with new digital activities.[16] These activities enable individuals to access previously un-seen media content and new forms of personal communications as well as even collaborative networks of smartphones. As smartphones have become ubiquitous this device shift, from PCs to mobile/touch devices,[17] seems to also be rapidly changing the way individuals are creating value from things surrounding them, including forests. While forest organisations can generate enormous amounts of data, such as multi-source forest inventory data released by Finnish Forest Research Institute, or open map information from the National Land Survey, this data by itself is mostly meaningless. For the individual user the significant value is created by offering accurate analytics of this data in their service proposals.[18] Finns continue to walk in the forests, pick berries and mushrooms, and pursue equilibrium/peace of mind forms of recreational activity. Driven by the rapid development of digitalisation, there are numerous new ways to support these nature-related activities. Further, there are new dimensions in the Opportunity Space that are largely un-tapped by commercial firms. Figure 7.4 and Box 7.1 describe some examples.

BOX 7.1   DIGITALISATION ENABLES NEW WAYS TO USE FORESTS – SOME EXAMPLES

NatureGate app[19] enables the person to identify berries and mushrooms, as well as other forest species according to their characteristics. Users may also save and share the observations and see what others have spotted.

Once the wild plants of the forests have been identified, *Villivihannekset*[20] ('Wild plants') app aims to inspire users to try to use these products naturally growing in the forest.

Tienoo[21] ('Region') app guides the users to freely roam in nature while being presented with the site-specific information on environmental phenomena along with other location based services.

Järviwiki[22] ('Lakewiki') a web service, which is built and maintained in cooperation by local communities. In Järviwiki there is basic information of each Finnish lake over 1 hectare in extent and tools for sharing observations and pictures.

Karttapullautin[23] ('Map pusher') can be used for navigation sport mapping (for example, orienteering, adventure racing, map making). Without arduous field checking, the app generates orienteering maps based on the laser scanning data and terrain modelling database released by the National Land Survey of Finland.

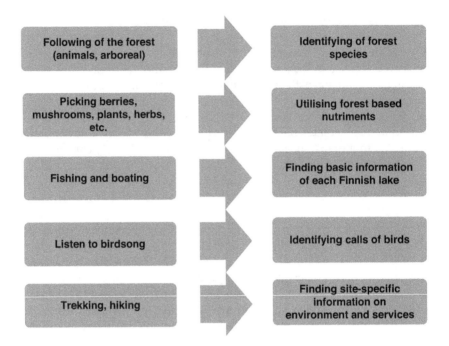

Figure 7.4   Examples of the data-driven activities that are enablers of new ways to utilise or enjoy forests

Due to the global trends of climate change and the resulting orientation towards sustainability, consumers are increasingly concerned about environmental, social and economic issues, related to raw material usage. As a result, an increasing number of consumers are willing, able and motivated to take action on these concerns. One effort into understanding these new types of consumers (that is, the green/ethical/sustainable customer) is based on studies on the group that that has been labelled as LOHAS consumers. LOHAS is an acronym for 'Lifestyles of Health and Sustainability'[24,25] – a segment of consumers concerned about issues such as sustainable living, the environment, health, and fitness. This thinking resonates with a wide range of industries, corporate activities, products and services, all designed to be environmentally conscious, sustainable, and/or socially responsible. In Finland, an estimated one-third[26] of the general population belongs to this part of a growing segment of the LOHAS consumers.[27]

As a consequence, consumers are paying attention to food that is nutrient-rich, and contain minerals and vitamins considered to be especially beneficial for the health and wellbeing of the consumer and the planet.

BOX 7.2 SUPERFOODS FROM FORESTS – HANDPICKED NORDIC WILD BERRIES

A Finnish food industry company Kiantama Ltd., producer of the Biokia® brand,[28] has seized an opportunity to create innovative ways for their customers to incorporate wild forest berries in everyday diet. The company is located deep in the heartlands of the Finnish berry-growing region producing safe, high-quality berry products for the retail market. The company's values are purity, health and fairness. Studies show that wild berries growing in northern latitudes are exceptionally rich in vitamins, flavonoids, carotenes, antioxidants and other beneficial components.[29,30] Because of these health effects, Nordic wild berries are regarded as highly nutritious superfood. The raw materials for Kiantama's products grow in the unpolluted wilderness and contain no artificial flavourings, preservatives or pesticides.

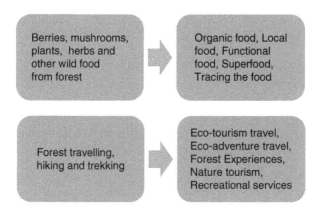

Figure 7.5   Examples of how the global trends of sustainability and climate change may contribute to a transformation towards high value-added products and services

Here the importance of wild food growing in the Finnish forests, such as berries, mushrooms, herbs, plants, as well as fish and hunted game will provide possibilities to widen the Opportunity Space.

Ecotourism and travel are also part of the growing LOHAS consumer movement covering everything that is focused on sustainable living, social justice, and personal development. Ecotourism can provide deep experiences in forests and support conservation efforts. Some ideas of these demands stemming from environmental change and resulting in new requirements for forest-related high value-added products and services are depicted in Figure 7.5.

Ageing, population growth, urbanisation, family size and structure, describe the effects of demographic changes that are likely to affect future consumption and consumer behaviour. For example, an ageing population will be likely to increase the need for welfare and nursing services. However, at the same time, citizens are increasingly recognising the health and welfare benefits of nature[31] and it can be argued that forests have a vast untapped potential that could be utilised for citizens' everyday wellbeing. While population growth is modest in Finland, on the global level, it may mean that the natural resources of Finnish forests could become a target of an increasingly bigger global demand[32] and it is important to better understand the value of this potential as a source of new Innovation Opportunities. Increasing urbanisation results in congested towns and cities and by 2030 approximately five billion people, that is, 70 per cent of the world's population, will live in cities. However, at the same time the way in which people live their lives will also change and Figure 7.6 illustrates how demographic changes may affect the need and requirements for forest-related high value-added products and services.

Outcome/aftershocks
In developing this case a comparison was made between the dominating forest industry industrial logic and emerging Innovation Opportunities. While the activities of the present incumbents are rational and a result of a long historical legacy they should not prevent the development of new Innovation Opportunities. Actions by the Forest Industry, such as focusing

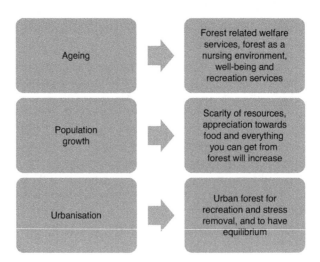

*Figure 7.6   Examples of how the societal changes may contribute to a
transformation towards high value-added products and services*

> ## BOX 7.3   SILENCE TOURISM
>
> A network of companies, entrepreneurs and societies in North Karelia of Finland has engaged in developing silence as a tourism asset.[33] Silence in this context does not mean a total lack of sounds but the possibility to relax – alone or in a group – in a unique quiet, slow-paced, environment. The aim of the Silence Travel Network is to develop innovative services and nature experiences based on developing activities where silence and listening play an important role. The direct beneficiaries of the network are entrepreneurs working in tourism – food/catering and adventure services. At present, these businesses offer services in a few pilot regions. Simultaneously, the indirect beneficiaries are all other entrepreneurs, travellers, larger economic regions as well as associations, training organisations, and other projects in North Karelia that overlap with this network.

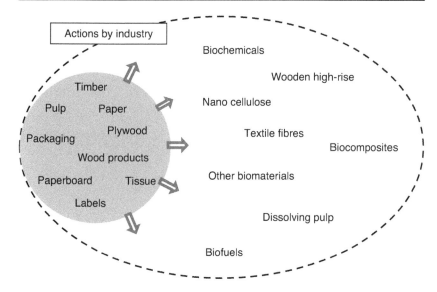

Figure 7.7   Traditional IOS of established firm in the Finnish forest sector

on (forest originating) biomass and a strict manufacturing perspective, are the result of a strong Dominant Logic emphasising bulk products with low added value, requiring little regenerational effort and limiting Innovation Opportunities. These kinds of actions create a situation where economic production happens in a low-risk comfort zone but where the potential for new growth based on innovation around new opportunities is limited. In this context staying within an industrial comfort zone results in marginal and conventional regeneration activities (see Figure 7.7). Describing the actions by the users on one hand, but also the actions of Forest Industry incumbents on the other, this case has highlighted the gap between current activities and the possible future potential. Working inside its comfort zone represents the traditional world of business thought and is mostly based on tangible value of the forests: mass produced paper, pulp and wood products.

In order to reach out to groups outside of its comfort zone, forest companies need the means to better comprehend their broader innovation context, and to examine what consumers are doing. By moving beyond the idea of goods towards the intangible value creation firms in the sector will have new opportunities to redefine the Innovation Opportunity Space within which they operate. The first point of departure is to focus on the intangible value generated within forests, in addition to the tangible one. The second point is the adoption of digitalisation enabling new ways of forest usage and responding to the growing demand for digital products and services. New forest-related services on the whole, such as wellbeing, nature travelling and recreation, represent the third point of departure from present operational mode (see Figure 7.8) and point the way to the shape and nature of the emerging Innovation Opportunity Space for Forests in Finland.

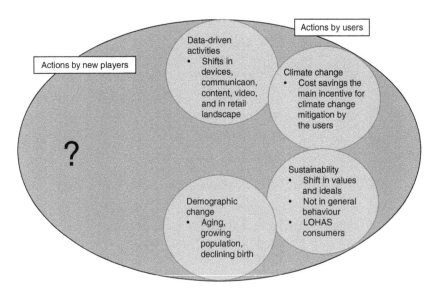

Figure 7.8   Service dominant IOS

7.3   A REVOLUTIONARY SERVICE DELIVERY MODEL – GIFFGAFF

This case study explores how it is possible for a commercial organisation to create a business model in which its users, or customers, effectively become a core part of its day-to-day operations. What is particularly interesting about giffgaff is that, first and foremost, it is a commercial organisation that was designed specifically to benefit from the interactive nature of the Internet (something that was once referred to as Web 2.0). It relies on its users undertaking many of the tasks previously done by staff in-house so that it looks very different to many other firms. It has now become quite common for firms to rely on their users for ideas, information sharing and feedback, but giffgaff has taken this to an entirely different level. Many firms will plug user ideas into their research and development operation or rely on them spreading the word on social media as part of their marketing operation. Giffgaff does all this as well but has taken this idea several steps further by drawing on a community of users to undertake core tasks like sales, marketing and customer service. This is a commercial organisation that has placed its users at the core of its operation.

7.3.1   Background: Giffgaff

Giffgaff is a mobile telephone operator based in the UK. Technically it is a Mobile Virtual Network Operator (MVNO) as it does not own its own mobile phone network infrastructure and rents bandwidth from firms that do, in this case O2. The term 'giffgaff' derives from an old Scottish word meaning mutual giving and giffgaff is a wholly owned subsidiary of Telefonica Group which also, at the time of writing, owns O2. That background aside, having been launched in late 2009 giffgaff is a relatively new entrant to a mobile phone market that has been dominated by large operators like Vodafone, T-Mobile and O2. Its key initial differentiator in this marketplace was its much lower cost, something achieved by their radically different organisational structure. The ambition behind this business structure is very simple: to build a commercial organisation in which many of the firm's operational activities will be undertaken by the users of the service. Although there are many examples of complex services created and operated by users on their own account (this book is full of them, but Wikipedia and Linux are good examples), at the time of giffgaff's creation there was no clear model for how this could be achieved in a traditionally commercial context. As result, giffgaff's operational model has evolved quite rapidly as ideas have been trialled and either adopted or discarded and a viable model has emerged through a rather Darwinian process.

However, it is important to see this trial-and-error approach as a strength rather than as a weakness as what was being attempted was the creation of a new type of organisation in which the business relied on the orchestration of the efforts of its users in order to operate. As has been seen, most organisations operate by employing their own staff, keeping important things in-house, and maybe incorporating some form of user input into their processes here and there. Giffgaff's approach is fundamentally different since the aim is to minimise their own employed staff and enable their users to perform many of the things that were usually done in-house. This was a fundamentally new approach and, as a result, not only did giffgaff have to learn how to build and maintain the large online user community required to run their operations, they also had to discover what worked in this new context. From a business perspective, they had to build a new set of organisational capabilities from the ground up. The following sections will explore the development of these capabilities and outline the many parts that users now play in giffgaff's operational model.

7.3.2 The Giffgaff Community

Giffgaff was built to be an online-only organisation in which the user community, composed of 'young, tech-savvy, digital native people',[34] played an essential role. This group, which continues to be its target market, now populate its community and form an important element of its operational structure and provide many of the support and other services that more traditional firms would keep in-house. As we will see, the giffgaff community is now highly integrated into the firm's operational structure.

The core idea is that individual giffgaff subscribers/members will be rewarded for participating in the community by recruiting new users, helping others, posting videos, suggesting ideas and so on, and that this reward can be translated into things like call credit or cash. Community members have the opportunity both to get involved in the operation of the business in some small way and also to obtain reward for their efforts. The opportunities for involvement have evolved since giffgaff launched in 2009, but social media platforms like Facebook, Twitter and Instagram, together with systems like YouTube are at the heart of how the community interacts. But this is an orchestrated community and giffgaff employs a Community Team to oversee how members interact. An important part of the Community Team are the group of Educators whose main role is to educate members and influence their behaviour through 'positive reinforcement, to ensure engagement is in the right tone when contributing'.[35] This important group are also a major conduit to the community for company news and decisions and are actively involved in the day-to-day operation of the community. Giffgaff has a number of ways of engaging members in its operational structure, including:

Customer Service is managed entirely online and almost entirely undertaken by the user community, although financial, technical and billing issues will be dealt with in-house by giffgaff staff. Community members are incentivised by being awarded Payback Points (see below), receiving kudos from other users, and being ranked in terms of the quantity and value of their help. This approach has proved to be very successful with average wait time for responses being as low as 90 seconds from the original request.[36] The participation levels amongst some members was very high with, at one stage, the top ten super-users spending more than nine hours a day on the community site.[37] Giffgaff have now created a quiz-based system that enables users to work through a tiered system that starts with individuals being labelled as either Experienced, Dedicated or Hardcore Helpers. This quiz-based approach allows individuals to build their knowledge and capabilities and, once successful, to earn more payback.

Giffgaff community knowledge base is a collection of responses to Frequently Asked Questions (FAQs) categorised by topic, author, kudos and date. This is a searchable resource and enables users to self-help when they have problems or challenges that they need assistance with. Actively curated by the internal team it is a valuable and developing knowledge resource largely created by giffgaff's users.

Payback is central to the operation of giffgaff with members being rewarded with Payback Points for recruiting new subscribers or providing help in one of the online forums. Payback is heavily weighted towards recruiting new subscribers and, subject to certain conditions, members are able convert their points to cash, call credit, or can simply donate the cash equivalent to a charity. Giffgaff now operates a Super Recruiter programme that focuses solely on building giffgaff's subscriber base, with members of the programme receiving strong financial incentives to recruit and retain new customers.

Giffgaff labs provides a mechanism for users to get involved in service development and is a structured and systematic approach to opening up the new service development process. Members of the giffgaff community (all of whom are also subscribers and users of the service) can propose new ideas, which are then voted on by other members. The number of votes acts as a signal to giffgaff's internal R&D team regarding the level of support within the community for the suggestion. The quickest route through the system takes just three stages of New idea > Working on it > Implemented, although it may also be that the idea is rejected as 'Not for us'. Of the 10,000 or so ideas that have been suggested in the first six years of operation, some 500 have been implemented.[38] Members do not receive any financial incentive for submitting ideas other than the prospect of 'giffgaff fame and glory', the opportunity to add an achievement to one's CV, make a difference to the wider giffgaff community, and learn more about different areas of the organisation. The success of an idea and its status is clearly published on the Ideas Board.

Giffgaff Unlockapedia is a directory of the information required for users to unlock contract mobile phones from their original service operator. When it was launched giffgaff only supplied the SIM (subscriber identification module) cards that their prospective customers could use in their existing mobile phones. Many existing mobile phones would have been obtained through a contract with an existing telecommunications provider and would be 'locked', preventing the user from moving to another provider. In order to facilitate this transfer giffgaff created Unlockapedia, a wiki-based system which was largely populated by users offering detailed advice and instructions on how a particular make and model of phone can be unlocked. The site now also allows users to rate firms that unlock mobile phones on a commercial basis.

Video Missions and giffgaff TV builds on the emergence of video guides on services like YouTube and is an initiative that draws on the expertise of the giffgaff community of users to create video guides that deal with specific needs. The final versions of these guides can be shared on giffgaff's own YouTube channel. Video Missions is 'a place for video makers, script writers and presenters to join forces and make fantastic tutorials for our Knowledge Base'.[39] Information is provided by the firm on the kind of equipment required to make video tutorials, together with advice on setting up shots and editing. Payback points are awarded according to the part played in the production (script, presenting, voice over or full video) and a list of Video Missions is shown, together with the roles that need to be filled. Users can also propose their own ideas, with the best productions being recognised on the Video Makers Wall of Fame.

P2P loans and lending. Since its launch in late 2009 as a SIM-only MVNO (Mobile Virtual Network Operator) giffgaff has slowly developed and began to sell mobile phones in late 2013. At the same time the company also partnered with an online P2P (peer-to-peer) finance company to offer loans to customers who wanted to borrow money to finance the purchase of their new phone. Subsequently giffgaff has developed its community knowledge base to include tips and advice about managing money, loans and borrowing.

Giffgaff is an interesting example of an organisation that has successfully based a commercial operation on phenomena previously only observed in a wide range of non-profit contexts like Wikipedia and Linux. The emergence into the mainstream of large-scale online communities that undertake complex tasks at no-cost provided the basis for an exploration of the commercial possibilities of this phenomenon. Giffgaff is one example of the move towards commercialisation and provides some useful insights into the potential and the limits of what can be achieved in this context. The following sections will explore giffgaff's Innovation Opportunity Space in more detail (Figure 7.9).

7.3.3 Giffgaff's Innovation Opportunity Space

Architecture
To begin the process of understanding the architecture of the Innovation Space within which giffgaff operates it is important to have some idea of the size and scope of the UK market for mobile phone services and the nature of the market for those services. The mobile telephony market in the UK could be considered to be mature, with around 93 per cent of the adult population owning or using a mobile phone[40] with the population of the UK estimated to be around 64.5 million.[41] Although it is hard to come up with a definitive figure, it is likely that the overall market for mobile telephony in the UK is very large indeed, standing at around 50 million individual consumers or users, resulting in around 90 million mobile phone subscriptions.[42] The UK is dominated by some very large providers who have been active in the mobile phone market for decades and have built highly effective structures that often rely on high-street retail sales and in-house call centre operations. This dominant model brings with it an associated cost structure that, if a way were to be found that resulted in dramatic reductions of this cost base, would provide an opportunity for low-cost providers to emerge. In creating an operational model that relies on its own customers to provide many of the services that are delivered by in-house staff by their competitors, this is exactly what giffgaff has done.

From an official regulatory perspective, this market is overseen by a large government approved regulator called OFCOM (Office for

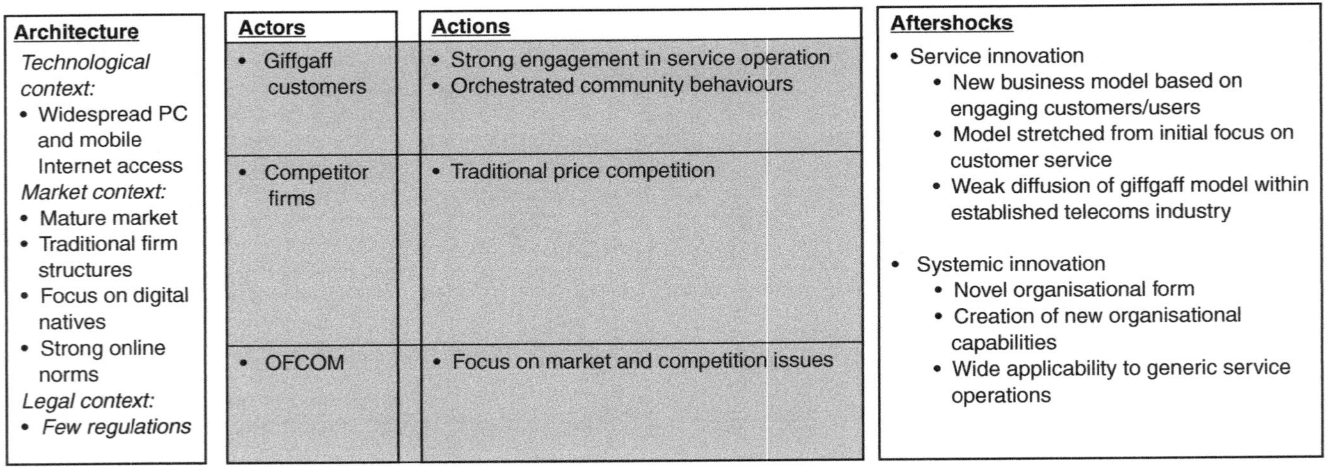

Architecture	Actors	Actions	Aftershocks

Technological context:
• Widespread PC and mobile Internet access
Market context:
• Mature market
• Traditional firm structures
• Focus on digital natives
• Strong online norms
Legal context:
• Few regulations
	• Giffgaff customers	• Strong engagement in service operation
		• Orchestrated community behaviours
			• Service innovation
			  • New business model based on engaging customers/users
			  • Model stretched from initial focus on customer service
			  • Weak diffusion of giffgaff model within established telecoms industry
			
			• Systemic innovation
			  • Novel organisational form
			  • Creation of new organisational capabilities
			  • Wide applicability to generic service operations

	• Competitor firms	• Traditional price competition	
	• OFCOM	• Focus on market and competition issues	

Figure 7.9   Innovation Opportunity Space – giffgaff

Communications) that is responsible for television, radio, post and telecommunications within the UK. As a UK government regulator it has a legal duty to represent the interests of consumers and promote competition within the markets it oversees and offers a range of services that are designed to hold commercial providers to account, including providing maps of service coverage, network speed checkers and complaint resolution processes. Like many regulators, OFCOM operates at quite a high level and its main focus means that innovative business models, like that being pioneered by giffgaff, may not fall within its remit.

The norms and behaviours associated with mobile phones have continued to evolve and, as smartphone ownership has grown, have merged with those found online. Online-only services that do not have call centres and a physical customer-facing presence are now commonplace and widely accepted and, as a result, many opportunities have begun to emerge for new entrants like giffgaff that wish to create new services or to disrupt 'old', mature markets. Many of the norms that emerged and were developed on the Internet – for example, interacting with others remotely, sharing experiences, ideas or knowledge, helping others – are now being drawn on and developed by those who wish to apply them to commercial contexts. Giffgaff is unusual in that it has drawn on these norms, developed them, and successfully applied to the pre-existing, 'traditional', context of mobile telephony. However, it is worth noting that these norms and behaviours were originally developed in the context of non-commercial activities, with the result that the legal obligations (for example, health and safety, duty of care) firms have in respect of their employees are not likely to apply to volunteer users who choose to perform tasks for their chosen commercial 'partner'. As a result the architecture of the Innovation Space that applies to users who choose to perform online 'work' for a firm on an ad-hoc, volunteer, basis is vague in the extreme. This is both an opportunity and a potential threat to commercial operators in this space.

Actors
There are four main types of actor within this Opportunity Space: OFCOM, competitors, giffgaff and the mobile phone users themselves. OFCOM, as has been noted above, operates at quite a high level for this marketplace and giffgaff's approach is likely to be at some distance from its main priorities. In contrast, giffgaff operates within a very crowded mature marketplace that has several rival suppliers with its own network infrastructure, plus a large number of MVNO (Mobile Virtual Network Operator) firms (of which giffgaff is one) that simply rent bandwidth from these large network operators. However, the scale of the UK market (see above) is such that it is likely that operators like giffgaff can target a particular niche and

still be able to develop a viable business. The key actor group in this context, however, is the user or customer. As we have seen, giffgaff's target market for its service were 'young, tech-savvy, digital native people'[43] who were likely to be comfortable with the sharing, community-based norms of the Internet. Giffgaff's strapline 'the mobile service run by you' captures this well, but also provides the basis for its service model and its low cost.

One of the items of received wisdom concerning the Internet is that only 1 per cent will be very active in any community, with 9 per cent active only sporadically, and 90 per cent being content to use the community without contributing.[44] This profile of use, sometimes termed the 90-9-1 model appears to be quite different in the context of giffgaff, with its community reportedly operating on a 74-25-1 basis.[45] The implication is that whilst giffgaff has only 1 per cent of highly active users within its community, at 24 per cent they have a much higher volume of occasional contributors. From a customer service perspective the results of this can be impressive and by 2010, a year after it had launched, the average response time for most of the 100,000 questions posed on its help forum was three minutes, with 95 per cent of the questions being answered within one hour.[46] However, in order to achieve this form of response it is important to have built and continually renew an online community so that it achieves the critical mass required. What this might mean in the context of mobile telephony remains unclear and although precise figures are hard to obtain and subject to continual fluctuation, giffgaff has well over 1 million users which (if the 74-25-1 community figures continue to apply) means, at a bare minimum, there will be 10,000 highly active, and 250,000 occasional, contributors within its user community.

Actions

Giffgaff was launched in 2009 as an experimental mobile phone service that offered low-cost services and was based on an innovative community-run business model. The Chief Executive stated 'When we started we were worried about the fact that we were a mobile phone operator that didn't have a call centre, it all sounded a bit bonkers' and saying that he was amazed that it had worked.[47] Its initial target group was a focused segment of the overall mobile phone market in the UK and it has grown its subscriber base to well over 1 million individual users. However, given that in the mature market it chose to enter those users would have largely been obtained by inducing them to switch from other providers, it was inevitable that other firms would react by cutting prices and improving their offer. However, giffgaff has won a series of industry awards and was named as Best Telecoms Provider by Which?,[48] a consumer advocate group in 2014 and 2015.

Aftershocks

Although the UK mobile telephony market continues to be very dynamic and attract new entrants, it is notable that giffgaff continues to be the only commercial mobile telephone provider in the UK that has adopted such an innovative, user-based, business model. The part(s) played by users within the giffgaff community have also evolved as it has become clear how best to match the resources that are available within its subscriber base with the needs of the business. However, it is clear that giffgaff has developed a new business model within a mature sector that has enabled it to create and occupy a small niche within the large UK market. However, despite having a subscriber base of well over 1 million users, the niche that giffgaff occupies is still tiny and it is likely to have only a very small percentage market share.[49]

Giffgaff has grown to its current size from being a start-up in 2009 and, for incumbents, it is likely that the challenge of reshaping their operational structures to incorporate contributions from users would pose too many organisational challenges and be far too difficult to attempt in the absence of a strong need. As a result giffgaff remains an outlier in the sector that has remained too small to make a significant impact on its major competitors to date. This may be an example of the limits of giffgaff's approach, or it may be the result of resistance within the sector, but it could be that giffgaff is a pioneer in creating a new model of business that could be applied to many other sectors outside of mobile telephony. Indeed, it could be argued that giffgaff has developed an operational model that is applicable to many other services that now depend on a traditional call-centre model. If so, it is likely that the learning from this experimental model will be applied to other sectors. However, it is also likely that a new regulatory framework to provide and protect the rights of any users who elect to 'work' in this way will be developed and enforced if this phenomenon continues to grow.

7.4 CONCLUDING REMARKS

This chapter has examined two quite different contexts, both of which concern innovation in mature, settled contexts. The Finnish forest sector case made clear the innovative potential of a long-established industry characterised by a focus on traditional outputs, but also made clear the huge challenges to current business structures and commercial models. In contrast, the giffgaff case explored how a new entrant to a mature industry created an entirely novel commercial model, developing a new set of organisational capabilities in the process. Both cases provide insights into the way in which organisations are able to recognise emerging innovation opportunities and either ignore or embrace them.

It is important to recognise that innovation is not without risk, and innovation in a settled context may be far more challenging given the apparent stability of the industrial landscape. One key message of these two cases is that the past may not be a reliable guide to the future, and history is littered with once-great firms that failed to recognise the changing nature of their innovation opportunities. The forests in Finland's case provide a detailed analysis of an industry that is ignoring the innovation opportunities that now surround it. The case is quite clear that the potential exists for new entrants to capture the value that is currently untapped by the forest industry. It may be that a new leisure industry will emerge and operate in parallel with traditional forestry operators, and this may be a rational position given the norms, behaviours and commercial logic of the forest industry. However, if this does occur, the traditional forest industry will need to ensure that such growth will have impacts on the commercial viability of their operation over time. Arguably a similar message emerges from the giffgaff case – that of a traditional industry in which the Innovation Opportunities offered by changes in their market context are ignored or resisted. Once again, firms may be able to sustain such a position in the short run but, in doing so, they run the risk that they leave the Innovation Opportunity Space open for others.

NOTES

1. Vargo, S. (2014) Insights on Innovation from an Institutional and Ecosystem Perspective. Keynote presentation at The 24th RESER Conference, 11–13 September 2014, Helsinki, Finland. Accessed on 24 March 2017 from http://www.reser2014.fi/docs/Vargo_RESER2014.pdf.
2. Prahalad, C.K. (2004) The blinders of dominant logic, *Long Range Planning*, vol. 37, no. 2, pp. 171–179.
3. Pätäri, S., Kyläheiko, K. and Sandström, J. (2011) Opening up new strategic options in the pulp and paper industry: case biorefineries, *Forest Policy and Economics*, vol. 13, no. 6, pp. 456–464.
4. Prahalad, C.K. (2004) The blinders of dominant logic, *Long Range Planning*, vol. 37, no. 2, pp. 171–179.
5. Prahalad, C.K. (2004) The blinders of dominant logic, *Long Range Planning*, vol. 37, no. 2, pp. 171–179.
6. Wilson, J.Q. (2000) *Bureaucracy: What Government Agencies Do and Why They Do It*, New York: Basic Books.
7. Krott, M. (2005) Forest users: owners, workers and employees, and the general population, in P. Glueck, V.B. Solberg and A.I. Tikkanen (eds), *Forest Policy Analysis*, 1st edition, Dordrecht: Springer, pp. 39–67.
8. Krott, M. (2005) Forest users: owners, workers and employees, and the general population, in P. Glueck, V.B. Solberg and A.I. Tikkanen (eds), *Forest Policy Analysis*, 1st edition, Dordrecht: Springer, pp. 39–67.

9.   Finnish Forest Association1. *Forest ownership*, accessed 24 March 2017 from http://www.smy.fi/en/forest-fi/finnish-forests-owned-by-finns/.
10.   Finnish Forest Association2. *Forestry*, accessed 24 March 2017 from http://www.smy.fi/en/forest-fi/forestry/.
11.   Hänninen, H., Karppinen, H. and Leppänen, J. (2011) Suomalainen metsänomistaja 2010. Vantaa: Working Papers of the Finnish Forest Research Institute 208, p. 94, accessed 24 March 2017 from http://www.metla.fi/julkaisut/workingpapers/2011/mwp208.pdf.
12.   Finnish Forest Association3. *Forest-based energy*, accessed 24 March 2017 from http://www.smy.fi/en/forest-fi/forest-based-energy/.
13.   In contrast to many countries, Finland has a law of 'everyman's rights' that permits Finnish citizens to roam freely even on privately owned land. The exceptions to this are only areas where houses are located or military areas. One can also collect the non-wood forest products (berries, mushrooms, etc.), if they are not deliberately grown for private or commercial purposes.
14.   The Forest Industry and Innovation. (2010) Helsinki: Finnish Forest Industries, p. 20, accessed 24 March 2017 from http://www.forestindustries.fi/mediabank/885.pdf.
15.   The Forest Industry and Innovation. (2010) Helsinki: Finnish Forest Industries, p. 20, accessed 24 March 2017 from http://www.forestindustries.fi/mediabank/885.pdf.
16.   Duncan, E., Hazan, E. and Roche, K. (2014) Digital disruption: six consumer trends and what businesses need to do now. *McKinsey on Marketing & Sales*, no. 3, accessed 17 February 2016 from http://www.mckinseyonmarketingandsales.com/digital-disruption-evolving-usage-and-the-new-value-chain.
17.   Duncan, E., Hazan, E. and Roche, K. (2014) Digital disruption: six consumer trends and what businesses need to do now. *McKinsey on Marketing & Sales*, no. 3, accessed 17 February 2016 from http://www.mckinseyonmarketingandsales.com/digital-disruption-evolving-usage-and-the-new-value-chain.
18.   Ohlhorst, F.J. (2013) *Big Data Analytics: Turning Big Data into Big Money*, New York: John Wiley & Sons.
19.   NatureGate (2015) NatureGate mobile, accessed 24 March 2017 from http://www.luontoportti.com/suomi/en/.
20.   Suomen Luonto (2015) Suomen Luonnon Villivihannekset-mobiilisovellusm accessed 24 March 2017 from http://www.suomenluonto.fi/sovellus/.
21.   Metsähallitus (2013) *Tienoo mobiilisovellus – Elämyksiä luonnossa*, accessed 24 March 2017 from http://www.metsa.fi/-/tienoo-mobiilisovellus-elamyksia-luonnossa.
22.   Lake & Sea Wiki (2012) Järviwiki: About, accessed 24 March 2017 from http://www.jarviwiki.fi/wiki/Järviwiki:About.
23.   Karttapullautin. *The award winning* Karttapullautin – toolbox/workflow for generating O training maps without field checking*, accessed 24 March 2017 from http://www.routegadget.net/karttapullautin/.
24.   Natural Marketing Institute (2008) *Understanding the LOHAS Market Report*. 6th edition, accessed 24 March 2017 from http://www.lohas.se/wp-content/uploads/2015/07/Understanding-the-LOHAS-Consumer-11_LOHAS_Whole_Foods_Version.pdf.
25.   *Environmental Leader* (2009) LOHAS forum attracts Fortune 500 companies, 22 June, accessed 24 March 2017 from http://www.environmentalleader.com/2009/06/22/green-forum-attracts-fortune-500-companies/.
26.   According to the report of the Natural Marketing Institute (2010) approximately 19 per cent of the adults in the US (41 million people) are considered to be LOHAS consumers.
27.   Tripod Research (2010) *Matkalla kestävämpään* (in Finnish), accessed 24 March 2017 from http://www.medialiitto.fi/files/1190/Vastuullinen_kuluttaja. . ...Martinez_tripod.pdf.
28.   Kiantama – Nordic Wild Berries. [online], accessed 23 March 2017, from https://www.youtube.com/watch?v=d8JKHV17my0.
29.   National Institute for Health and Welfare. Berries, accessed 24 March 2017 from http://www.fineli.fi/foodclass.php?classif=igclass&class=berry&lang=en.

30. Halvorsen, B.L., Holte, K., Myhrstad. M.C., Barikmo, I., Hvattum, E., Remberg, S.F., Wold, A.-B., Haffner, K., Baugerø, H., Andersen, L.F., Moskaug, J.Ø., Jacobs, D.R. and Blomhoff, R. (2002) A systematic screening of total antioxidants in dietary plants, *Journal of Nutrition*, vol. 132, no. 3, pp. 461–471.
31. Nielsen, T.S. and Hansen, K.B. (2007) Do green areas affect health? Results from a Danish survey on the use of green areas and health indicators, *Health & Place*, vol. 13, no. 4, pp. 839–850.
32. Rissanen, R., Rehunen, R., Kalenoja, H., Ahonen, O., Mäkelä, T., Rantala, J. and Pöllänen, M. (2013) *Alli Atlas – The Development Scenario of Finland's Regional Structure and Transport System* (in Finnish). Helsinki: Publication of Ministry of Environment, accessed 18 February 2016 from http://www.tut.fi/verne/wp-content/uploads/ALLI_kartasto_2013.pdf.
33. VisiKarelia.fi – North Karelia in Finland. *Silence Travel*, accessed 24 March 2017 from http://www.visitkarelia.fi/en/Travelling/Your-vacation/Silence-Travel.
34. FigaroDigital, giffgaff case study, accessed 12 May 2016 from http://figarodigital.co.uk/case-study/giffgaff/.
35. giffgaff blog: Meet The Community Team, posted 29 January 2013.
36. Crowdsourcing customer service: Another giffgaff brainwave, Telefonica Digital Hub, downloaded 13 June 2013.
37. Buchanan, L. (2010) Giffgaff – a case study of customers in control, 9 December 2010, accessed 13 May 2016 from http://thecustomerevolution.blogspot.co.uk/2010/12/giffgaff-case-study-of-customers-in.html.
38. giffgaff labs: how it works, accessed 13 March 2016 from https://labs.giffgaff.com/how.
39. Welcome to Video Missions, giffgaffwebsite, accessed 13 May 2016 from https://community.giffgaff.com/t5/Contribute/New-Video-Missions-come-and-get-involved/td-p/18427981.
40. OFCOM estimates relating to 2014, accessed 23 May 2016 from http://media.ofcom.org.uk/facts/.
41. ONS estimate relating to 2014, accessed 23 May 2016 from https://www.ons.gov.uk/peoplepopulationandcommunity/populationandmigration/populationestimates.
42. OFCOM estimates relating to 2015, accessed 23 May 2016 from http://media.ofcom.org.uk/facts/.
43. FigaroDigital, giffgaff case study, accessed 12 May 2016 from http://figarodigital.co.uk/case-study/giffgaff/.
44. For more on this please refer to http://community.lithium.com/t5/Science-of-Social-blog/The-90-9-1-Rule-in-Reality/ba-p/5463, accessed 9 February 2017.
45. Figures reported in Buchanan, L. (2010) *The Customer Revolution*, accessed 23 May 2016 from http://thecustomerevolution.blogspot.co.uk/2010/12/giffgaff-case-study-of-customers-in.html.
46. Kite, L. (2011) Peer power, *CRM Magazine*, June, accessed 23 May 2016 from http://www.destinationcrm.com/Articles/Editorial/Magazine-Features/Peer-Power-75310.aspx.
47. Fairman, M., quoted in Burn-Callander (2015) Giffgaff, the 'bonkers' mobile network proves that the crowd can run your business for you, *Daily Telegraph*, 26 May, accessed 23 May 2016 from http://www.telegraph.co.uk/finance/newsbysector/mediatechnologyandtelecoms/telecoms/11630738/Giffgaff-the-bonkers-mobile-network-proves-that-the-crowd-can-run-your-business-for-you.html.
48. Which? Is a UK-based consumer's organisation.
49. Four years after launch in 2013 it was estimated that giffgaff had a market share of some 2 per cent – for more information see http://www.statista.com/statistics/279993/market-share-of-mobile-phone-operators-in-the-united-kingdom-uk/, accessed 23 May 2016.

8. Emerging business models in frontier contexts

Juha Arrasvuori, Pirjo Yli-Viitala, Arja Kuusisto and Jose Christian

8.1 FRONTIER CONTEXTS FOR INNOVATION OPPORTUNITIES

As argued throughout this book, the creation and adaptation of new technologies will always tend to open up new Innovation Opportunities, as will changes in regulations or consumer behaviour. A 'frontier context' is an Innovation Opportunity Space where a number of factors are in place:

1. A new technology has emerged and is increasingly being adopted;
2. There is a regulation in place that facilitates (or least doesn't hinder) a wide-scale adaptation of this technology;
3. There are businesses or consumers motivated to do new things with this technology, and;
4. There are people motivated to use the new technology.

All these factors have to exist in order for a new Innovation Space to emerge. In a frontier context for Innovation Opportunities, the sheer novelty of the context may stimulate innovation. People innovating in this context may be motivated by being 'the first' to achieve something in this context or to do something that 'has not been done before'. In other words, to be pioneers of the frontier context. There is potential to create new businesses or at least obtain venture capital and other research and development funding. Alternatively, the new context may offer ways to improve the common good. Excitement and buzz about the possibilities of the frontier context may leak outside the immediate context and enter the mainstream media, which will make further people curious about its possibilities and draw new actors into the context. From past examples, the first Internet boom of the mid-1990s was just such a frontier context, as was the Web 2.0 boom of ten years later, and the Sharing Economy later still – each of these shifts in the frontier of innovation had an effect in every corner of the globe and impacted on established media and ways of doing business. In this chapter, we examine three examples of frontier contexts: open data, the Internet of Things and the User Organisation.

The open data movement which emerged in the early years of the 2000s is both a technology, that is, digital data in a machine-readable format whose publishing is driven through regulation, and a resource in particular for users (such as activists) to exploit such as for developing new digital applications and achieving service innovation or even innovation at a social or systemic level. Several examples from the open data movement will be discussed through this chapter. Although open data is by definition free of charge to use, we present examples of value-adding activities to open data resources that aim to provide commercial applications and services.

The Internet of Things (IoT) is another frontier context for Innovation Space discussed in this chapter. Internet of Things is the network of physical objects or devices embedded with various electronics, sensors, software and connectivity to enable objects to collect and exchange data with any other device connected to the Internet. IoT is a frontier context for Innovation Opportunities that combine hardware and software with the physical environment and the people inhabiting it. Technologies and applications for IoT are currently being developed by large multinational firms like General Electric as well as by enthusiastic individual users. In this chapter, we present examples of users innovating in the IoT space through using open data and open hardware resources.

The emergence of a new context for Innovation Opportunities is likely also to cause conflict between the actors operating in the space, for example between non-profit and for-profit interests. With emerging Innovation Opportunities, conflict may focus on attempts to annex and defend key segments of the new Space, with the aim of future exploitation and monetisation. Due to such potentially conflicting interests between actors in an IOS, a collaborative project that may have started as a non-commercial activity may over time be steered by some of the actors towards the field of commercial application. To conclude this chapter on frontier contexts, CyanogenMod is discussed as an example of a project that emerged from the Open Source Software scene as a cooperative non-commercial user-based venture that has morphed over time into something far more commercial.

8.2   OPEN DATA, THE INTERNET OF THINGS

8.2.1   Defining Open Data

Open data is data collected, authored and owned by an organisation that publishes this data for others to use without limitation and charge. The use of open data may include analysing, modifying, combining, augmenting, presenting and using it in a product or service provided for free or for profit. Possibly the most prominent open data resources originate from government-funded organisations all over the world, thus being called 'government data'. The rationale for releasing such data freely is that as it has been produced with the taxpayers' money, the data should also be freely available for the taxpayer to benefit from it. Also some private research organisations, businesses, and open source collaborative projects (for example, OpenStreetMap) publish open data. Some open data resources may be a direct alternative to commercial data, for example, OpenStreetMap is an open data replacement to proprietary map data such as Google Maps.[1]

Figure 8.1 illustrates the relation between different types of data. Some of the open data is so-called 'open government data', in other words, data owned and produced by governments. 'My data' is confidential data about an individual (for example, medical history, transaction data), which the individual has the right to access and review. Some of 'my data' can be

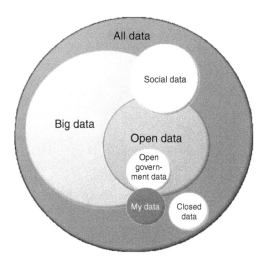

Figure 8.1   The relation between open data and other types of data. The figure is adapted from Manyika et al. (2013).[2] The size of the circles does not represent the relative sizes of these data types

published as open data, for example, in an anonymised or composite form so certain data items cannot be traced back to any individual. 'Social data' is the data created by users of social media, such as Facebook and Twitter. Some data is closed, such as proprietary data owned by businesses.

In the context of open data, a 'dataset' is a collection of data related to a specific topic, which is published and managed by a single source. Examples of datasets include the bus schedules in a city, the amount of rainfall in a region, or the real-time location of snow ploughs in a town. A dataset may be downloaded (in a file format such as text, HTML, Excel or CSV spreadsheet) for use, or it may be accessed 'live' from a server through an API, thus obtaining the latest published version of the data. Depending on the implementation, an updated dataset may also be 'pushed' to a user who has subscribed to it.

Based on the definitions given by Project Open Data, which is a US government funded action to promote the use of open data, the seven defining characteristics of open data are summarised in Table 8.1.

Table 8.1   Characteristics of open data as defined by Project Open Data[3]

Open data characteristic	Definition
Public	Government agencies must favour openness to the extent permitted by law and subject confidentiality
Accessible	Data is machine-readable, i.e. published in modifiable and open formats that can be retrieved, downloaded, indexed, and searched by computer software
Described	Providing sufficient information for understanding the strengths, weaknesses, limitations and security requirements of a dataset
Reusable	Data made is available under an open license placing no restrictions on its use
Complete	Data is published with the finest possible level of granularity practical and permitted by law and other requirements (i.e. the published data must not hurt the privacy of an individual or jeopardise the operation of an organisation)
Timely	Data is published as quickly as necessary to preserve its value
Managed post-release	A point of contact must be nominated for providing assistance with the use of a data set and for responding to complaints about disregard of open data requirements. The point of contact is responsible for correcting errors in the data

Table 8.2   Types of open data (based on definition by The Open Knowledge Foundation[4])

Domain	Examples
Finance	Data such as government accounts (expenditure and revenue) and information on financial markets (stocks, shares, bonds, etc.)
Statistics	Data produced by statistical offices such as the census and key socio-economic indicators
Weather	Data on past and current weather conditions, as well as data for understanding and predicting the weather and climate
Environment	Data on natural environment such as level of pollutants in air and water
Transport	Data such as timetables, routes, on-time statistics, and reports on traffic conditions
Geospatial	Maps of different types, descriptions of points of interest and other location annotations
Cultural	Data about cultural works and artefacts, e.g. titles and authors
Science	Data that is produced as part of scientific research

Many kinds of open data have been published in various domains of knowledge. Some of these are summarised in Table 8.2.

Access to open data resources has been predicted to enable innovation and business growth particularly in domains such as education, transportation, energy (electricity, oil and gas), healthcare, finance, nature (ecosystems), climate, agriculture, manufacturing, safety, consumer products, and business (goods and services). For example, a McKinsey Global Institute analysis proposes that in certain business domains combined, open data can help unlock up to $3 trillion in economic value annually.[5] In addition to creating new business, open data may assist governments, organisations, enterprises and individuals to save money by identifying from the data excessive spending or ineffective use of resources. Use of open data may also create social benefits and impact, such as improved social services and transparency in government decision making and public spending. Access to open data may also lead to scientific discovery through the efforts of citizen science, where an enormous set of data is split into smaller subsets provided with instructions for a 'layman' on how to analyse the data subset. Furthermore, also the data collection activity may be distributed to individuals who openly publish the data they have collected (as exemplified in the case of OpenStreetMap).

BOX 8.1   DATA.GOV – A SINGLE POINT FOR ACCESSING US GOVERNMENT'S OPEN DATA

As part of the US Open Data Initiatives, thousands of government data resources across different fields of knowledge (for example, health and medicine, education, energy, public safety, global development, and finance) have been posted in machine-readable form for free public use on the website www.data.gov. It is to enable entrepreneurs and innovators to develop a wide range of new products and businesses based on these public information resources so as to improve the lives of Americans in many ways, and create jobs in the process. On the data.gov site, data is published by many US government departments and agencies.

8.2.2   Publishing and Managing Open Data

Releasing open data is done by government organisations responsible for collecting, creating and storing certain types of data. Government data in many countries have been collected into portals, that is, single points of access such as Data.gov in the United States and Data.gov.uk in the United Kingdom. By 2013, there were more than 40 countries with government open data platforms and more than 1 million datasets had been made open worldwide.[6]

Different types of data are in the process of being prepared for release by governments all over the world. To speed up the process of businesses and individuals obtaining relevant datasets, feedback channels have been set up between citizens/applications developers who can request a certain dataset to be released, and the government organisation responsible for keeping that type of data. Typically, the government organisations releasing the data can be, for example, national institutes (responsible for handling state-wide data) or municipalities (responsible handling local data).

Managing open data includes updating it, correcting errors, transferring it into new formats for securing future access, and so on. These activities have also been called 'data curating'.

8.2.3   Architecture, Actors, Actions and Aftershock: Open Data as an Innovation Opportunity Space

Next we examine open data as an Innovation Opportunity Space. In Figure 8.2 we summarise the Architecture, Actors, Activities and Aftershocks of the open data IOS.

Architecture	Actors	Actions	Aftershocks
Technological context: • PC and mobile Internet access • Data in machine-readable formats	• Citizens/users • Open data activists	• Use open data through apps and services; act upon it; give feedback to Governments, Developers and Firms; • Request release of open data sets	**Service innovation** • New for-profit services based on providing added value to open data
	• Developers • Firms	• Develop apps that use open data; • Develop business by combining open and proprietary data, storing, aggregating, analyzing, reformatting, representing data; • Request release of open data sets	**Social innovation** For example, apps and services for: • Solving societal challenges; • Helping the common good; • Solving needs of special groups
Legal context: • Data is licensed so that it can be reused freely	• Governments	• Release and manage open data resources; • Stimulate the use of open data (e.g. by arranging competitions and events)	**Systemic innovation** For example, solutions for: • Improving transparency in government; • Improving effectiveness of public spending; • Tackling climate change

Figure 8.2   Open data as an Innovation Opportunity Space

171

Architecture

In this abstraction, the architecture of the open data Innovation Opportunity Space includes a technological context and a legal context. The technological context includes the 'era of digitalisation' discussed earlier in section 8.1, where users connect with their PC and mobile devices (for example, smartphones) to the Internet, and use various software applications and online services. The legal context includes the licenses under which open data is published, which allow anyone to use the data freely and potentially in for-profit purposes. For example, the Open Knowledge Foundation offers a set of Open Data Common Licenses for publishing open data.[7] Such licenses clarify the rules for innovating in this space.

Actors and actions

As shown in Figure 8.2, we can identify three main clusters of actors in this Innovation Opportunity Space (IOS). Each cluster is associated with specific activities in the open data IOS.

The first cluster of the open data IOS includes the citizens/users. They use open data through apps and services to help their everyday life tasks, such as using public transport, obtaining background information for buying a property, attempting to save energy, or doing research on tax incentives. A specific subgroup in this cluster is open data activists, who promote the opening of data reserves and the potential of open data (by arranging events such the annual Apps4Finland competition, discussed below), but do not necessarily develop apps or services themselves. Citizens/users and open data activists give feedback to developers and firms on the apps/services using open data, and to governments on the data and their interpretations of it. Users/citizens also can request government representatives to publish specific datasets, when it becomes clear that a particular set of data is not available. A user/citizen can take the role of a developer when that person gets involved in developing an app or a service that uses open data. Although it may start as a hobby, developing an app or a service may eventually become a business, essentially making the developer a very particular type of entrepreneur.

The second cluster of the open data IOS includes developers and firms who create apps and services that use open data. Some developers may do this without financial objectives, but commercial firms may aim to develop profitable business from utilising open data resources. They do this, for example, by aggregating open data from multiple sources, by combining open data with proprietary data, by offering new knowledge obtained through analysing the data, by presenting the data in informative (and possibly interactive) ways, by storing data, and so on. In other words, developers and in particular firms provide added value to the open data, and we will examine some open data business models in a later part of this section.

The third cluster of the open data IOS is the governments and organisations that create, publish and manage the data. Additionally, governments can stimulate the utilisation of open data by users/citizens, developers and firms by organising competitions and sharing knowledge about the potential uses for open data.

Aftershocks

As suggested in Figure 8.2, actions done in the open data IOS can produce a broad range of aftershocks. In the following sections, we discuss three kinds of aftershocks, namely the impacts open data make in service innovation, social innovation, and systemic innovation.

Aftershocks I: service innovation   open data can be an enabler of service innovation, in particular, the development of new digital service products. Typically, these online services are accessed by their users through PCs or smartphones and aim to provide value to their users and profit for the businesses developing them.

As outlined earlier, open data resources can be a basis for developing a for-profit business. However, although open data is available for free to anyone, the format in which it is published may have a range of limitations that make it less useful to an average user. In some cases, a 'layperson' may not know from where to find a dataset or how to interpret it to obtain insight from it. Thus, a common trait of these businesses utilising open data is that they provide some added value to their users. Some of the ways of adding value to open data are summarised in Figure 8.3.

The added value may come, for instance, from assisting the user to find particular information from a dataset, from a clear presentation of the data (as in the example 'Tax tree', Figure 8.4), from more insightful data created by aggregating data from multiple open data sources (as in the example 'Trulia'), or from obtaining unique data created by combining open data with proprietary data (as in the example 'BillGuard'), or by performing deep analysis of the data (as in the example 'Cloud'N'Sci.Fi'). In other words, the added value comes from the firm turning open data into information, knowledge or insight relevant to the user. Here, the 'user' of the data can be a private person, a business, or an official.

Aftershocks II: social innovation Social innovation has been seen as an extension of the innovation concept, as a new innovation paradigm embedded in the shift from the industrial to the knowledge society.[8] Social

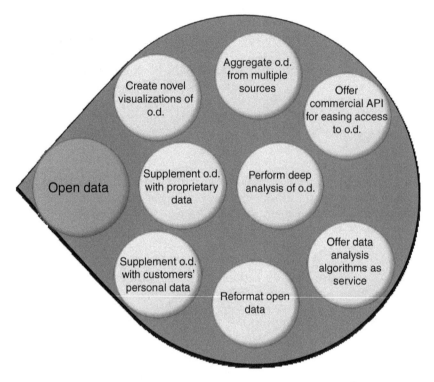

Figure 8.3   Extending the open data IOS – and creating for-profit business
            from open data – by various value adding activities (in small
            circles)

innovation addresses new concepts or measures to meet social demands or
societal challenges of all kinds. In particular, social innovations are solutions to challenges that the market or public sector have not been able to
solve adequately. The concept of social innovation has moved from marginal to centre stage during the past decade due to the difficulty of existing
structures and policies to solve urgent societal challenges such as urban
safety, social inequality, and accessibility for disabled people.

   Despite the attention the idea has attracted in recent years, the concept
of 'social innovation' has not yet been established in the scholarly field.
Depending on the approach of the scholar, social innovation has been
examined as the *effort* of developing new tools that support groups in
achieving improved wellbeing;[9] as the *new solutions* that meet a social
need of a group more effectively than existing solutions, lead to improved
capabilities, lead to better use of resources, and enhance a society's capability to act;[10] and as the *changes in attitude, behaviour or involvement* of a

BOX 8.2 TAX TREE – CREATING BUSINESS FROM A NOVEL DATA VISUALISATION

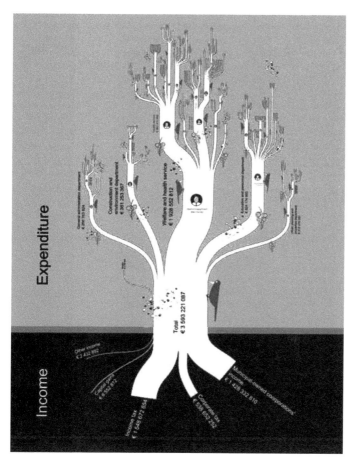

Figure 8.4   *Tax tree[11] was an initial application for visualising the multiple branches of public income and expenditures, in other words, where tax money comes from and where it goes. It won first prize in the first Apps4Finland open data application competition in 2009. The visualisation method of Tax tree was later adapted into commercial products, such as an interactive visualisation of government budgets that is used by Finnish civil servants, parliament members and citizens[12]*

BOX 8.3   TRULIA – REAL-ESTATE INFORMATION SERVICE PROVIDING ADDED VALUE THROUGH AGGREGATING OPEN DATA

Trulia[13] is a service for real estate professionals and private home buyers in the United States. Trulia combines open data from various sources to present supplemental information about a property that is on the market for sale or rent. For their services, Trulia gets a fee from the property sellers. Trulia uses open data resources to show the property's information from public records, the area's house price trend information, nearby businesses and services, local schools and their ratings (from GreatSchools.com), and reported criminal activity and predicted crime risk (from CrimeReports.com, EveryBlock.com, SpotCrime.com). These open data sets are updated continuously and automatically, so the information presented for a piece of property is always up to date. Trulia launched in 2004 as a start-up company. A decade later, in 2014, the real estate database Zillow announced that it had acquired Trulia for $3.5 billion.[14]

BOX 8.4   BILLGUARD – AGGREGATING PERSONAL TRANSACTION DATA WITH OPEN DATA

BillGuard[15] is a US-based personal finance security company tackling the problem of erroneous credit card transactions. The company aggregates information from all its users on credit card transactions that have been identified as unwanted, erroneous, or fraudulent. BillGuard combines this data from its users with open data from the US Consumer Financial Protection Bureau consumer complaint database.[16] The aggregated information is used to screen all transactions of BillGuard users for identifying payments that typically are erroneous. The user interface to the service is an iPhone or Android app.

---

group that lead to new ways of collaborative action.[17] Social innovations can be found at the overlapping areas between these three views, as suggested in Figure 8.6.

As discussed earlier in this chapter, open data has been recognised as offering significant opportunities for developing new products and services. This potential can be especially significant for developing social innovations, for which the use of proprietary data may be limited due to cost and licensing issues. The digital applications and services that are social innovations can be developed for non-profit or for profit purposes.

In this section we present illustrative cases where open data apps and services have become social innovations by helping to solve a societal challenge such as improving the independent mobility of visually impaired users (see case on BlindSquare) and optimising the maintenance of public infrastructure (see case on FixMyStreet).

BOX 8.5   CLOUD'N'SCI – DATA ANALYSIS ALGORITHMS AS A SERVICE

To obtain any deep insight and knowledge from a dataset requires analysing and refining the raw data. Analysing vast amounts of data can be a complicated process requiring special skills and experience. Cloud'N'Sci[18] is a Finnish company offering data analysis algorithms as a service. The firm offers a marketplace for data analysis algorithm developers to make their algorithms globally available to a broad range of applications. The principle of their service is that customers input data and get analysis results as output from the service; in other words, the analysis algorithms are not visible to the customers but remain protected IP. Potential customers for the service are application developers who can get new analysis and other data refinement functionality to their apps at a lower cost compared to developing the analysis algorithms by themselves. Cloud'N'Sci.Fi has devised an entire 'ecosystem' based on various actors' interests related to open data analysis (see Figure 8.5).

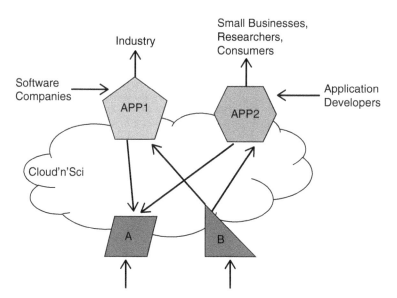

Figure 8.5   Actors in the Cloud'N'Sci ecosystem.[19] *In the figure, 'A' and 'B' are analysis algorithms developed by parties such as research groups or specialised algorithm programmers. One application can use different algorithms developed by different parties. Through the Cloud'N'Sci ecosystem, these algorithms are utilised by software developers in applications that are used, for example, by industry, small businesses, or even consumers*

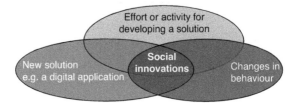

Figure 8.6   Social innovations are the result of developing a new solution, the solution/tool itself, and the changes in the users' behaviour caused by taking the solution/tool into use

---

BOX 8.6   BLINDSQUARE

BlindSquare[20] is a smartphone application for improving the independent mobility of visually impaired people. BlindSquare uses open data resources such as OpenStreetMap, FourSquare and public transport schedules to provide accurate navigation guidance to its users. By 2015, BlindSquare had more than 10,000 users in 130 countries. Users from all over the world have contributed to the application, for example, by making translations into 25 languages and presenting suggestions for improving its eyes-free user interface. The feedback from several of the visually impaired users has been that BlindSquare has empowered their lives because they have become more confident to move independently in unfamiliar locations.[21]

BlindSquare is an illustrative example of a social innovation project aiming to solve a societal challenge (in this case, increasing the accessibility for visually impaired users), as the application has been programmed by a single developer who has skilfully coordinated the global user tests, translations and other localisations.

BOX 8.7   FIXMYSTREET

The public infrastructure including the condition of streets and tidiness of parks affects every citizen. Municipalities have the responsibility of taking care of the public infrastructure. However, it is the citizens living in a neighbourhood who first notice a problem in the public infrastructure, such as a hole in the road, a missing street sign or a broken streetlight. A challenge is how can citizens report such problems to municipal organisations responsible for solving them. The citizens may not know which municipal organisation is responsible for each particular problem.

FixMyStreet[22] is an application for citizens to inform their local authority of problems needing attention, such as bumps in the road, broken streetlamps, drainage, and so forth. Filing a report optionally includes uploading a photo of the described problem. FixMyStreet allows seeing reports already filed by citizens and notifications on when the problems have been fixed. The main interface of the application is based on open data maps. The FixMyStreet software platform has been published as open source, and has been adapted into local use in more than 14 countries.[23]

BOX 8.8   A FINNISH APPROACH TO ORCHESTRATE
INNOVATION BY PROMOTING OPEN DATA
USE – THE PÄÄSTÖT.FI APPLICATION

In the context of open data, various competitions are one form of crowdsourcing to find new ideas and inspiring ways to leverage open data for innovations. In Finland, the annual competition called 'Apps4Finland' encourages the creative use of open data and open data sources. Since 2009, the competition has brought about a wide range of extraordinary apps, visualisations and other competition entries. The organisers of the competition (Forum Virium Helsinki, Open Knowledge Finland and the Finnish Association for Online Democracy) sought to influence the innovative behaviour of the crowd of users so as to channel their creative energies into an outcome that will generate economic, promotional, or reputational value. Here, the orchestrated innovation takes the form of activities where the final outcomes tend to be less controllable and defined than in a managed user innovation context.

In the sixth edition of Apps4Finland competition in 2014, the total sum of prize money exceeded 40,000 euros. In addition to this, a number of awards were given by partners who proposed specific challenges to be solved by the competition entries. The first prize was awarded to the data visualisation, 'Päästöt.fi'[24] (meaning 'Emissions.Finland'), which was also voted to receive the Grand Prix of the entire competition in 2014. The awards in the Visualise competition category were given for presenting complex data in an easy-to-understand visual format.

Potentially harmful emissions are a major global environmental as well as societal problem. Päästöt.fi is a service meant for the use by any individual who is interested in obtaining an overview of the emission sources in the surrounding area or within Europe. The website shows the EU's biggest polluters on an illustrative, interactive map. It allows the user to focus on a specific area or look at the biggest polluters in all of Europe. The Apps4Finland jury praised the lucidity and the visual appeal of the app. What's more, it helps a 'layperson' to comprehend emissions-figures by putting them in local, national and Europe-level perspectives. Further, it becomes possible to compare environmental protection between the different countries.

Often the innovative process is triggered by personal frustration. This was the case also with the developers of the Päästöt.fi service. One of it's two developers wanted to be informed of the biggest polluters in Finland. At first, he could not find any information since the authority compiling climate emissions-related statistics did not publish/release the data. However, he realised that the compiled statistics were reported forwards to the European Environment Agency. Very soon he found an extensive database, which covered plant-specific emission data not only on the level of Finland but also on all EU countries. A decision by the EU Parliament in 2006 ordered the establishment of a centralised registry and made public information accessible to all.[25] Surprisingly, this huge data repository was largely unexploited at the time.

Open data may add value socially and commercially through improved accessibility of the relevant datasets. The more transparent society is, the more aware citizens are about their living environment, which makes it easier for them to participate and allows them, for example, to monitor the actions of the plants in the surrounding area. Opening up data enables citizens not only to be better informed

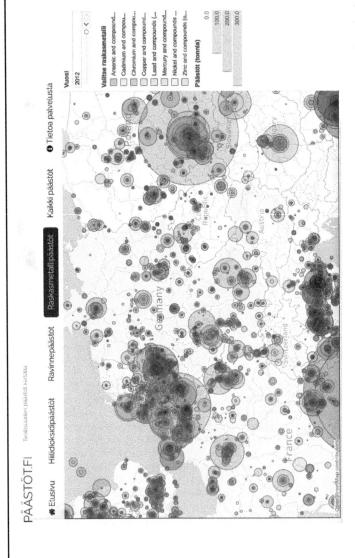

Figure 8.7   Example of Päästöt.fi (www.paastot.fi) visualisation of heavy metal emissions (e.g. arsenic, cadmium, chromium) from the industry in central Europe. The visualisations are presented on top of maps from OpenStreetMap

of potentially harmful emissions, but they can also evaluate the magnitude of emissions, and thus be able to evaluate the impact of natural disasters, for example. Further, the service opens a new window to the European Pollutant Release and Transfer Register (E-PRTR) and enables users to explore the greatest sources of pollution locally or on a European scale.

Päästöt.fi is the web service that allows people to see the biggest polluters near their home or anywhere in Europe with an interactive map interface. The map reveals, for example, the main emitters of carbon dioxide, nutrients and heavy metals (Figure 8.7).

Even if the Päästöt.fi service was originally targeted at individuals, it may also encourage civic organisations and businesses to get involved in the protection of the environment and make practical actions to drive for the reduction of emissions.

Aftershocks III: from standalone solution development to systemic innovation Systemic innovation has emerged as an important topic through the rising awareness of a range of technological and societal transformations that are globally interconnected. As a process, systemic innovation addresses complex challenges, which can be related, for example, to the environment (for example, climate change), resources (for example, energy, housing) or society (for example, education, healthcare, transparency of governance, inclusion of disabled people). Such challenges can rarely be tackled by a single organisation or sector, but working towards solving them involves an interaction of public policy, reforms to legislation, transformations to business cultures and practices, and changes in attitudes and behaviour or citizens. As a solution, a systemic innovation is a set of interconnected parts like technical, economic, product, service, process and social innovations, where each is dependent on the other. To create a solution on the systemic innovation level involves innovation both in the separate parts of the system and in the ways the parts interact with each other.

As discussed in the previous section, social innovations typically tackle less complex societal challenges. However, a combination of smaller social innovations may help to tackle a broader complex problem. The applications and services that are part of systemic innovation can be developed for non-profit or for profit purposes. There must not necessarily be any appointed actor coordinating the different partial solutions for the systemic innovation. The systemic innovations may emerge by different people working – possibly unbeknownst to each other – to develop solutions within the domain of a complex challenge. At some point, some actor may realise how to connect the different dots (of the partial solutions produced globally) into a systemic innovation that helps to solve the bigger picture of the complex problem. There is a broad space for such innovation opportunities with open data resources.

**BOX 8.9   MYSOCIETY – TRANSPARENCY OF GOVERNANCE
AND INVOLVEMENT OF CITIZENS**

mySociety[26] is an e-democracy project run by UK Citizens Online Democracy that
aims to build 'socially focused tools with offline impacts'. mySociety has organised the development of apps and services such as TheyWorkForYou, WhatDo
TheyKnow, PledgeBank, WriteToThem, and the aforementioned FixMyStreet.
mySociety can be seen as a systemic innovation providing different solutions for
improving governance and fulfilment of democracy. For example, TheyWorkFor
You tracks speeches and activities of UK Members of Parliament. WhatDoThey
Know is a website for helping citizens write Freedom of Information requests and
automatically publishing the responses, in other words, it assists citizens to find
out what the British government and public services are doing. PledgeBank is a
website for publishing pledges and solving problems of collective action, thus
working for the public good.

   Several of these apps and services have been adapted into use in other countries in addition to the UK. By having access to government data, citizens can
become more informed of and involved in the decision making in their states.
Citizens can for example analyse the data and may come to different conclusions
about future actions than what the government officials or hired consultants have.
New tools and methods developed by citizens and firms can ease the budget pressure in the public services by reducing reliance on outside experts. For example
in the US, the states of California and Texas have reported to have identified millions of dollars in savings per year by releasing budgetary information and enabling
citizens to spot potential opportunities to cut costs.[27]

---

mySociety is an illustrative case where using open data applications and
services have contributed to systemic innovation.

8.3   CONTRIBUTING TO BUILDING THE INTERNET
OF THINGS THROUGH OPEN SOFTWARE AND
HARDWARE

The Internet of Things (IoT) can be seen as a systemic innovation
involving many technologies and areas of life and business on a global
scale. Internet of Things (IoT) is also a significant frontier context for
Innovation Opportunities: it has generated lots of buzz and great expectations have been directed towards it.

   Internet of Things (IoT) is the network of physical objects or devices
embedded with various electronics, sensors, software and connectivity to
enable objects to collect and exchange data potentially with any other device
connected to the Internet. Each device is uniquely identifiable on the Internet.
These objects can 'sense' properties of the environment – including the

people – around them and through pre-programmed rules and instructions, they can change their behaviour automatically. Furthermore, data describing the 'sensed' environment can be sent to the owner of the device, who can then react accordingly, for example, by instructing the device to change its behaviour or perform some other action. Yet another use scenario for IoT is that a first device can instruct a second device to change its behaviour. These three scenarios illustrate how IoT creates a vast space of creating opportunities for integration between the physical world and digital systems, resulting in, for example, improved efficiency and economic benefit. Cisco and Dell estimated in a report released in 2015 that that the IoT will consist of up to 50 billion connected 'things' by the year 2020.[28]

8.3.1 The IoT as an Innovation Opportunity Space

Next we examine the Internet of Things as an Innovation Opportunity Space. In Figure 8.8 we summarise the Architecture, Actors, Activities and Aftershocks of this Innovation Opportunity Space.

Architecture

In the abstraction presented in Figure 8.8, the architecture of the IoT Innovation Opportunity Space consists of a technological context. The technological context includes connected sensors, data analysis methods, application development environments (for example, software development kits or 'devkits'), smartphones, tablets and PCs, and the existing Internet infrastructure (supplemented by 3G/4G/5G mobile networks and local networks, for example WLAN). Through connected sensors and appropriate programming, even mundane devices and objects (see example of Enevo below) can become 'smart' connected objects.

Actors and actions

As shown in Figure 8.8, we identify three main clusters of actors in the Internet of Things Innovation Opportunity Space, namely 'developers', 'utilisers' and 'enablers'. Each cluster of actors is associated with sets of specific actions and activities. Starting from the group up, 'enablers' are the people and organisations creating the basic hardware and software components that enables the creation of IoT smart objects, as well as the information network providers. Some of this software and hardware is distributed by open principles. 'Developers' are users and businesses who implement various IoT products, such as hardware objects and the associated software. 'Utilisers' of IoT include consumers, service businesses and the industry who use these products to solve practical problems, develop new business, or to improve their manufacturing or delivery processes.

Architecture	Actors	Actions	Aftershocks

Technological context:
• Inexpensive, connected sensors
• Data analysis methods
• Application development environments
• Smartphones, PCs
• Existing Internet infrastructure
	Developers:
	• Users
	• Businesses
	
	Utilizers:
	• Consumers
	• Service businesses
	• Industry
	
	Enablers:
	• Sensors and other HW developers
	• Infrastructure providers
		• Develop various Internet of Things products (software and/or hardware)
		• Stimulate development of IoT applications e.g. by arranging hackathons
		
		• Use IoT applications to solve practical problems or improve everday life
		• Develop new service business based on IoT (e.g. data analysis)
		• Use IoT improve manufacturing processes or to renew the industry
		
		• Develop the hardware enabling Internet of Things
		• Provide the necessary infrastructure for IoT (e.g. network connectivity and data security management)
			• Product innovations
			  • SW / Apps
			  • Smart devices
			
			• Service innovations
			  • Digital services
			  • New business models based on IoT
			
			• Process innovations
			  • E.g. new ways to manufacture, monitor or deliver

Figure 8.8   The Internet of Things as an Innovation Opportunity Space

BOX 8.10 ENEVO

Waste management has been an important function of societies ever since the first human settlements were established. Today, activities related to waste management are estimated to be annually a 1 trillion US dollar business. The Internet of Things brings new opportunities to innovate in this domain.

Enevo is a Finnish company that provides smart wireless sensors, which are used to measure and forecast fill-levels in ordinary waste containers.[29] More specifically, Enevo provides a comprehensive waste logistics solution, which 'uses smart fill-level sensors, advanced analytics and a cloud based dynamic scheduling and routing engine to provide the most efficient waste collection operations for entire cities.'[30] The concept of Enevo emerged when two business partners were discussing their living expenses, in particular the costs of waste disposal. The business idea is to optimise waste collection routes and schedules for waste trucks based on the data Enevo's sensor network sends to its servers (Figure 8.9). The smarter collection plans based on Enevo's service, have saved up to 50 per cent in direct costs for its customers in their waste logistics. The company reports to have 145 clients in 35 countries (June 2015).[31]

Enevo's battery-powered sensor device is an ultrasound sonar that measures the level of waste in a trash container and transmits this data wirelessly to Enevo's severs. The first proof-of-concept hardware of Enevo's sensor was reportedly hacked together with duct-tape in a month by the two partners developing the start-up.[32] When the sensor device had been perfected for mass-production, the service software with the analytics and route planning was developed.

Enevo rents its sensors for a monthly fee to its customers. Since it is Enevo who's collecting and managing the data, the business has great opportunities to extend its business further, for instance, by using the data the sensors measure in new ways, or, by measuring new types of data either within trash containers or in other locations.[33]

Above all, Enevo is a great example of how a traditional industry can be transformed by changing the way we think about it, and, by the technological opportunities of IoT. Enevo's innovative business is based on adding smart features (sensors with wireless connectivity) to what is a most mundane object, a trash container, together with providing the smart analytics that generates optimal routes and schedules for waste collection. Undoubtedly, Enevo's 'Smart City waste logistic system' is a truly disruptive innovation, which is saving time, money and environment to an extent that has not been experienced in the waste management industry before.

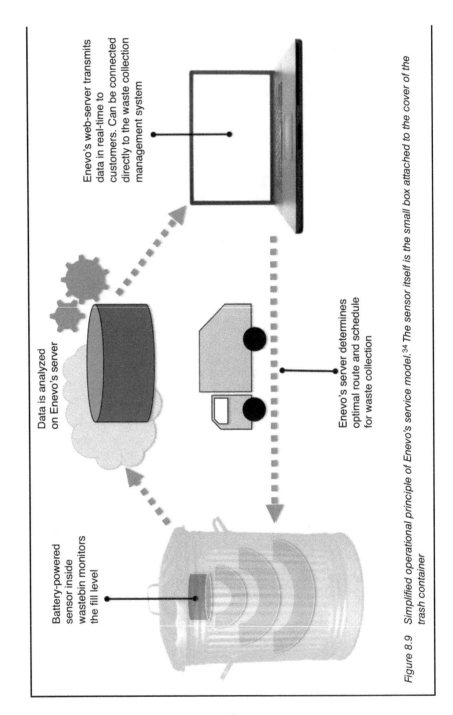

Battery-powered sensor inside wastebin monitors the fill level

Data is analyzed on Enevo's server

Enevo's web-server transmits data in real-time to customers. Can be connected directly to the waste collection management system

Enevo's server determines optimal route and schedule for waste collection

Figure 8.9   Simplified operational principle of Enevo's service model.[34] The sensor itself is the small box attached to the cover of the trash container

The aftershocks in the IoT IOS are the new products, services, and pro-cesses – or clever combinations of these three as in the example of Enevo – and the societal and economic benefits caused by their use.

Aftershocks I: innovation through IoT in an established domain
In addition to inventing new products, services and processes, Internet of Things enables making innovations in established domains.

Aftershocks II: user innovation in the IoT Innovation Opportunity Space with open hardware and software
Developing the Internet of Things is a major global undertaking in which businesses ranging from industrial giants like General Electric to small start-ups, various other organisations and individual users participate on different levels of activity. Building from scratch the hardware for an IoT application can be practically impossible for most users. However, inex-pensive generic hardware components have been made available for users to develop their own 'smart' objects for the Internet of Things. Such IoT development platforms include, for example, Arduino, BeagleBone Black, the BBC micro:bit and Raspberry PI (see Box 8.11). These platforms have been distributed on the open software and open hardware principle. The BBC micro:bit has even been given away for free and creating applications for it are taught in schools in the UK.

As a whole, the Internet of Things can be seen as a systemic innovation (as discussed earlier in this chapter) that is constructed bit-by-bit (in this case, connected application by connected application) by large corpora-tions as well as innovative individuals.

8.4 CYANOGENMOD: THE EMERGENCE OF THE USER ORGANISATION

CyanogenMod (CM) is a complex user-led Open Source project that spe-cialises in modifying and redistributing a community developed version of the Android operating system. According to recent figures CyanogenMod, has over 12 million installations in over 400 different models of smart-phone and tablets and has been translated into over 140 different lan-guages worldwide. The project has been seen by many as a very successful user-based initiative that has attracted a significant amount of interest and investment from established companies, including Microsoft. What is most significant about the CyanogenMod project, however, is that all of its products and services and all the enhancements made to the software were made by a wide range of volunteers. These groups of users are able

---

BOX 8.11　RASPBERRY PI

The Raspberry Pi is a series of small-sized computer boards developed in the UK by the Raspberry Pi Foundation. The intent of the foundation has been to promote the teaching of computer science through inexpensive hardware. The price of the basic Raspberry Pi board has been between $25 and $35. A later generation version, Raspberry Pi Zero, was made available for sale in 2015 for as little as $5 and was even given away for free with an issue of the MagPi magazine. Although the basic component is essentially a credit-card sized computer board with CPU and memory but without display or keyboard, Raspberry Pi has the necessary connections for extending it to a full-fledged computer with Internet connectivity as well as for obtaining data from various external sensors and for controlling various actuator devices. Multiple parties have produced various add-on hardware modules, such as the RaZberry module that enables controlling Z-Wave compatible home automation systems with Raspberry Pi applications. Raspberry Pi applications are programmed with open source software based on the Linux operating system. Available programming languages range from those intended for beginners (for example, Basic, Python, and Ruby) to those for experienced programmers (for example, C++).

The inexpensive price and broad extendibility have made Raspberry Pi popular: by February 2017, more than twelve million Raspberry Pi units had been sold.[35] As the low retail price and barebones appearance of Raspberry Pi suggest, most of the value of this platform is created by its users. Raspberry Pi user communities offer online support, program code, schematics and practical hints for making 'hacks' on the platform. Thus, instead of just a device, Raspberry Pi can be seen as a full-fledged ecosystem for developing novel products and solutions, for example, for the Internet of Things. Furthermore, Raspberry Pi can be seen as one manifestation of the recent maker movement, also known as maker culture, which promotes the do-it-yourself creation of physical devices, rather than just software applications.

---

to contribute to the project allowing CM to have a wide range of supporting products and services, including complementary software to facilitate usage, the documentation of key processes, and even its translation.

CyanogenMod presents an emergent Innovation Opportunity Space, characterised by an architecture that facilitates diverse groups of actors to contribute to the project through a range of practices (Figure 8.10). In addition, the actions of these actors, particularly the project leaders, have led to significant aftershocks in Open Source collaborative development, where non-programming contributions are acknowledged to provide great value to the final product.

8.4.1　CyanogenMod's Origins and XDA Forum

The CyanogenMod project can be described as an embodiment of a hacker[36] community that is motivated by both freedom and scepticism.

Architecture	Actors	Actions
Technological context: • Widespread Android use • Based on Open technology	• CM groups	• Strong commitment to project • Highly structured community activity
Market context: • New market • Attractive to digital natives • Strong online norms	• Google	• Able to set the pace for development
Legal context: • Few regulations	• Smartphone firms	• Able to facilitate or make user involvement more difficult

Aftershocks

- Service innovation
  - New organisational model based on engaging customers/users
  - Ongoing diffusion of aspects of the model within the software industry

- Systemic innovation
  - Novel organisational form
  - Creation of new organisational capabilities in a developing commercial context
  - Potential applicability to the creation of complex software products

Figure 8.10   Innovation Opportunity Space – CyanogenMod

Freedom in terms of ownership and control of their hardware and software in order to satisfy complex individual needs; scepticism in terms of distrusting authority, resisting commercialisation, and overcoming restrictions imposed by commercial actors. True to this philosophy, CyanogenMod has aimed to provide users greater control over their devices through customisation and improved security features, including ad blockers and stronger encryption. Most significantly, CyanogenMod is part of a generation of hackers that focus on smaller devices that make use of specialised software, such as smartphones, 3D printers, drones, and SBCs (Single Board Computers) like the Raspberry Pi. While being part of a new generation of open source hackers, the CyanogenMod project has strong links – and owes much of its early success – to proprietary software. The project's owner, Steve Kondik, and its leaders met in the XDA Developers forum, where they would swap ideas, solutions, and modified ROMs. The story of CyanogenMod therefore begins with Windows Mobile and the XDA Developer's forum.

8.4.2   From Windows Mobile To The Android Open Source Project

The story of CyanogenMod and its developers can be traced back to the mid-1990s, with the introduction of the Pocket PC. At the 1996 COMDEX conference in Las Vegas, Bill Gates demonstrated Microsoft's new operating system, Windows CE (later to be renamed Windows Mobile). A significant aspect of Windows CE was the fact that it provided users the ability to connect to the Internet using mobile networks. This capability came as a commitment from Microsoft to provide a hand-held operating system with near PC desktop functionality (Microsoft, 1996[37]). In addition, Microsoft's business model made it possible to increase the operating system's adoption by licencing it in the same way as they had with their Windows PC operating system. A wide range of manufacturers licenced Windows Mobile and released their own devices, one of the most notable of these being the XDA line of pocket PCs manufactured by HTC for O2.

The XDA's popularity led to the creation of the XDA Developers' website and its forum, where programmers and enthusiasts could find and exchange information. The website contains reviews and news from the mobile industry, including written articles, podcasts, and videos. The forum, on the other hand, contained threads about modifying Windows Mobile, where users would change the way it looked, add new features, and then redistribute these modified versions. Because of its closed-source nature and commercial licenses, the practice of redistributing modified versions of Windows Mobile was met with a number of issues, including a cease and desist order by Microsoft in 2009. This tension between the hacker communities and Microsoft disappeared with the introduction of the Android Operating System.

There were two key events that facilitated the move away from Windows Mobile, first was Android's Open Source license, allowing hackers to modify and redistribute the software, and second was a change in policy within the XDA forum, lifting a ban on non Windows Mobile discussions. When releasing the operating system, Google decided to use Open technology in order to make sure that all users and all manufacturers wanting to use Android would be able to modify it as they wished (Android.com, 2008[38]). In accordance, Android makes use of Open Source technology, most importantly the Linux kernel and a Java script implementation. In addition, the software itself is released with an Apache Software Licence 2.0, allowing both modification and redistribution[39] of the software.

With the growth in popularity in Android in 2008, the XDA Developers website decided to relax community rules and allow people to openly discuss Android issues. This change in rule would bring about the introduction of a wide range of projects based on modified versions of Android, while retaining many of the practices developed during the Windows Mobile days. For instance, many of the projects would be led solely by individual forum members, who would use their own usernames to re-brand the modified operating system. This practice, which started with Windows Mobile, was passed on to Android leading to a wide range of XDA Forum-based projects run by users such as *JesusFreke* and *Cyanogen*. Many of these early projects were small in terms of user-base and contributors, with only a few well-known projects gaining large following, one of which was JesusFreke.

The JesusFreke modified ROM, maintained by Ben Gruver, was one of the most popular projects with an estimated 5,000 users and would play an important role in the success of CyanogenMod. In October 2009, Gruver decided to stop the development of his custom ROM and instead asked his users to switch to another customised ROM run by Steve Kondik, whose XDA user name was *cyanogen* (Gruver, 2009[40]). Following the endorsement, CyanogenMod's user-base increased significantly to become the largest Android-based project in the XDA Forum. The ever-increasing number of users and downloads during 2009 and 2010 prompted the project owner and leaders to establish a dedicated infrastructure with the aim of supporting the wide user-base and contributions.

8.4.3 Community Development and Work

In 2010, the CyanogenMod project established its own ICT infrastructure, with a new website, a wiki, a forum, and repository. Due to the rapid growth of the project during its time in the XDA forum, users were contributing to the project through a number of different practices, including programming, translation, documentation, and user-to-user assistance. The new ICT infrastructure was therefore established to facilitate the coordination of these diverse types of contributions, allowing project leaders to control contributions made to the project by establishing and implementing rules at both project and group level, something that would have not otherwise been possible. From 2010 to 2013 the project's popularity increased, with approximately 11.6 million installs, with 74,665 contributors making a total of 585,375 contributions to the project. These contributions were not just limited to software development of the ROM, but included documentation, translations, and supporting services.

With its own ICT infrastructure, the project developed complex rules and procedures that guided behaviour for the general contributors (those who are not part of the leadership team). This included rules that determine what tools to use, the evaluation process for each contribution, and the timing of the contributions. In addition, the project established a formal development process that had been previously used by companies such as Google and Mozilla, and that gives contributors a location for experimentation and another location for fine-tuning. To understand the processes, however, it is first important to determine how users can contribute to the project.

8.4.4   User Contributions

There is a general assumption that only programmers and hackers are involved in Open Source projects, where the only way to contribute is through complex programming activities. This assumption is further reinforced by the complex and sometimes overwhelming documentation that is available for Open Source projects, focusing on the technical aspects of the software. What has to be emphasised, however, is that software is a multidisciplinary endeavour, where a wide range of skills is needed in order to produce a usable consumer good. CyanogenMod is one of the first Open Source projects to acknowledge this and fully support it.

The first and most important group within the project were those of the programmers who are responsible for the key things and the new implementation of ideas at the level of the software. This type of contribution was carried out by the original group of developers that met and socialised in the XDA forum, amounting to less than ten individuals in total. These core contributors were software engineers that had some knowledge of the ROM modification and were therefore able to contribute to the project through programming. Most of their activities related to the design and implementation of new features, including a service that could track the location of your phone, and an automatic installer which would facilitate the process of software installation. In addition, the majority of the programming contributions would also be authorised and checked by them, with their serving as gate keepers and controlling what was placed in the overall system.

However, other valuable forms of contribution came from the non-specialist, general, users who were able to give project leaders access to other resources and provide them with relevant tools for performing important tasks. Another important contribution is that of additional software that facilitates the usage of the operating system, such as the ClockworkMod, which helps people manage and install different ROMs, as well as other tools such as installer apps that provide the simplification of the process of installing the operating system without having to deal with the technical complexities. In addition, there is also the porting of the operating system to other devices: as each device is different in the components it uses, there are a few things that need to be taken into account, and access to those devices is needed in order for them to work. General contributors are therefore important in this respect, as it is they who will port the operating system. This activity would be difficult to do otherwise as project leaders may have a limited access to the resources needed to port to all the devices.

In addition to the programmers, local language translators proved to be another key group, making a wide range of translations and making the project available in over 50 languages, from Afrikaans to Zulu. This is provided by a much wider range of individuals, with some 137 individual contributors taking responsibility for translating the software into a local language. The translation contributions even have their own page where people are able to coordinate their activities and are able to tell each other what needs to get done. These typically take place in private Internet Relay Chat (IRC) channels that people need to be invited to and then speak to each other and also a website that allows individuals to monitor how much of the project has been translated and how much needs to still get done.

Finally, an important part of the project is the documentation, which aims to instruct the people who will install the software how to do various things, all of these are found in the wiki. The documentation for the project is unique because it provides information to users and potential users on how to prepare the mobile phone for installation, how to install the operating system, and also how to modify the software and contribute to the project. The documentation provides information about key activities that are essential to installing and then using the software, all the way to programming and adding new contributions to the repository. In addition, each of these guides would be specific to each device and would also have instructions on how to unlock, delete the operating system, and install CyanogenMod. The documentation also features rules and guidelines that stated where, when and how users could contribute to the project. This documentation was more than important when it came to encouraging a wider group of people to contribute and become involved in the development of the operating system.

8.4.5 Project Governance

The primary question when it comes to a complex project like this, where users contribute to the project in a wide variety of ways, is about coordination and how these people actually work together to produce something. This is something that is particularly tricky when it comes to a voluntary organisation, where individuals are able to come and leave as they please. This is also something that, in the study of Open Source development, typically falls under the issue of community governance.[41] This is particularly tricky within the CyanogenMod project as each type of contribution may require a different way depending on availability of skills and resources as well as the ICT through which it was being carried out.

One of the key aspects was the fact that the programmers were restricted in their contributions only in terms of how these were evaluated and compared to the objectives of the project. For instance, while all contributors were able to change the code and introduce new features, not many of these were actually included in the final release of the software. This is because all contributions were then reviewed by the core developers, and were approved or rejected based on whether they were consistent with the project's outcome and what they wanted to do. In addition, although all contributions were to be reviewed, this was not possible for all translations, as there would be no other person who would be able to verify particular languages.

In addition, rules on participation were developed and enforced at both project level and community level, therefore creating a distinction on how people should contribute based on the type of contribution being made. This was based on two main ways, for instance, contributions to the wiki were based on templates, which would limit and restrict the type of information that each page contained. In a different way, porting the ROM to new devices would be less restricted, and would allow developers greater flexibility. This difference in rules would be set up after consultation with the contributors, but the final decision would be made by the project leaders.

8.4.6 Development Process

As important as project governance is to the coordination of contributions, the project's development process established by the project leaders would also have an impact on the overall direction of the project. The development process takes place in three parallel stages, Nightly Builds, Release Candidate, and Stable Release. These three stages were similar to what has been used in other open source projects, such as Mozilla's Firefox, and each stage represents both a level of stability in the software, and the implementation of new features. This is to say, the Nightly Builds were generally unstable as these would be the location where developers could experiment with the implementation of new features. The Release Candidate builds were a bit more stable than the nightly ones but still had a few bugs to solve. Finally, the Stable Release would be the final stable version that would be given and distributed to users in general. In addition to the difference in terms of builds, another important characteristic was the type of users that were able to contribute at each stage.

The key to the different stages is that these represent locations where users can carry out a specific set of changes to the software. For instance, the Nightly Build is the places where most of the experimental development is done, providing a separate area where other releases will not be affected and serving as a signal to state that the build is not stable. Similarly, the Release Candidate is the location where the majority of bug fixing and fine-tuning takes place, and the central location where general users are encouraged to contribute. It is also important to understand that these releases are not sequential but are instead parallel to each other, and all three are being worked on constantly.

Another effect that this has is that the project leaders and the general contributors are active in different geographical locations, and this will therefore have an effect on the innovation process. The key thing is that normally we look at users and assume that they contribute throughout the project's life cycle. CyanogenMod, however, showed that the timing of the contribution was significant in terms of the direction of the project. This is because, as can be seen, all new features were implemented during the Nightly Builds, where only a selected few were able to contribute. Once the new features were implemented and placed in the project, general contributions would then be involved throughout the Release Candidate stage. In addition, this would mean that the roles and the purpose of their contributions would be limited to testing and improving what was already there, rather than to implement new features.

8.4.7 CyanogenMod as an Innovation Opportunity Space

The CyanogenMod project is very clearly an emerging Innovation Opportunity Space as it was brought about by the different application of an existing technology. The emergence of the Android operating system and the mass acceptance of smartphones were both important factors.

Architecture
The architecture has three dimensions that aid in structuring and facilitate innovation: the software license, the ICT, and project rules. The legal aspects deal with Android and the technology that was set up in order to promote collaborative development of the software. Google deliberately focused on the Open technologies that would enable and empower their platform partners to modify and differentiate the platform to suit their own needs. These permissions, however, also facilitated innovation by individual users, allowing the modification and redistribution of the software and giving them the permission to modify the software without further committing them to other strict agreements.[42] This architecture, as with others in Open Source, gives users the right to view, change and redistribute, but it also makes it easier to develop skills on something that is Open and can be found in a wide range of locations, such as documentation on the Linux kernel and on Java programming.

The second perspective of architecture is that which is found within the project, dealing with the infrastructure that facilitates coordination of activities. For instance, the dedicated IRC channels allow individuals to discuss the tasks that need to be carried out and to determine what requires doing. Equally, the review software facilitated the discussion essential to develop a shared understanding on the direction of development. Equally, the Wiki served as the tool that lowered the barriers of participation to any potential user or contributor, providing detailed instructions as to how to install the software and how to contribute. Finally, the rules of contributing to the project also facilitated and focused user contributions. It facilitated contributions by providing a clear understanding on how users will contribute, making it possible for contributors to have a clear and transparent view as to how their contributions will be evaluated. At the same time, however, it focused contributions by stating where and when they are to take place, limiting the way in which general users contribute and allowing the project leaders to retain overall control.

Actors
The actors in the CyanogenMod project are groups that are both internal and external to the project. The actors that are internal to the project are

mainly the contributors and the group of leaders that oversee contributions. Each type of contribution within the project generates its own community of practice, with its own rules and ways of behaving. This therefore makes it important for the project leaders to determine how these actors are going to be managed. The difference being that some of the programming contributions will go through significantly different forms of management than the translators and the people that do the documentation. In addition, a second group of actors are the project leaders, of which the project owner is part of, and they are responsible for making sure the groups are run properly and about the direction of the film.

The external actors include Google, the platform owner, and the device manufacturers, who can make it easy or more difficult for users to modify their devices. Google has been proven to be a very important actor in this space, being able to dictate and hold power over the user-modified ROMs and further setting the pace of development through their yearly releases. In addition, device manufacturers have also played an important role by facilitating or by making it more difficult for users to unlock the device and install their own ROM, as well as by making the related hardware component drivers available to the general public, therefore facilitating its modification.

Actions

Actions within the project go along the lines of the development of software, but also include and extend to the development and maintenance of supporting products and services. The key to the CyanogenMod project is that software development forms just a small fraction of all the activity that takes place within the project. An interesting aspect of the project is the fact that it looks at a number of things that include the development of other related software to the operating system that allows and facilitates the usage of the main software, such as installers and ROM managers. The project leaders, therefore, have been able to apply their knowledge by creating tools that lower barriers of entry to other non-technical potential users.

In addition, the related services and actions include things that are not completely important to the development of the software, but that add value to the project, such as the documentation and the translation to other languages. The availability of the software in other languages opens the possibility of its adoption in other geographical locations that may not have been possible otherwise. These translations have been carried out by the general contributors for their own benefit. Finally, the documentation proves to be an important activity within the project as it can teach others how to contribute and how to be part of the project by setting and making the rules of the project explicit and more transparent. The actions of the actors in this Innovation Opportunity Space are therefore broad and not limited to software development but on a wider range of actions that increase the project's value.

Aftershocks

The outcomes of the actions include the recognition that user-led projects are much more complex that traditional perspective of Open Source. In turn, this opens the possibility of being able to view individual users as much more than one-trick ponies, but instead (much as we have seen with the giffgaff case in Chapter 7) to view them as a diverse group of individuals with multiple resources and talents. The actions taken by the project leaders led to the creation of an architecture of collaboration that was both conducive and supportive of the diversity of skills possessed by the contributors. This led to a much fuller project that had a wide range of contributions in separate locations, therefore tapping into innovation from users for its use in the software and related services.

Finally, the architecture of collaboration in this project produced something that can be applied into a wide range of mobile devices and even to other contexts, reducing the cost of development and offering the potential of creating entirely new commercial models. By introducing the novel architecture of collaboration and creating a wide range of development tools and documentation, the project itself has also been able to lower the barriers of entry and get a wider pool of users to contribute to the project, therefore providing a wide range of skills and resources, such as languages and devices that would otherwise not be available to the project leaders. The aftershocks are therefore significant in that it has facilitated the creation of a project whose governance and structure resembles more a formal organisation than a community of hackers, and one whose potential for commercialisation made it a reality.

8.5　CONCLUDING REMARKS

This chapter has presented a range of examples of new technologies, novel organisational forms and emerging business models in different kinds of frontier contexts. Understanding and analysing an Innovation Opportunity Space is likely to be far more challenging in this context as matters are likely to be far more fluid and subject to challenge and change. However, standing back to examine an Innovation Opportunity Space as a whole will provide a far greater appreciation of the range of Opportunities that are in the process of emerging, something that will be of great value to strategic managers.

Technological shifts will always create a range of new Innovation Opportunities, and the cases on open data and the Internet of Things provide detailed insights into the developing context of their respective Innovation Opportunity Spaces. Clearly, such Opportunity Spaces can potentially overlap and new and unforeseen interactions can lead to a range of quite different innovation pathways. Generally, it is wise to assume that if it can be imagined, it will likely have been already attempted somewhere in the world. As a result, it is often not about being the first to do something, rather it is about being the first to do something well in your chosen context or market, as illustrated by the CyanogenMod case study.

The CyanogenMod case study is valuable because it is the first in-depth study to show that Open Source projects, hitherto the domain of geeks and hackers, can become mainstream activities. Central to this evolution is the novel architecture of participation that was developed in the project that welcomed (and structured) contributions from many different types of contributor, technical and non-technical. Much like the giffgaff case study in Chapter 7, what we see here is an organisation creating a new way for different kinds of user to get involved in a large-scale activity. What this shows us is that, potentially, users and others can create or get involved in large-scale virtual organisations that have been established to create and support highly complex products. This is unprecedented and shows the way to the development of entirely new, and entirely virtual, organisational forms and structures. Like many of the new non-commercial ideas that have emerged and been developed by users and online communities on the Internet, it is likely that this knowledge will be found in a commercial form in the near future.

NOTES

1. A concept related to open data is 'open knowledge', which can be seen as an umbrella term for open data, and includes, e.g. open content (media such as literature published by Project Gutenberg) and free access to scientific research publications. However, the focus of this chapter is on open data.
2. Manyika, J., Chui, M., Bughin, J., Dobbs, R., Bisson, P. and Marrs, A. (2013) *Disruptive Technologies: Advances that Will Transform Life, Business, and the Global Economy* (vol. 180). San Francisco, CA: McKinsey Global Institute, p. 4.
3. http://project-open-data.github.io/principles/ accessed 24 August 2015.
4. https://okfn.org/opendata/ accessed 25 February 2016.
5. Manyika et al. (2013).
6. Manyika et al. (2013).
7. http://opendatacommons.org/licenses/odbl/ accessed 25 February 2016.
8. Hochgerner, J. (2013) Social innovations and the advancement of the general concept of innovation, *Social Innovation: New Forms of Organization in Knowledge-Based Societies*, pp. 12–28.

9. Dawson, P. and Daniel, L. (2010) Understanding social innovation: a provisional framework, *International Journal of Technology Management*, vol. *51*, no. 1, pp. 9–21.
10. Caulier-Grice, J., Davies, A., Patrick, R. and Norman, W. (2012) Defining social innovation. *A deliverable of the project: 'The theoretical, empirical and policy foundations for building social innovation in Europe' (TEPSIE)*, European Commission–7th Framework Programme, Brussels: European Commission, DG Research.
11. http://www.hri.fi/fi/sovellukset/tax-tree/ accessed 24 August 2015.
12. http://hahmota.fi/ accessed 25 February 2016.
13. http://www.trulia.com accessed 25 February 2016.
14. http://www.bloomberg.com/news/articles/2014-07-28/zillow-to-acquire-trulia-for-3-5-billion-in-stock accessed 25 February 2016.
15. https://www.billguard.com accessed 24 August 2015.
16. http://catalog.data.gov/dataset/consumer-complaint-database accessed 25 February 2016.
17. Neumeier, S. (2012) Why do social innovations in rural development matter and should they be considered more seriously in rural development research? Proposal for a stronger focus on social innovations in rural development research, *Sociologia ruralis*, vol. 52, no. 1, pp. 48–69.
18. http://www.cloudnsci.fi accessed 25 February 2016.
19. Figure is based on: http://www.slideshare.net/CloudNSci/the-smarter-way-to-commercialize-algorithms, slide 10 accessed 9 February 2017.
20. http://blindsquare.com accessed 25 February 2016.
21. http://mashable.com/2012/06/01/blindsquare-app/#T3hpTtZHxPq8 accessed 25 February 2016.
22. https://www.fixmystreet.com accessed 25 February 2016.
23. Meijer, A.J. (2012) The do it yourself state, *Information Polity*, vol. 17, no. 3–4, pp. 303–314.
24. www.paastot.fi accessed 25 February 2016.
25. More than 30,000 industrial plants across Europe, from coal plants to piggeries, are obliged by EU legislation to report the harmful emissions of 91 substances into air, soil and water.
26. https://www.mysociety.org accessed 25 February 2016.
27. Manyika, J., Chui, M., Bughin, J., Dobbs, R., Bisson, P. and Marrs, A. (2013) *Disruptive Technologies: Advances that Will Transform Life, Business, and the Global Economy* (vol. 180). San Francisco, CA: McKinsey Global Institute.
28. http://www.dhl.com/content/dam/Local_Images/g0/New_aboutus/innovation/DHL_TrendReport_Internet_of_things.pdf accessed 25 February 2016.
29. https://en.wikipedia.org./wiki/Enevo accessed 24 August 2015.
30. http://www.enevo.com/news/smart-city-waste-logistics-system-provider-enevo-receives-15-8-million-funding-led-foxconn-ginko-ventures-mistletoe-japan/ accessed 1 September 2015.
31. http://www.enevo.com/news/smart-city-waste-logistics-system-provider-enevo-receives-15-8-million-funding-led-foxconn-ginko-ventures-mistletoe-japan/ accessed 1 September 2015.
32. http://www.tekes.fi/tekes/tulokset-ja-vaikutukset/caset/2014/enevo-oy-kaikuluotain-roskissessa-saastaa-luontoa-ja-rahaa/ accessed 1 September 2015.
33. www.forbes.com/sites/federicoguerrini/2014/09/10/from-espoo-to-new-york-city-how-finnish-startup-enevo-is-trying-to-disrupt-the-waste-management-industry accessed 24 August 2015.
34. Illustration is based on http://reset-lehti.fi/wp-content/uploads/2014/08/Enevo_muokattu_reset.jpg accessed 1 September 2015.
35. http://www.wired.co.uk/article/raspberry-pi-future accessed 23 March 2017.
36. Taken from Eric Raymond's revision of the Jargon File, a hacker is defined as 'A person who enjoys learning the details of programming systems and how to stretch their capabilities, as opposed to most users who prefer to learn only the minimum necessary.'

37. Microsoft Announces Broad Availability of Handheld PCs With Windows CE. Read more at https://news.microsoft.com/1996/11/19/microsoft-announces-broad-availability-of-handheld-pcs-with-windows-ce/#x0X1BpcX3lg5FDGl.99.
38. Android.com (2008). The android source code; governance philosophy. http://source.android.com/source/index.html (accessed 28 February 2017).
39. Google Apps and Services are proprietary license and are not covered by the Apache license. As a result, all modified ROMs can only be redistributed without these.
40. Gruver, B. (2009). Calling it quits. http://goo.gl/RZ2KMV (accessed 28 February 2017).
41. See O'Mahony, S. (2007) The governance of open source initiatives: what does it mean to be community managed? *Journal of Management & Governance*, vol. 11, no. 2, pp. 139–150.
42. Google specifies and compares the Apache Software License 2.0 with the Lesser General Public License (LGPL), which forces individuals to release the software in both binary and open source. This comparison can be found at https://source.android.com/source/licenses.html accessed 9 February 2017.

9. Capturing the Innovation Opportunity Space

Stephen Flowers, Martin Meyer and Jari Kuusisto

9.1 INTRODUCTION

This book has been an exploration of the business models developed in response to the new forms of innovation that have emerged over the last few years. These new forms of innovation may be driven by commercial firms but also by individuals, online communities and the crowd and many types of organisation, both commercial and communitarian, have developed strategies for creating and capturing the value that flows from these relationships. Understanding these new forms of innovation, and the business models that have been developed, are key to those seeking to capture the value that is created in these relationships. This is not easy as the traditional approach towards innovation tends to place the commercial firm and things like products, patents and copyright at the centre of the process. Although this remains an important part of the innovation landscape, the case studies contained in this book make it very clear that this landscape contains many other important groups. An important new feature of the developing innovation landscape is the ease with which different groups are now able to communicate and link up and the recognition that, given the right circumstances, it is possible to access the ideas, skills and experience of users, online communities and the crowd that are essential to create new products and services. Innovation has changed.

Considering the summary of the cases outlined in Table 9.1, it is clear that we have predominantly focused on the commercially driven activities that draw on resources outside the firm within both their innovation and operation processes. In some cases commercial firms act as intermediaries between those who wish to offer their resources for a financial return and their market (for example, Airbnb, BlaBlaCar, Fixura), whilst in other cases firms seek to utilise external expertise within their internal innovation

Table 9.1   Summary of selected case studies

Case study	Initial Innovation Driver	Operating model	Resource Locus
Airbnb	Commercial	C2C	Hybrid
Audacity	Communitarian	C2C	Users
BlaBlaCar	Commercial	C2C	Hybrid
Boeing 747	Commercial	B2B	Firm
Chinese Online.com	Commercial	B2C	Hybrid
CyanogenMod	Communitarian	C2C	Users
Destiny video game	Commercial	B2C	Firm
DIY skate parks	Communitarian	C2C	Users
Fixura	Commercial	C2C	Users
Forests in Finland	Commercial	B2B	Hybrid
giffgaff	Commercial	Hybrid	Hybrid
GeekBridge	Commercial	B2C	Hybrid
Innovation Mill	Commercial	B2B	Firm
Intellectual Ventures	Commercial	B2B	Firm
Machinima	Communitarian	C2C	Users
Moodle	Commercial	B2B	Hybrid
OpenStreetMap	Communitarian	C2C	Users
Project Gutenberg	Communitarian	C2C	Users
QIYI	Commercial	B2C	Hybrid
Swapstyle	Commercial	C2C	Users
Thingiverse	Communitarian	C2C	Users
Uber	Commercial	B2C	Hybrid
VacationRentals	Commercial	C2C	Hybrid
Vuze	Communitarian	C2C	Users

process (for example, Boeing, Destiny). Other cases have shown how groups have been able to undertake complex non-commercial innovations by drawing on a wide range of external resources that are freely given by a wide range of actors (for example, Safecast, OpenStreetMap, Parkrun). Perhaps the most sophisticated approaches have required the creation of a complex hybrid operational model that draws on both internal and external resources within a new form of organisational structure and business model (for example, giffgaff, Moodle). What emerges strongly from this new and shifting innovation landscape are the opportunities that are open to firms able to embrace this new way of working, and the significant benefits that may be achieved. This chapter will outline the steps that firms should take in order to create new value and capture an Innovation Opportunity Space in this way.

9.2   FOCUSING ON RESOURCES AND VALUE

The case studies show that the business models built around the new forms of innovation are about Resources and Value as firms have worked out how to create commercial value from external resources. To recap, Resources are things like time, money, knowledge, experience, practised routines and processes, but can also include things like ideas, suggestions, proposals, prototypes, comments and videos. Value can be commercial (for example, it may relate to a direct or indirect financial outcome), but may also be social, communitarian or reputational. Distilling the Resource/Value distinction further (Resources: are they held by the firm, or are they obtained externally?; Value: commercial or non-commercial) allows the creation of the 2x2 matrix introduced in Chapter 2 and shown in Figure 9.1.

You'll recall that this 2x2 matrix provides the basis for the distinction between Old and New forms of innovation, with Old Form Innovation being an approach to the creation of new and improved goods and services based on the producer's ownership and control of the necessary resources. By contrast, New Form Innovation makes use of a wide range of external

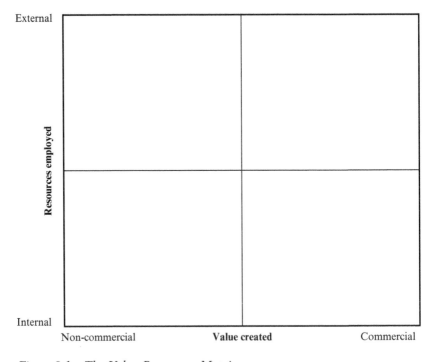

Figure 9.1   The Value-Resources Matrix

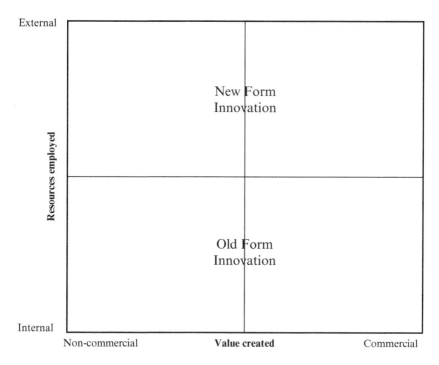

Figure 9.2   Mapping forms of innovation on the Value-Resources Matrix

resources in order to create new goods and services, with these resources being provided by external groups like users, online communities and members of the crowd. The major distinction between Old and New forms of innovation was introduced in Chapter 2 but is shown again in Figure 9.2.

As we have seen throughout this book, these new models of innovation can create a huge amount of value for those involved, but they may not necessarily be designed to operate commercially. In some areas – for example, digital information-based systems – the skills and technologies required are now widespread, and the barriers to entry relatively low, with the result that there are many examples of New Form innovations that are non-commercial, as shown in Figure 9.3. Although the systems in the top-left quadrant of Figure 9.3 (Non commercial/External resources employed) may appear self-sufficient they draw on a range of external resources for their ongoing operation. Wikipedia, perhaps the biggest of them all, is a great example of this since it is totally reliant on external 'workers' to maintain its many pages of information. It is important to note that Figure 9.3 presents a snapshot in time and all

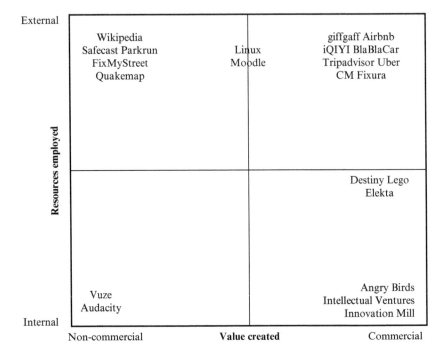

Figure 9.3   Mapping organisations on the Value-Resources Matrix

systems will evolve over time and, as a result, may move between different quadrants over time. For example, it could be argued that Linux started life as an Internally resourced, Non-Commercial innovation, migrated to the External Resources/Non-commercial quadrant as the wider online community became involved in its development, and with the development of a large commercial services industry around it is now a hybrid non-commercial/commercial system. The same could be argued for Moodle. In stark contrast, giffgaff is an organisation created from the outset as a commercial entity, but which shares many similarities with other organisations that draw on external resources in order to operate.

The New Form Innovation organisations described in this book have all managed to develop an operational model that relies on a range of external resources. In some cases firms like Airbnb, Uber, Swapstyle and BlaBlaCar draw on the physical resources like accommodation, clothes and vehicles, whilst in others (for example, Wikipedia, Ushahidi, TripAdvisor) it is information, and still others (for example, Kickstarter) it is money. Exceptionally, a wide range of knowledge, financial, technical, information and other resources may be drawn on (for example, Safecast).

These examples have been selected in order to illustrate how it is possible to draw on a wide range of external resources within an innovation process. These examples are not held up as the only future of innovation, rather they contain ideas and insights that illustrate how innovation is evolving and how organisations of all types can learn to benefit from external resources.

The next section will examine how organisations can begin to engage with the new ideas, new thinking, and new ways of working that are required to explore the value of New Form Innovation in their own context. It is important to make clear that what is proposed is more likely to supplement rather than replace existing innovation processes. Indeed, Old Form Innovation remains the mainstay of industrial economies around the world and has stood the test of time. However, New Form Innovation offers an entirely novel way to extend and develop existing ways of working and to create the entirely new sources of value that can sit alongside more traditional forms of innovation.

9.3   CAPTURING THE INNOVATION OPPORTUNITY SPACE

Recognising that a New Form of innovation has emerged and taking action on that knowledge are two quite different things, and many organisations around the world are struggling with the implications of this shift for their operating models. Silicon Valley, and its associated Venture Capital funders, has become a crucible for start-up firms that wish to turn this insight into commercial gain, and at the same time it has never been easier to create a non-commercial, communitarian, organisation. However, this section is focused on the challenges that face existing organisations based on Old Form Innovation that are aware that New Form Innovation may offer many advantages that have hitherto been closed to them. The stages outlined below present a logical, systematic approach to dealing with one of the major challenges that will face all Old Form Innovation firms in the coming years: how can firms draw on New Form Innovation to support and extend their business model? Organisations are complex entities and the stages outlined below are intended to provide the top-level headlines to indicate the nature of the activities within each stage. It is for the leaders, managers and staff within each organisation to work together to apply each of these headline stages to their own organisational, competitive and commercial context. The four stages outlined below are designed to provide a simple structure for focusing action (Figure 9.4).

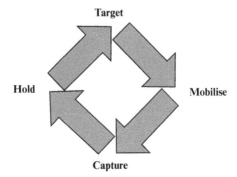

Figure 9.4   Stages in capturing the Innovation Opportunity Space

Target – Mobilise – Capture – Hold

Target: Identifying and targeting an Innovation Opportunity Space; identifying the source(s) and nature of the external resources required.

Mobilise: Mobilising the resources required (both external and internal) to move on the Innovation Opportunity Space.

Capture: Capturing the Innovation Opportunity Space by the effective use of external and internal resources.

Hold: Maintaining the organisational position that has been achieved in the Innovation Opportunity Space.

9.3.1   Stage 1: Target

Targeting an Innovation Opportunity Space
The targeting of an Innovation Opportunity Space requires the firm to have a clear goal in mind and a good understanding of the Innovation Space itself, the potential Opportunities that exist within it, and the source(s) of the required resources. This first stage will focus on the Innovation Space and the Opportunity, with subsequent stages focusing on identifying and securing the necessary resources and the actions required for capture to be achieved.

(a) Develop initial goal
This is the first part of the process in which strategic managers and others explore what they wish to achieve. It may be that they wish to extend

Table 9.2   The Innovation Opportunity Space

Architecture	Norms, practices, behaviours, rules, and regulations that govern the Opportunity Space.
Actors	Individual users, online communities, firms and other bodies (e.g. regulators) that are active in the Opportunity Space.
Actions	Individual and collective activities taken by the individual users, online communities, firms and other bodies that are active in the Opportunity Space.
Aftershocks	The impact and outcomes of the actions taken by the actors within the Opportunity Space.

BOX 9.1   NOVEL CATEGORY ERROR

The Novel Category Error arises when you are trying to collect data on a matter, product or service that does not currently exist, is unfamiliar, or is poorly understood. Things which do not yet exist are good examples of such errors, as are topics or issues that have been reframed or reinterpreted to fit a new context. Collecting useful data in these areas is very difficult, with the result that any data should be viewed with some caution. For example, the concept of an app is now very familiar, as are app-based services like Uber, but was quite alien before smartphone adoption became widespread. As a result, just a few years ago attempts to collect data on app-based services would have been problematic, and any findings tentative in the extreme. In general, derivative ideas are simpler to understand and collect useful data on anything that is really new, and the likelihood of a Novel Category Error diminishes. However, whilst this may be a good thing from a data collection point of view, it is less likely to be a good thing if one is searching for the really new idea.

---

their existing business model or else find out what may be possible in their Opportunity Space. It may be that they wish to achieve first-mover advantage, they need to react to a competitor's actions, or else have been prompted by some other change in their Innovation Opportunity Space. Whatever the motivation, it is essential to develop a clear idea of what is to be achieved, what success would look like, and the time period that will be allowed for this initiative to begin to bear fruit. The first stage in this process is to undertake a detailed review of the Innovation Opportunity Space, as outlined below and in Table 9.2.

(b) Reviewing the Innovation Opportunity Space
Using this framework it is important to collect as much data as possible to inform the analysis, remembering that much of the data (for example,

Table 9.3   Types of Innovation Space

Stable Innovation Space	Characterised by mature products and services that are well known and understood by those who use them, a small number of dominant suppliers, and clear and enforced norms and practices around use (possibly enforced by regulation). Innovation pathways will be apparent, clearly communicated and widely accepted.
Unstable Innovation Space	Occurs when the guiding assumptions that make apparently mature products and services attractive are called into question. Dominant suppliers may be challenged by new entrants, norms and practices around use may be set aside or widely questioned, regulation may be ignored or challenged. Innovation pathways are no longer clear and different versions and visions of the future compete for dominance.
Emerging Innovation Space	Existing norms, practices or regulation are being questioned or set aside as new technologies, or novel applications of existing technologies, are being created. There is fertile ground for the creation of a range of new products, services, norms and practices that are likely to lead to unpredictable innovation outcomes. Many innovation pathways appear to be possible and there are many voices and visions of how things may develop, often on the basis of very little firm evidence.

concerning sectors, specific markets, social media and so on) will have been collected using a different frame of reference and with other purposes in mind. As a general rule, the closer your Innovation Opportunity is to what already exists, the more use currently available data will be. By the same token, the newer your Innovation Opportunity, the less use any existing data will be in effectively informing decision making. It is always important to guard against the Novel Category Error.

It is also important to develop a clear idea of the nature of the Opportunity Space itself (see Table 9.3).

(c) Assess relevant resource levels within the Opportunity Space
This should explore the relevant resources that are within the organisation as well as those that are external to it. You'll recall that resources include things such as time, money, knowledge, experience, practised routines and processes, but can also include things like ideas, suggestions, proposals, prototypes, comments and videos. Translating this into an organisational context it would be expected that there will an ongoing market intelligence

---

BOX 9.2   EXTERNAL RESOURCES: FINDING THE SIGNAL IN THE NOISE

This is a world in which resources are often deployed in less formal contexts, where huge numbers of volunteers can be jointly engaged in a complex community endeavour, and where the ideas or other contributions of a single individual can change everything. In such contexts the traditional notions of diffusion may have little meaning as everyone is likely to be either an Innovator or an Early Adopter,[1] with ideas, suggestions and technologies being shared and refined far faster than they can be within a traditional organisation. This is at its most widespread and advanced in B2C digital contexts (for example, software, consumer electronics) but has been reported in many other areas, including B2B contexts. However, this does raise the issue that the results of an external scan will be highly dependent on the nature of the organisation's business, the nature of its customers or clients and its location within the larger (and more complex) supply chain. For example, component suppliers located within a supply chain for a large and complex final product would find a very different external resource environment to a firm that produces vehicles or consumer electronics. Although the former context will be sparse and harder to find in comparison to the latter, it will still be a source of valuable resources, if they can be located and accessed. Typically, B2B contexts will present a significant challenge in this respect as firms, and the individuals within them, will often have strong legal, warranty and competitive disincentives to share their ideas and innovations. As a result, firms in such B2B contexts will often require far more sensitive and considered approaches to their innovation resource intelligence gathering. By contrast, in the world of B2C, innovative activity is often highly visible on social media and image and video sharing sites.

---

process, a New Product Development (NPD) process, together with mechanisms for reviewing operational and financial performance. Externally, it would also be expected that similar organisations that operate within the same space will have similar processes and associated resources, all of which are likely to be largely or entirely closed to any analysis. Other organisations, for example service companies, trade and policy groups, regulators, are only likely to possess highly specialised resources that relate to their particular interests. All these resources will likely be located within some sort of traditional organisational structure, governed by lines of authority and control and answerable to investors, stakeholders or trustees. In other words, they will be governed by the Architecture of their own Opportunity Space. In contrast, the wider diaspora or individual users, online communities and those that form the crowd tend to be governed by quite a different set of norms and practices and inhabit a quite different world. As a result, the resources that may be available in these contexts are likely to vary widely and accessing them is likely to require a range of different approaches to be deployed, implying the need

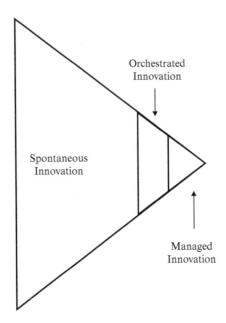

Figure 9.5   Mapping external resources

for different organisational capabilities and routines to be created and developed.

For simplicity, external innovation resources may be observed in three types of activity, as shown in Figure 9.5 and explained in more detail below.

Spontaneous innovation activity

Spontaneous activity occurs when innovation around a product, service or product/service combination leads to novel outcomes which are valued by one or more actors. These novel outcomes may be in the form of ideation for future versions or the commercially produced item, modifications (minor or major), extensions to the item, or else new uses that lay outside the original designer's intentions. Exceptionally, some users will spontaneously create their own entirely novel product, service or product/service combination. The key innovation management challenge in this context is how firms should react and how/if there is any value in seeking to transition user activity to an orchestrated or managed mode.

Orchestrated innovation activity

Orchestrated activity occurs when a firm seeks to *influence* the innovative behaviour of external groups in order to channel their creative energies into an outcome that will generate firm-level value. Such value may be economic, but may also be promotional or reputational in nature. Orchestration takes the form of activities that seek to harness the resources found within some online communities in order to generate value, but in which the final outcomes tend to be less controllable and defined (for example, opening up, or closing, product architecture in order to encourage or influence innovative activity). The key innovation management challenge in this context is the direction in which firms should seek to orchestrate external activity, how they should react to unexpected developments, and if there is any value in seeking to transition such activity to a managed mode.

Managed innovation activity
Managed activity occurs when a firm seeks to manage the innovative behaviours of external groups in order to channel their creative energies into an outcome that will generate firm-level value. Such value may be economic, but may also be promotional or reputational in nature. In this context firms will seek to build a managed framework around activity that feeds directly into a firm's own value stream.

This structured approach to external resources can be applied at the organisational level by applying the IOS External Resource Scanning Framework, shown in Table 9.4.

This framework should be employed to assess the scale and scope of the external resources that may be available within the Opportunity Space that has been targeted. The framework presents a particular lens through which it is possible to explore four things: (1) the external innovation activities around one or more products or services; (2) the extent to which these activities are organised, if at all; (3) the results of such innovation activities, and finally; (4) the nature of the organisational responses to such external innovation activities. In this way it becomes possible to obtain insights into the scale and scope of such resources and to assess the extent to which they may be influenced in particular directions (Table 9.5).

In order to get maximum benefit from this exercise it is important that organisations undertake a systematic analysis of their targeted Opportunity Space, but also look to draw on an exemplar case that can be used to focus and mobilise internal discussions and analysis. For example, just as it has been reported that one of the inspirations for giffgaff was Wikipedia, organisations may develop their own exemplar cases or draw on any of the case studies in this volume.

Within this analysis it is important to acquire both data concerning the external resources that surround the organisation (individual measurements of activity) and to develop metrics (measurements from data that has been analysed and summarised to provide insight into a particular aspect

Table 9.4   The IOS External Resource Scanning Framework – 1

	Spontaneous Innovation	Orchestrated Innovation	Managed Innovation
Episodic, uncoordinated, individualistic innovation activity	Explore and assess	–	–
Emergent community-based innovation	Explore and assess	Explore and assess	–
Community-based innovation:	Explore, catalogue, assess	Explore, catalogue, assess	Explore, catalogue, assess
Activities Ideation Minor mods Major mods Novel uses Novel products Novel services			
Outcomes	Assess	Assess nature, success and direction of influences	Assess nature, success and direction of managed behaviours
The crowd	–	Assess scale, scope, focus and likely success	Assess scale, scope, focus and likely success

Table 9.5   The IOS External Resource Scanning Framework – 2

	Spontaneous Innovation	Orchestrated Innovation	Managed Innovation
Firm intelligence gathering Scale Scope Actors Duration Outcomes	Anecdotal?	Linked into innovation operation?	Systematic, linked into innovation operation?
Firm posture and responses Unclear Uncoordinated Unmanaged Structured Coordinated Managed	Likely unclear, uncoordinated unmanaged?	Likely structured and coordinated?	Likely highly structured, coordinated and managed?
Competitor New Form Innovation analytics	Likely few?	Structured?	Structured, linked to MIS?

of activity). For example, the data may show that there are upwards of 10,000 individuals within an innovation community, but a metric showing that there are 23 per cent active at any one time, 7 per cent who have been active continuously in any six-month period, or 2 per cent active on a continuous basis provides a much more useful insight indicating the scale and scope of the resource available within such a community. Although such communities are a potentially large reservoir of innovative resources, it is likely that the level of Effective Resource (that is, the actual amount of innovation resources available at any one time) is relatively small, with the corresponding level of Latent Resource (that is, the innovation resources that are potentially available) being relatively high. This presents two challenges for organisations who wish to draw on this reservoir of innovation resources: (1) to develop mechanisms to draw on Effective Resources, and: (2) to further mobilise the Latent Resources so they become active. These challenges are considered further in the next section.

It is also necessary to be clear about the organisation's readiness to open up and begin the process of exploring the landscape of external resources. This is likely to be a challenging and potentially difficult process and it is no surprise that the majority of the case studies within this volume were founded with this business model in mind. However, the many case studies in this volume demonstrate that established firms can successfully open up parts of their innovation process to users, online communities and the crowd.

Review

Following the collection and analysis of resources available, both external and internal, and a detailed assessment of the innovation readiness it is important that the initial goal is reviewed to ensure that it is feasible and achievable. This is a simple Go/No-Go decision that should be taken following a detailed review of the evidence and an assessment of the strategic context in which the organisation finds itself. If a 'Go' decision is agreed, then it is a simple matter of proceeding to Stage 2: Mobilise. If it is a No-Go decision it may be necessary to maintain a watching brief or to return to the beginning of the process. However, it may also be necessary to seek to deny access to the external resources identified by competitors by engaging in different forms of participation.

9.3.2 Stage 2: Mobilise

It is most important to re-confirm the intended goal as it is likely that events both inside and outside of the organisation will have changed the Opportunity Space. In addition, it is important at this stage to be clear concerning the proposed role to be played by external resources and how they may be drawn into the organisational innovation process. Drawing on the cases presented in this book, it can be seen that there are three potential business or operating models that have emerged from the analysis, each of which will now be considered.

Communitarian new form

This operating model draws on a range of external resources in order to operate, but does so for communitarian rather than directly commercial purposes. This is not to say that commercial business models may not be built around this approach, and there are many examples (for example, Linux, Moodle, mySociety) in which commercial offerings are linked in some way to the core, non-commercial, system.

Hybrid new form

This hybrid form combines communitarian and commercial elements. In the cases of both Linux and Moodle a range of external groups and individuals contribute to the development of the core system, with a range of commercial services based on the core system also being available.

Commercial new form

This emerges from this analysis as the dominant approach to drawing on external resources. In this model of business and innovation a range of external resources are drawn on within a wider commercial activity. Although their precise method of operation varies, all of the firms in this grouping draw on a range of external resources as part of their business model. Firms may act as intermediaries for individuals to share their resources (for example, Airbnb, Swapstyle) or to channel money (for example, Fixura), with the most sophisticated drawing on a wide range of external resources and incorporating them into many aspects of their operation (for example, giffgaff). The two things that they all have in common is that they have built a commercial model around the use of external resources and they retain total control of business and innovation decisions.

Hybrid old form

This is an extension to traditional, Old Form Innovation approaches and, at its simplest, involves harvesting user suggestions, drawing on ideas or involving users in new product testing (for example, Lego, Destiny). In common with commercial approaches control is maintained over the business and innovation decisions.

It should come as no surprise that the businesses that are located in the top-right corner of the matrix, the Commercial New Form businesses, were all founded relatively recently and have emerged from a start-up culture around new forms of innovation. Traditional businesses, and indeed the overwhelming majority of commercial enterprises in modern economies, are based on a model in which the resources they require to operate and innovate are located within the firm itself. In contrast, the enterprises that occupy the top right corner of the matrix all require access to external resources in order to operate, something that requires a different set of internal skills, routines and processes but most of all, a different mindset. It is notable that this quadrant contains many intermediary businesses, with complex service or production organisations represented.

The route for more traditional Old Form Innovation organisations are perhaps best illustrated by the firms located in the Hybrid Old Form grouping. These firms all maintain complete internal resources but have developed processes to be able to draw on external ideas, knowledge and experience in a controlled manner. Such firms have created strong and clear links between their own internal NPD processes and the external resources they can call on as they need to. Although this is clearly a more controlled and measured response to the opportunities presented by the large reservoir of external resources that exists outside commercial firms, the adoption of such an approach will present its own organisational challenges.

It is also important to recognise that access to external resources – the resources that surround the organisation, but which it does not necessarily own or control – will differ in B2B and B2C contexts. Considering Figure 9.6 it is clear that the overwhelming majority of the cases are concerned with B2C relationships and commercial firms have developed approaches that enable them to gain access to consumer resources. These resources, which include things like ideas, knowledge, experience together with a range of physical items like vehicles, clothing and accommodation, are all made available in a relatively straightforward manner. In some cases the provision of such resources effectively side-steps existing regulations, whilst in others firms rely on the acquiescence of consumers to the arrangements they offer. The success of their business models relies upon them being able to capture the Innovation Opportunity Space in their particular area. Business to business relationships that seek to access and create value from the resources held by other organisations will tend to be more complex and those involved more constrained in the actions by legal, procedural and other structures.

However, considering Figure 9.6 it is clear that there are examples of such arrangements in both the Hybrid New Form and Hybrid Old Form business models. Considering the Hybrid New Form cluster, it is clear

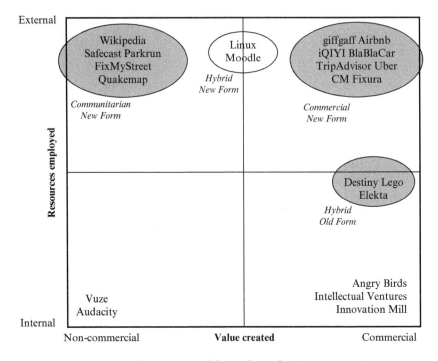

Figure 9.6   Mapping business models on the Value-Resources Matrix

that the business model has developed around the commercial services that are supplied to support the use of Linux or Moodle, whilst the software is freely available as Open Source and its development continues to be undertaken at no cost by a wide range of external groups and individuals. In direct contrast to this approach Elekta collaborates on the development of its new medical technologies with a small number of teaching hospitals, with clear arrangements covering the IP that is created in this process. Organisations that wish to develop processes that enable them to draw on external resources in some way will need to be very clear how they will do this and how the value that is jointly created will be shared.

(a) Mobilise external resources
In moving to begin the process of mobilising external resources it is important to draw on the analysis undertaken within the previous stage to start to characterise the scale, scope and nature of the external resources that may be open to the organisation. The simple form shown in Table 9.6 is an illustration of what such a high-level analysis might look like. This simple

Table 9.6   *Framework for mapping resources across different sources of external innovation*

	Spontaneous external Innovation	Orchestrated external Innovation	Managed external Innovation
Latent Resource Pool			
Episodic, uncoordinated, external innovation activity	–	–	–
Emergent Resource Pool			
Emergent community-based external innovation	–	–	–
Vibrant Resource Pool			
Community-based external innovation:	–	–	–
Targeted Resource Pool			
Crowd-base external innovation	–	–	–

table should be underpinned by a wealth of detailed analysis that starts by examining the entire Innovation Opportunity Space, before drilling down to the firm and product level and include an analysis of the ways in which exemplar, competitor and comparator firms make use of external resources.

In addition, organisations will need to consider what form of organisational model would be best suited to the context that is being targeted. Although there are many examples of B2C organisations who have had success in this area, firms providing B2B products or services will likely prefer to build from their core strengths and explore how this can be exploited in their particular B2B context. However, it is also important to characterise the nature of the resource pool and its potential for collaboration. For example, if the external innovation is primarily transgressive in nature (think illegal streaming, file downloading, and so on) then collaboration could present major challenges. In contrast, if the external innovation is more fan-based, then it might be more amenable to some form of collaboration or recognition.

However, it is vital that any moves to mobilise external resources is undertaken in an as open and authentic manner as possible, with value being generated on both sides of the relationship. Engaging with external groups in this manner is fundamentally different from other, more traditional, innovation processes and in order to create a successful and sustainable relationship firms need to recognise that this requires a different more 'Open' approach to value and innovation.

(b) Mobilise internal resources

At the same time internal processes, routines and approaches will need to be developed to enable the ideas, suggestions, knowledge, experience and artefacts obtained from outside of the organisation to be plugged into the NPD process. Processes for recognition and value-sharing will also need to be put in place, as will processes for supporting this new form of resource. Once all of these internal issues have been dealt with it is then much easier to relate to external groups in an effective and productive manner.

Bearing in mind that organisations, and the individuals within them, can often become very 'fixed' in their way of seeing the world and doing things, mobilising internal resources may be very difficult indeed. The very idea of New Forms of innovation taking place outside the firm, often led by enthusiasts who do not conform to the profile of traditional industry professional, can be quite threatening or disorientating to individuals who have spent their lives in commercial innovation. As a result, this work is likely to be a major effort in its own right as it will require an internal audit or relevant processes, staff capability, timelines and funding streams. An understanding of internal and external timelines and responsiveness will need to be developed and any potential bottlenecks in processes identified. Any need for staff training and development will also be identified and put in place in good time.

9.3.3   Stages 3 and 4: Capture/Hold

These stages focus on the capture and holding of the targeted Innovation Opportunity Space by effectively drawing on a range of external resources. They will require the creation and maintenance of systems and processes to effectively engage with those external to the organisation and to bind them (as far as may be possible) to internal R&D and NPD processes. This will necessarily be a dynamic process, will require constant care and maintenance and organisations will also need to continuously scan their wider environment for shifts and changes in the Opportunity Space. Organisations should develop some sort of Innovation Scoreboard that enables them to develop a high-level view of the way in which external resources are being accessed and deployed in both their, and adjacent, Opportunity Spaces. Such a scoreboard could take the form of Table 9.7.

It should be emphasised that the notion of permanent Capture may be misleading and its meaning will vary according according to the nature of product, service, sector and its end-user. For example, many of the firms who are active in Commercial New Form innovation have focused on B2C relationships in which the resources they require and depend on are provided by the volunteers (most commonly, individual consumers)

Table 9.7   Mapping resources across different sources of external innovation

	Spontaneous external Innovation	Orchestrated external Innovation	Managed external Innovation
Latent Resource Pool			
Episodic, uncoordinated, external innovation activity	Y	–	–
Emergent Resource Pool			
Emergent community-based external innovation	Y	Y	–
Vibrant Resource Pool			
Community-based external innovation:	Y	Y	Y
Targeted Resource Pool			
Crowd-base external innovation	–	–	Y

who possess the resources. If this group of volunteers lose interest in their involvement, their circumstances change, or they just get a better offer from a competitor, collaborating organisations may struggle. In this context it is likely that elements of this group will be lost over time, with new members needed to be recruited to replace them. This process, sometimes termed 'churn', and the processes put in place to mitigate its effects, will likely be a consistent feature of this form of business going forward. In contrast, it is likely that B2B relationships will be far more stable over time although churn may also be a feature in this area.

The Hold stage is always likely to be qualified and it should always be assumed that retaining any position will require continual work and maintenance. Arguably, the Hold phase will require the most resources of all over time. As a result, organisations will need to put strong processes in place so that it is possible to both hold their hard-won position in the Opportunity Space, to make an informed judgement if they should expand or withdraw the position. In such a dynamic context resources will continue to evolve and develop and any capture is only ever likely to be provisional and temporary. Any success will impact all Actors in an Innovation Space and affect competitors, collaborators, customers, users, online communities and the crowd – and potentially, what worked well today may not work in the same way tomorrow. Developing effective strategies for accessing external resources are likely to be ever more necessary for organisations that wish to achieve competitive advantage. However, over time although such strategies will become ever more necessary, they will not be sufficient in themselves and will need to form part of a wider palette of organisational responses to a changing competitive environment.

In order to be effective the Hold stage will require routine refreshing of the various tools and techniques that have been employed to capture the Innovation Opportunity Space. As a result, resource scanning and any associated analytics will need to be refreshed on an ongoing basis according to the dynamics of the Opportunity Space. At the same time long-term scanning of the Innovation Space, its Architecture, Actors, Actions and Aftershocks will also need to be undertaken in order to inform management action. It may be that such information can be added to existing management information processes, or a new IOS dashboard may be developed to convey such information in an easily accessible format. However, the key issue is that the Hold stage requires ongoing care and attention if it is to persist.

NOTE

1. The term Early Adopter was coined by Everett Rogers within his work on the diffusion of innovations. This theory explores the speed at which new ideas and innovations diffuse in a market or other context. Rogers proposed five groups that should be considered, of which the Early Adopter is one. The five groups, together with their proportions, are as follows: Innovators (2.5 per cent), Early Adopters (13.5 per cent), Early Majority (34 per cent), Late Majority (34 per cent), Laggards (16 per cent). Although this is a highly influential theory and its terms and concepts are often employed in everyday use, it is unclear how they apply to the innovation dynamics of online contexts.

SUMMARY AND KEY QUESTIONS

1 Setting the Scene

How would you characterise your organisation? (Old/New Form Innovation)

How would you describe the current business model?

How would you describe your organisational readiness to engage with New Forms of Innovation?

2 Target

What is your goal? (extend business model, assess feasibility, etc.)

How would you describe your Innovation Opportunity Space?

> Architecture
>
> Actors
>
> Actions
>
> Aftershocks

In what type of Innovation Opportunity Space do you find yourself?

> Stable
>
> Unstable
>
> Emerging

What are the resource levels within the Innovation Opportunity Space, as indicated by the types of observable innovation activity?

> Spontaneous
>
> Orchestrated
>
> Managed

How likely is it that you will make a Novel Category Error in your investigations?

3 Mobilise

Is your original goal still valid?

Have you clarified the implications of proposals for the wider organisation?

What kind of operating model are you proposing?

> Communitarian New Form
>
> Hybrid New Form
>
> Commercial New Form
>
> Hybrid Old Form

How would you describe your organisational readiness?

What needs to be put in place before you can proceed?

> Training
>
> Development
>
> Revised processes
>
> Etc.

How would you describe potential external resources?

> Latent resource pool
> Emergent resource pool
> Vibrant resource pool
> Targeted resource pool

How do you propose to mobilise external resources?
How is the Innovation Opportunity Space changing?
What impact are your actions likely to have?
Have you put in place necessary items, including:

> A detailed plan of action, with a clear goal and success criteria
> Appropriate financial resources
> Training and development for relevant staff
> Internal processes placed in a state of readiness
> Innovation Opportunity Space scoreboard to assess and communicate own progress

Innovation scoreboard to assess activity in adjacent IOS

4 Capture/Hold

How is the Innovation Opportunity Space changing?
What impact are your actions having?
How is the innovative behaviour in the Innovation Opportunity Space changing?
How are the resource profiles in the Innovation Opportunity Space evolving?
How have the Actors in the Innovation Opportunity Space changed?
What are the relevant Actions of those Actors?
What are the Aftershocks of organisations seeking to access the resources that exist within the Innovation Opportunity Space?
How will this impact on your operational model?
Review and update:

> Detailed plan of action, goal and success criteria
> Required financial resources
> Relevant training and development needs
> Internal processes
> Innovation scoreboard to assess own progress
> Innovation scoreboard to assess activity in adjacent IOS

Index